THINK *and* GROW RICH

THE MASTER MIND VOLUME

JEREMY P. TARCHER/PENGUIN

a member of Penguin Group (USA) Inc.

New York

THINK *and* GROW RICH

THE MASTER MIND VOLUME

NAPOLEON HILL

with

JOEL FOTINOS & AUGUST GOLD

JEREMY P. TARCHER/PENGUIN
Published by the Penguin Group
Penguin Group (USA) Inc., 375 Hudson Street, New York, New York 10014, USA • Penguin Group (Canada),
90 Eglinton Avenue East, Suite 700, Toronto, Ontario M4P 2Y3, Canada (a division of Pearson Penguin Canada Inc.) •
Penguin Books Ltd, 80 Strand, London WC2R 0RL, England • Penguin Ireland, 25 St Stephen's Green, Dublin 2,
Ireland (a division of Penguin Books Ltd) • Penguin Group (Australia), 250 Camberwell Road, Camberwell,
Victoria 3124, Australia (a division of Pearson Australia Group Pty Ltd) • Penguin Books India Pvt Ltd,
11 Community Centre, Panchsheel Park, New Delhi–110 017, India • Penguin Group (NZ), 67 Apollo Drive,
Rosedale, North Shore 0632, New Zealand (a division of Pearson New Zealand Ltd) • Penguin Books (South Africa)
(Pty) Ltd, 24 Sturdee Avenue, Rosebank, Johannesburg 2196, South Africa

Penguin Books Ltd, Registered Offices: 80 Strand, London WC2R 0RL, England

Excerpt from *The Power of Decision: A Step-by-Step Program to Overcome Indecision and Live Without Failure Forever*
by Raymond Charles Barker, copyright © 1968, 1988 by the Estate of Raymond Charles Barker. Copyright © 2011
by Richard Collins. Used by permission of Jeremy P. Tarcher, an imprint of Penguin Group (USA) Inc.

Part IV, "Creating Your Master Mind," is abridged from the Penguin e-book
Creating Your Think and Grow Rich Master Mind by Joel Fotinos.

Most Tarcher/Penguin books are available at special quantity discounts for bulk purchase for sales promotions,
premiums, fund-raising, and educational needs. Special books or book excerpts also can be created to fit specific
needs. For details, write Penguin Group (USA) Inc. Special Markets, 375 Hudson Street, New York, NY 10014.

Library of Congress Cataloging-in-Publication Data

Hill, Napoleon, 1883–1970.
Think and grow rich : the master mind volume / Napoleon Hill ; with Joel Fotinos and August Gold.
p.   cm.
"Think and Grow Rich was first published in 1937"—T.p. verso.
ISBN 978-1-58542-896-0
1. Success in business.   2. Carnegie, Andrew, 1835–1919.   I. Fotinos, Joel.   II. Gold, August.   III. Title.
HF5386.H57   2011   2011027803
650.1—dc23

Printed in the United States of America
1   3   5   7   9   10   8   6   4   2

BOOK DESIGN BY NICOLE LAROCHE

CONTENTS

I.

INTRODUCTION

Welcome to the Master Mind Volume of *Think and Grow Rich*, the ultimate study edition of Napoleon Hill's great classic bestseller, which has sold millions of copies and helped countless people find not only financial riches but also riches of life, passion, and joy. You hold in your hands a book that can change your life—and will, if you dive into the ideas and concepts it contains.

The book itself is cited by many financial experts, business titans, and other self-help gurus as one of the books that helped to shape their lives. Why has this book struck such a chord, and continued to be one of the bestselling books published since its initial publication, in 1937? We believe the concepts and exercises put forth in *Think and Grow Rich* work.

Charged by the great steel magnate and philanthropist Andrew Carnegie to learn if there was a commonality in beliefs and actions among the wealthiest self-made millionaires in America, Napoleon Hill spent twenty years studying these men and women. He found that there were ideas and actions that were common among them, and originally published his thoughts in 1926 in a series of books called *The Law of Success* (now beautifully published in one complete volume in the Tarcher Success Classics series). He later distilled those ideas into one compact volume, called *Think and Grow Rich*, and now generation after generation has been impacted by his philosophy.

Napoleon Hill found that there were "thirteen steps to riches"—these are the thirteen principles that make up his Think and Grow Rich philosophy. You'll notice something interesting about these thirteen steps—not one of them mentions words like "money," or "wealth," or "finances." These thirteen steps, which include desire, auto-suggestion, and imagination, were revolutionary in that they identify the steps to financial riches, as well as riches of whatever it is we desire greatly. In fact, people have used *Think and Grow Rich* to actually think and grow whatever it is they want more of in their lives. The principles are universal and can be used by anyone of any background, at any age, in any place.

We believe one of the reasons *Think and Grow Rich* has succeeded for all of these years and why so many people read and love this book is that it is a book that places the responsibility for one's life firmly where it belongs—with each individual. When you read the book and then begin to actually take the actions that the book requires, something amazing happens. Suddenly you are actively engaged in your own life. You are now taking an active part in your own success. You are creating your present and future experiences.

We've heard countless stories of people who have begun to read *Think and Grow Rich* and take the actions that Napoleon Hill suggests, and they not only achieve their desires but also begin to see that their success was within their grasp the entire time. When they begin to spend more time using this philosophy in their lives than they do procrastinating and avoiding their lives, their whole lives open up and they can see that anything they truly desire, they can have.

We've also noticed something else as we've experienced and taught this philosophy to thousands of people over the years, and that is this: We generally want to control the process of how our good comes to us. We want what we want, when we want it. But when we read *Think and Grow Rich* correctly, we discover that when we create a goal, based on our burning desire, we enter into a contract with Life. Our part of our contract with Life does not include the "how" our goal comes to us. That is Life's part of the contract. Instead, our part of the contract is geared to keep us focused on those aspects of the journey that we alone are responsible for, such as creating a burning desire, using the principles of auto-suggestion constantly, being consistent and persistent in our daily positive actions, and so on.

Over the years, we've seen that when we begin to read *Think and Grow Rich* and do the exercises, we enter into what we call a "Think and Grow Rich journey"—that is, we begin an adventure in which we become conscious of our actions, beliefs, and our responsibilities in our own success and happiness. It is a journey, one that is filled with overcoming our self-imposed limitations and living a life that is larger, more abundant, and more joyous than before. That doesn't mean the journey doesn't have challenges and difficult moments— it will—but it does mean that you will now see these challenges and difficulties for what they are: necessary adjustments on our road to success. When we can view everything that happens to us as either a blessing or a blessing in disguise, we are "seeing rightly." Struggles become opportunities, and blocks become stepping stones.

This edition of *Think and Grow Rich* is unique and exciting. It contains, first and foremost, the original 1937 edition of Napoleon Hill's classic book. The original edition is, in our opinion, the most powerful and potent. This larger format allows for an easier reading experience, and also allows for larger margins. Take advantage of these larger margins to write down notes, thoughts, and other inspirations. We've also added lines at the bottom of each page so that you can keep track of any of Hill's ideas that inspire you, and perhaps inspire ideas in you.

We've also added more than two hundred quotes on success from many of history's most important thinkers, as well as from many contemporary figures. These quotes are meant to augment the main text, and to ignite you further. At the bottom corners of many pages, we've also highlighted certain quotes from the text of *Think and Grow Rich*, to draw special attention to many of Napoleon Hill's most important concepts. We like to call these "memorization quotes" because when we memorize important quotes from texts like *Think and Grow Rich*, they live inside our minds and can be useful for us when we need them the most.

At the end of each chapter, we've added some questions about that chapter to ask yourself, to think about, and even to discuss with your Master Mind. Allow these questions to help you ingest the information more fully. Following each set of chapter questions, we've also included a short checklist called Your Success Steps. After each chapter, make a list of what that chapter has motivated you to take action on, and then take that action. Once you complete the action, check the box next to it. In this way the book goes from mere ideas to actual ideas-in-action in your life.

Following the 1937 text are several features that need to be emphasized. First is a chapter on creating a Master Mind in your life, whether it be a Master Mind Group or a Master Mind Partner. Master Minds are essential, Hill tells us, to increasing our success. Use that section to help you create a Master Mind that works for you.

Following "Creating Your Master Mind" is a section of additional inspirational material. In this section we have included excerpts from six well-known and time-tested success classics: *The Science of Being Great* and *The Science of Getting Rich* by Wallace D. Wattles, *As a Man Thinketh* by James Allen, *How to Live on 24 Hours a Day* by Arnold Bennett, *The Power of Decision* by Raymond Charles Barker, and *The Pathway of Roses* by Christian Larson. These excerpts can provide further inspiration, motivation, and instruction as you move through your Think and Grow Rich journey.

Immediately after those six insightful excerpts, we've added a Success Classics Reading List. This is a list of other books on success that can enhance your journey to riches. These are provided to help you become what Hill calls a "lifelong learner." Learning is growing, and growth brings success.

If you are wondering what the best way to approach reading *Think and Grow Rich* is, you'll also find another unique tool at the back of this book—a Think and Grow Rich 90-Day Journey checklist. This list will break out the book into a 90-day program (well, actually it's 91 days . . .). Instructions will guide you through how to read *Think and Grow Rich*, one chapter at a time, and then keep you on track so that each week you are maximizing your experience of the material you are reading.

Finally you will find a series of blank lined pages. Use these pages to keep your Success Notes—fill these pages with ideas for actions, projects, and businesses; insights, sketches, and anything else that will support your Think and Grow Rich journey. They are designed to give you a place to think outside of the box.

A couple of final notes before you begin your journey. Throughout this book, we've left the material from Napoleon Hill, and the other authors, largely intact. That is, we've left the text essentially as they wrote it, including the use of male pronouns, capital letters, and certain words and spellings that were more commonly used at the time the pieces were written. Other than a few minor grammatical corrections made for ease of reading, you are reading the original *Think and Grow Rich* and other works as the authors intended. We felt it was important to keep the material as close to the original as possible.

The added material and format we've used are meant to supplement and enhance what is the main reason for buying and reading this book, which is Napoleon Hill's magnum opus *Think and Grow Rich*, not to replace it in any way. Use whatever of the additional material works for you, and don't use whatever doesn't. However, it's important to note that the additional material and tools were selected with great care and based on years of teaching these ideas, so we would suggest that using most or all of the additional material and tools will be using this edition of *Think and Grow Rich* to the utmost.

We also bring to your attention two other tools that you may consider using in conjunction with this Master Mind Volume edition of *Think and Grow Rich*. *The Think and Grow Rich Workbook* takes the exercises, suggestions, and ideas of *Think and Grow Rich* and puts them (along with a couple of exercises inspired by the book) in a workbook format. The workbook follows *Think and Grow Rich* chapter by chapter, so you can read a chapter of *Think and Grow Rich* and then use *The Think and Grow Rich Workbook* to write out the exercises. It's a useful tool that we developed after years of using a three-ring binder to keep track of each exercise—our workbook is much handier, and will accelerate your journey.

Similarly, *The Think and Grow Rich Success Journal* will amplify your efforts. It's a journal in which you can record your Think and Grow Rich journey, track your action steps, and create a place where all of your ideas, thoughts, and actions can come together in one volume. The printed edition also contains a bonus CD with selections of *Think and Grow Rich* quotations and success affirmations, which you can use to listen to the ideas as well as read them.

And now it is time to begin your own Think and Grow Rich journey. Enter into this journey with an open mind, a willingness to do what Napoleon Hill suggests, and a newfound commitment to take actions until you have reached your goal. Don't stop until you have created the very life you desire. Make this journey as creative, meaningful, and enjoyable as you can. This is your journey—this is your life—and the keys to transformation can be found starting on the very next page . . .

—Joel Fotinos & August Gold

II.

STATEMENT OF
DESIRE CONTRACT

Write out a clear, concise statement of the amount of money you intend to acquire, name the time limit for its acquisition, state what you intend to give in return for the money, and describe clearly the plan through which you intend to accumulate it.

See page 40 for Napoleon Hill's concise instructions for filling out your Statement of Desire.

MY STATEMENT OF DESIRE

The exact amount of money I desire is:

$_____

I intend to give _____

_____

in return for the money I desire.

I intend to possess this money by:

_____

My plan of action is:

    1. _____

    2. _____

    3. _____

Signed: _____

Date: _____

III.

THINK AND
GROW RICH

(Original 1937 Text)

CONTENTS

PUBLISHER'S PREFACE

This book conveys the experience of more than five hundred men of great wealth, who began at scratch, with nothing to give in return for riches except thoughts, ideas, and organized plans.

Here you have the entire philosophy of money-making, just as it was organized from the actual achievements of the most successful men known to the American people during the past fifty years. It describes what to do, also, how to do it!

It presents complete instructions on how to sell your personal services.

It provides you with a perfect system of self-analysis that will readily disclose what has been standing between you and "the big money" in the past.

It describes the famous Andrew Carnegie formula of personal achievement by which he accumulated hundreds of millions of dollars for himself and made no fewer than a score of millionaires of men to whom he taught his secret.

Perhaps you do not need all that is to be found in the book—no one of the five hundred men from whose experiences it was written did—but you may need one idea, plan, or suggestion to start you toward your goal. Somewhere in the book you will find this needed stimulus.

The book was inspired by Andrew Carnegie, after he had made his millions and retired. It was written by the man to whom Carnegie disclosed the astounding secret of his riches—the same man to whom the five hundred wealthy men revealed the source of their riches.

In this volume will be found the thirteen principles of money-making essential to every person who accumulates sufficient money to guarantee financial independence. It is estimated that the research which went into the preparation, before the book was written, or could be written—research covering more than twenty-five years of continuous effort—could not be duplicated at a cost of less than $100,000.

Moreover, the knowledge contained in the book never can be duplicated, at any cost, for the reason that more than half of the five hundred men who supplied the information it brings have passed on.

Riches cannot always be measured in money!

Money and material things are essential for freedom of body and mind, but there are some who will feel that the greatest of all riches can be evaluated only in terms of lasting friendships, harmonious family relationships, sympathy and understanding between business associates, and introspective harmony which brings one peace of mind measurable only in spiritual values!

All who read, understand, and apply this philosophy will be better prepared to attract and enjoy these higher estates which always have been and always will be denied to all except *those who are ready for them.*

Be prepared, therefore, when you expose yourself to the influence of this philosophy, to experience a changed life which may help you not only to negotiate your way through life with harmony and understanding, but also to prepare you for the accumulation of material riches in abundance.

—The Publisher

AUTHOR'S PREFACE

In every chapter of this book, mention has been made of the money-making secret which has made fortunes for more than five hundred exceedingly wealthy men whom I have carefully analyzed over a long period of years.

The secret was brought to my attention by Andrew Carnegie, more than a quarter of a century ago. The canny, lovable old Scotsman carelessly tossed it into my mind, when I was but a boy. Then he sat back in his chair, with a merry twinkle in his eyes, and watched carefully to see if I had brains enough to understand the full significance of what he had said to me.

When he saw that I had grasped the idea, he asked if I would be willing to spend twenty years or more, preparing myself to take it to the world, to men and women who, without the secret, might go through life as failures. I said I would, and with Mr. Carnegie's cooperation, I have kept my promise.

This book contains the secret, after having been put to a practical test by thousands of people, in almost every walk of life. It was Mr. Carnegie's idea that the magic formula, which gave him a stupendous fortune, ought to be placed within reach of people who do not have time to investigate how men make money, and it was his hope that I might test and demonstrate the soundness of the formula through the experience of men and women in every calling. He believed the formula should be taught in all public schools and colleges, and expressed the opinion that if it were properly taught it would so revolutionize the entire educational system that the time spent in school could be reduced to less than half.

His experience with Charles M. Schwab, and other young men of Mr. Schwab's type, convinced Mr. Carnegie that much of that which is taught in the schools is of no value whatsoever in connection with the business of earning a living or accumulating riches. He had arrived at this decision, because he had taken into his business one young man after another, many of them with but little schooling, and by coaching them in the use of this formula, developed in them rare leadership. Moreover, *his coaching made fortunes for every one of them who followed his instructions.*

In the chapter on faith, you will read the astounding story of the organization of the giant United States Steel Corporation, as it was conceived and carried out by one of the young men through whom Mr. Carnegie proved that his formula will work *for all who are ready for it.* This single application of the secret, by that young man—Charles M. Schwab—made him a huge fortune in both money and opportunity. Roughly speaking, this particular application of the formula was worth *$600 million.*

These facts—and they are facts well known to almost everyone who knew Mr. Carnegie—give you a fair idea of what the reading of this book may bring to you, provided you *know what it is that you want.*

Even before it had undergone twenty years of practical testing, the secret was passed on to more than one hundred thousand men and women who have used it for their personal benefit, as Mr. Carnegie planned that they should. Some have made fortunes with it. Others have used it successfully in creating harmony in their homes. A clergyman used it so effectively that it brought him an income of upwards of $75,000 a year.

Arthur Nash, a Cincinnati tailor, used his near-bankrupt business as a "guinea pig" on which to test the formula. The business came to life and made a fortune for its owners. It is still thriving, although Mr. Nash has gone. The experiment was so unique that newspapers and magazines gave it more than a million dollars' worth of laudatory publicity.

The secret was passed on to Stuart Austin Wier, of Dallas, Texas. He was ready for it—so ready that he gave up his profession and studied law. Did he succeed? That story is told too.

I gave the secret to Jennings Randolph, the day he graduated from college, and he has used it so successfully that he is now serving his third term as a Member of Congress, with an excellent opportunity to keep on using it until it carries him to the White House.

While serving as Advertising Manager of the LaSalle Extension University, when it was little more than a name, I had the privilege of seeing J. G. Chapline, President of the University, use the formula so effectively that he has since made the LaSalle one of the great extension schools of the country.

The secret to which I refer has been mentioned no fewer than a hundred times, throughout this book. It has not been directly named, for it seems to work more successfully when it is merely uncovered and left in sight, where those who are ready, and searching for it, may pick it up. That is why Mr. Carnegie tossed it to me so quietly, without giving me its specific name.

If you are ready to put it to use, you will recognize this secret at least once in every chapter. I wish I might feel privileged to tell you how you will know if you are ready, but that would deprive you of much of the benefit you will receive when you make the discovery in your own way.

While this book was being written, my own son, who was then finishing the last year of his college work, picked up the manuscript of chapter two, read it, and discovered the secret for himself. He used the information so effectively that he went directly into a responsible position at a beginning salary greater than the average man ever earns. His story has been briefly described in chapter two. When you read it, perhaps you will dismiss any feeling you may have had, at the beginning of the book, that it promised too much. And, too, if you have ever been discouraged, if you have had difficulties to surmount which took the very soul out of you, if you have tried and failed, if you were ever handicapped by illness or physical affliction, this story of my son's discovery and use of the Carnegie formula may prove to be the oasis in the Desert of Lost Hope, for which you have been searching.

This secret was extensively used by President Woodrow Wilson, during the world war. It was passed on to every soldier who fought in the war, carefully wrapped in the training received before going to the front. President Wilson told me it was a strong factor in raising the funds needed for the war.

More than twenty years ago, Hon. Manuel L. Quezon (then Resident Commissioner of the Philippine Islands), was inspired by the secret to gain freedom for his people. He has gained freedom for the Philippines, and is the first President of the free state.

A peculiar thing about this secret is that those who once acquire it and use it find themselves literally swept on to success, with but little effort, and they never again submit to failure! If you doubt this, study the names of those who have used it, wherever they have been mentioned; check their records for yourself, and be convinced.

There is no such thing as something for nothing!

The secret to which I refer cannot be had without a price, although the price is far less than its value. It cannot be had at any price by those who are not intentionally searching for it. It cannot be given away, it cannot be purchased for money, for the reason that it comes in two parts. One part is already in possession of those who are ready for it.

The secret serves equally well all who are ready for it. Education has nothing to do with it. Long before I was born, the secret had found its way into the possession of Thomas A. Edison, and he used it so intelligently that he became the world's leading inventor, although he had but three months of schooling.

The secret was passed on to a business associate of Mr. Edison. He used it so effectively that, although he was then making only $12,000 a year, he accumulated a great fortune, and retired from active business while still a young man. You will find his story at the beginning of the first chapter. It should convince you that riches are not beyond your reach, that you can still be what you wish to be, that money, fame, recognition, and happiness can be had by all who are ready and determined to have these blessings.

How do I know these things? You should have the answer before you finish this book. You may find it in the very first chapter, or on the last page.

While I was performing the twenty-year task of research, which I had undertaken at Mr. Carnegie's request, I analyzed hundreds of well-known men, many of whom admitted that they had accumulated their vast fortunes through the aid of the Carnegie secret; among these men were:

Henry Ford	Theodore Roosevelt
William Wrigley Jr.	John W. Davis
John Wanamaker	Elbert Hubbard
James J. Hill	Wilbur Wright
George S. Parker	William Jennings Bryan
E. M. Statler	Dr. David Starr Jordan
Henry L. Doherty	J. Odgen Armour
Cyrus H. K. Curtis	Charles M. Schwab
George Eastman	Harris F. Williams
Dr. Frank Gunsaulus	Daniel Willard
King Gillette	Ralph A. Weeks
Judge Daniel T. Wright	John D. Rockefeller
Thomas A. Edison	Frank A. Vanderlip
F. W. Woolworth	Col. Robert A. Dollar
Edward A. Filene	Edwin C. Barnes
Arthur Brisbane	Woodrow Wilson
Wm. Howard Taft	Luther Burbank
Edward W. Bok	Frank A. Munsey
Elbert H. Gary	Dr. Alexander Graham Bell
John H. Patterson	Julius Rosenwald
Stuart Austin Wier	Dr. Frank Crane
George M. Alexander	J. G. Chapline
Hon. Jennings Randolph	Arthur Nash
Clarence Darrow	

These names represent but a small fraction of the hundreds of well-known Americans whose achievements, financial and otherwise, prove that those who understand and apply the Carnegie secret reach high stations in life. I have never known anyone who was inspired to use the secret who did not achieve noteworthy success in his chosen calling. I have never known any person to distinguish himself, or to accumulate riches of any consequence, without possession of the secret. From these two facts I draw the conclusion that the secret is more important, as a part of the knowledge essential for self-determination, than any which one receives through what is popularly known as "education."

What is education, anyway? This has been answered in full detail.

As far as schooling is concerned, many of these men had very little. John Wanamaker once told me that what little schooling he had, he acquired in very much the same manner as a modern locomotive takes on water, by "scooping it up as it runs." Henry Ford never reached high school, let alone college. I am not attempting to minimize the value of schooling, but I am trying to express my earnest belief that those who master and apply the secret will reach high stations, accumulate riches, and bargain with life on their own terms, even if their schooling has been meager.

Somewhere, as you read, the secret to which I refer will jump from the page and stand boldly before you, if you are ready for it! When it appears, you will recognize it. Whether you receive the sign in the first or the last chapter, stop for a moment when it presents itself, and turn down a glass, for that occasion will mark the most important turning-point of your life.

We pass now, to chapter one, and to the story of my very dear friend, who has generously acknowledged having seen the mystic sign, and whose business achievements are evidence enough that he turned down a glass. As you read his story, and the others, remember that they deal with the important problems of life, such as all men experience. The problems arising from one's endeavor to earn a living, to find hope, courage, contentment, and peace of mind; to accumulate riches and to enjoy freedom of body and spirit.

Remember, too, as you go through the book, that it deals with facts and not with fiction, its purpose being to convey a great universal truth through which all who are ready may learn, not only *what* to do, but also *how* to do it! and receive, as well, the needed stimulus to make a start.

As a final word of preparation, before you begin the first chapter, may I offer one brief suggestion which may provide a clue by which the Carnegie secret may be recognized? It is this—*all achievement, all earned riches, have their beginning in an idea!* If you are ready for the secret, you already possess one half of it; therefore, you will readily recognize the other half the moment it reaches your mind.

—The Author

CHAPTER 1

INTRODUCTION

The Man Who "Thought" His Way into Partnership with Thomas A. Edison

Truly, "thoughts are things," and powerful things at that, when they are mixed with definiteness of purpose, persistence, and a burning desire for their translation into riches, or other material objects.

A little more than thirty years ago, Edwin C. Barnes discovered how true it is that men really do think and grow rich. His discovery did not come about at one sitting. It came little by little, beginning with a burning desire to become a business associate of the great Edison.

One of the chief characteristics of Barnes' desire was that it was *definite*. He wanted to work *with* Edison, not *for* him. Observe, carefully, the description of how he went about translating his desire into reality, and you will have a better understanding of the thirteen principles which lead to riches.

When this desire, or impulse of thought, first flashed into his mind he was in no position to act upon it. Two difficulties stood in his way. He did not know Mr. Edison, and he did not have enough money to pay his railroad fare to Orange, New Jersey.

These difficulties were sufficient to have discouraged the majority of men from making any attempt to carry out the desire. But his was no ordinary desire! He was so determined to find a way to carry out his desire that he finally decided to travel by "blind baggage," rather than be defeated. (To the uninitiated, this means that he went to East Orange on a freight train.)

If we did all the things we were capable of doing, we would literally astound ourselves.

—Thomas Edison

Truly, "thoughts are things," and powerful things at that, when they are mixed with definiteness of purpose, persistence, and a burning desire for their translation into riches, or other material objects.

We may divide thinkers into those who think for themselves and those who think through others. The latter are the rule and the former the exception. The first are original thinkers in a double sense, and egotists in the noblest meaning of the word.

—Schopenhauer

He presented himself at Mr. Edison's laboratory, and announced he had come to go into business with the inventor. In speaking of the first meeting between Barnes and Edison, years later, Mr. Edison said, "He stood there before me, looking like an ordinary tramp, *but there was something in the expression of his face which conveyed the impression that he was determined to get what he had come after.* I had learned, from years of experience with men, that when a man really desires a thing so deeply that he is willing to stake his entire future on a single turn of the wheel in order to get it, he is sure to win. I gave him the opportunity he asked for, *because I saw he had made up his mind to stand by until he succeeded.* Subsequent events proved that no mistake was made."

Just what young Barnes said to Mr. Edison on that occasion was far less important than *that which he thought.* Edison, himself, said so! It could not have been the young man's appearance which got him his start in the Edison office, for that was definitely against him. It was what he thought that counted.

If the significance of this statement could be conveyed to every person who reads it, there would be no need for the remainder of this book.

Barnes did not get his partnership with Edison on his first interview. He did get a chance to work in the Edison offices, at a very nominal wage, doing work that was unimportant to Edison, but most important to Barnes, because it gave him an opportunity to display his "merchandise" where his intended "partner" could see it.

Months went by. Apparently nothing happened to bring the coveted goal which Barnes had set up in his mind as his definite major purpose. But something important was happening in Barnes' mind. He was constantly intensifying his desire to become the business associate of Edison.

Psychologists have correctly said that "when one is truly ready for a thing, it puts in its appearance." Barnes was ready for a business association with Edison; moreover, he was determined to remain ready until he got that which he was seeking.

He did not say to himself, "Ah well, what's the use? I guess I'll change my mind and try for a salesman's job." But, he did say, "I came here to go into business with Edison, and I'll accomplish this end if it takes the remainder of my life." *He meant it!* What a different story men would have to tell if only they

I had learned, from years of experience with men, that when a man really desires a thing so deeply that he is willing to stake his entire future on a single turn of the wheel in order to get it, he is sure to win.

would adopt a definite purpose, and stand by that purpose until it had time to become an all-consuming obsession!

Maybe young Barnes did not know it at the time, but his bulldog determination, his persistence in standing back of a single desire, was destined to mow down all opposition, and bring him the opportunity he was seeking.

When the opportunity came, it appeared in a different form, and from a different direction than Barnes had expected. That is one of the tricks of opportunity. It has a sly habit of slipping in by the back door, and often it comes disguised in the form of misfortune, or temporary defeat. Perhaps this is why so many fail to recognize opportunity.

Mr. Edison had just perfected a new office device, known at that time as the Edison Dictating Machine (now the Ediphone). His salesmen were not enthusiastic over the machine. They did not believe it could be sold without great effort. Barnes saw his opportunity. It had crawled in quietly, hidden in a queer-looking machine which interested no one but Barnes and the inventor.

Barnes knew he could sell the Edison Dictating Machine. He suggested this to Edison, and promptly got his chance. He did sell the machine. In fact, he sold it so successfully that Edison gave him a contract to distribute and market it all over the nation. Out of that business association grew the slogan "Made by Edison and installed by Barnes."

The business alliance has been in operation for more than thirty years. Out of it Barnes has made himself rich in money, but he has done something infinitely greater: he has proved that one really may "Think and Grow Rich."

How much actual cash that original desire of Barnes' has been worth to him, I have no way of knowing. Perhaps it has brought him $2 or $3 million dollars, but the amount, whatever it is, becomes insignificant when compared with the greater asset he acquired in the form of definite knowledge that *an intangible impulse of thought can be transmuted into its physical counterpart* by the application of known principles.

Barnes literally *thought* himself into a partnership with the great Edison! He thought himself into a fortune. He had nothing to start with, except the capacity to know what he wanted, and the determination to stand by that desire until he realized it.

Difficulties are the things that show what men are.

—Epictetus

What a different story men would have to tell if only they would adopt a definite purpose, and stand by that purpose until it had time to become an all-consuming obsession!

He had no money to begin with. He had but little education. He had no influence. But he did have initiative, faith, and the will to win. With these intangible forces he *made himself* number one man with the greatest inventor who ever lived.

Now, let us look at a different situation, and study a man who had plenty of tangible evidence of riches, but lost it, *because he stopped* three feet short of the goal he was seeking.

Action is the foundational key to all success.

—Pablo Picasso

THREE FEET FROM GOLD

One of the most common causes of failure is the habit of quitting when one is overtaken by *temporary defeat*. Every person is guilty of this mistake at one time or another.

An uncle of R. U. Darby was caught by the "gold fever" in the gold-rush days, and went west to dig and grow rich. He had never heard that *more gold has been mined from the brains of men than has ever been taken from the earth*. He staked a claim and went to work with pick and shovel. The going was hard, but his lust for gold was definite.

After weeks of labor, he was rewarded by the discovery of the shining ore. He needed machinery to bring the ore to the surface. Quietly, he covered up the mine, retraced his footsteps to his home in Williamsburg, Maryland, told his relatives and a few neighbors of the "strike." They got together money for the needed machinery, and had it shipped. The uncle and Darby went back to work the mine.

The first car of ore was mined, and shipped to a smelter. The returns proved they had one of the richest mines in Colorado! A few more cars of that ore would clear the debts. Then would come the big killing in profits.

Down went the drills! Up went the hopes of Darby and Uncle! Then something happened! The vein of gold ore disappeared! They had come to the end of the rainbow, and the pot of gold was no longer there! They drilled on, desperately trying to pick up the vein again—all to no avail.

Finally, they decided to quit.

Barnes literally thought *himself into a partnership with the great Edison! He thought himself into a fortune. He had nothing to start with, except the capacity to know what he wanted, and the determination to stand by that desire until he realized it.*

They sold the machinery to a "junk" man for a few hundred dollars, and took the train back home. Some "junk" men are dumb, but not this one! He called in a mining engineer to look at the mine and do a little calculating. The engineer advised that the project had failed because the owners were not familiar with "fault lines." His calculations showed that the vein would be found just three feet from where the Darbys had stopped drilling! That is exactly where it was found!

The "junk" man took millions of dollars in ore from the mine because he knew enough to seek expert counsel before giving up.

Most of the money which went into the machinery was procured through the efforts of R. U. Darby, who was then a very young man. The money came from his relatives and neighbors, because of their faith in him. He paid back every dollar of it, although he was years in doing so.

Long afterward, Mr. Darby recouped his loss many times over, *when he made the discovery* that desire can be transmuted into gold. The discovery came after he went into the business of selling life insurance.

Remembering that he lost a huge fortune because he stopped three feet from gold, Darby profited by the experience in his chosen work, by the simple method of saying to himself, "I stopped three feet from gold, but I will never stop *because men say 'no'* when I ask them to buy insurance."

Darby is one of a small group of fewer than fifty men who sell more than a million dollars in life insurance annually. He owes his "stickability" to the lesson he learned from his "quitability" in the gold mining business.

Before success comes in any man's life, he is sure to meet with much temporary defeat, and, perhaps, some failure. When defeat overtakes a man, the easiest and most logical thing to do is to quit. That is exactly what the majority of men do.

More than five hundred of the most successful men this country has ever known told the author their greatest success came just one step *beyond* the point at which defeat had overtaken them. Failure is a trickster with a keen sense of irony and cunning. It takes great delight in tripping one when success is almost within reach.

The key to every man is his thought. Sturdy and defiant though he look, he has a helm which he obeys, which is the idea after which all his facts are classified. He can only be reformed by showing him a new idea which commands his own.
—Ralph Waldo Emerson

One of the most common causes of failure is the habit of quitting when one is overtaken by temporary defeat.

A FIFTY-CENT LESSON IN PERSISTENCE

Shortly after Mr. Darby received his degree from the "University of Hard Knocks," and had decided to profit by his experience in the gold mining business, he had the good fortune to be present on an occasion that proved to him that "No" does not necessarily mean no.

One afternoon he was helping his uncle grind wheat in an old-fashioned mill. The uncle operated a large farm on which a number of colored sharecrop farmers lived. Quietly, the door was opened, and a small colored child, the daughter of a tenant, walked in and took her place near the door.

The uncle looked up, saw the child, and barked at her roughly, "What do you want?"

Meekly, the child replied, "My mama says send her fifty cents."

"I'll not do it," the uncle retorted. "Now you run on home."

"Yes sir," the child replied. *But she did not move.*

The uncle went ahead with his work, so busily engaged that he did not pay enough attention to the child to observe that she did not leave. When he looked up and saw her still standing there, he yelled at her, "I told you to go on home! Now go, or I'll take a switch to you."

The little girl said, "Yes sir," *but she did not budge an inch.*

The uncle dropped a sack of grain he was about to pour into the mill hopper, picked up a barrel stave, and started toward the child with an expression on his face that indicated trouble.

Darby held his breath. He was certain he was about to witness a murder. He knew his uncle had a fierce temper. He knew that colored children were not supposed to defy white people in that part of the country.

When the uncle reached the spot where the child was standing, she quickly stepped forward one step, looked up into his eyes, and screamed at the top of her shrill voice, *"My mama's gotta have that fifty cents!"*

The uncle stopped, looked at her for a minute, then slowly laid the barrel stave on the floor, put his hand in his pocket, took out half a dollar, and gave it to her.

The child took the money and slowly backed toward the door, never taking her eyes off the man *whom she had just conquered.* After she had gone, the uncle sat down on a box and looked out the window into space for more than ten minutes. He was pondering, with awe, over the whipping he had just taken.

Mr. Darby, too, was doing some thinking. That was the first time in all his experience that he had seen a colored child deliberately *master* an adult white person. How did she do it? What happened to his uncle that caused him to lose his fierceness and become as docile as a lamb? What strange power did this child use that made her master over her superior? These and other similar questions flashed into Darby's mind, but he did not find the answer until years later, when he told me the story.

Strangely, the story of this unusual experience was told to the author in the old mill, on the very spot where the uncle took his whipping. Strangely, too, I had devoted nearly a quarter of a century to the study of the power which enabled an ignorant, illiterate colored child to conquer an intelligent man.

As we stood there in that musty old mill, Mr. Darby repeated the story of the unusual conquest, and finished by asking, "What can you make of it? What strange power did that child use, that so completely whipped my uncle?"

The answer to his question will be found in the principles described in this book. The answer is full and complete. It contains details and instructions sufficient to enable anyone to understand, and apply the same force which the little child accidentally stumbled upon.

Keep your mind alert, and you will observe exactly what strange power came to the rescue of the child; you will catch a glimpse of this power in the next chapter. Somewhere in the book you will find an idea that will quicken your receptive powers, and place at your command, for your own benefit, this same irresistible power. The awareness of this power may come to you in the first chapter, or it may flash into your mind in some subsequent chapter. It may come in the form of a single idea. Or, it may come in the nature of a plan, or a purpose. Again, it may cause you to go back into your past experiences of failure or defeat, and bring to the surface some lesson by which you can regain all that you lost through defeat.

After I had described to Mr. Darby the power unwittingly used by the little colored child, he quickly retraced his thirty years of experience as a life insurance salesman, and frankly acknowledged that his success in that field was due, in no small degree, to the lesson he had learned from the child.

There are people everywhere who have decided to expand their lives. These people are willing to be temporarily uncomfortable in order to achieve expanded consciousness and reach new goals.

—Raymond Charles Barker

*More than five hundred of the most successful men this country has ever known told the author their greatest success came just one step **beyond** the point at which defeat had overtaken them.*

Success is to be measured not so much by the position that one has reached in life as by the obstacles which he has overcome.

—Booker T. Washington

Mr. Darby pointed out: "Every time a prospect tried to bow me out, without buying, I saw that child standing there in the old mill, her big eyes glaring in defiance, and I said to myself, 'I've gotta make this sale.' The better portion of all sales I have made were made after people had said 'No.'"

He recalled, too, his mistake in having stopped only three feet from gold. "But," he said, "that experience was a blessing in disguise. It taught me *to keep on keeping on,* no matter how hard the going may be, a lesson I needed to learn before I could succeed in anything."

This story of Mr. Darby and his uncle, the colored child and the gold mine, doubtless will be read by hundreds of men who make their living by selling life insurance, and to all of these, the author wishes to offer the suggestion that Darby owes to these two experiences his ability to sell more than a million dollars of life insurance every year.

Life is strange, and often imponderable! Both the successes and the failures have their roots in simple experiences. Mr. Darby's experiences were commonplace and simple enough, yet they held the answer to his destiny in life; therefore they were as important (to him) as life itself. He profited by these two dramatic experiences, because *he analyzed them,* and found the lesson they taught. But what of the man who has neither the time nor the inclination to study failure in search of knowledge that may lead to success? Where, and how, is he to learn the art of converting defeat into stepping stones to opportunity?

In answer to these questions, this book was written.

The answer called for a description of thirteen principles, but remember, as you read, the answer *you* may be seeking, to the questions which have caused you to ponder over the strangeness of life, may be found *in your own mind,* through some idea, plan, or purpose which may spring into your mind as you read.

One sound idea is all that one needs to achieve success. The principles described in this book contain the best, and the most practical of all that is known, concerning ways and means of creating useful ideas.

Before we go any further in our approach to the description of these principles, we believe you are entitled to receive this important suggestion. . . . When riches begin to come, they come so quickly, in such great abundance, that one wonders where they have been hiding during all those lean years. This

"That experience was a blessing in disguise. It taught me to keep on keeping on, *no matter how hard the going may be, a lesson I needed to learn before I could succeed in anything."*

is an astounding statement, and all the more so when we take into consideration the popular belief that riches come only to those who work hard and long.

When you begin to think and grow rich, you will observe that riches begin with a state of mind, with definiteness of purpose, with little or no hard work. You, and every other person, ought to be interested in knowing how to acquire that state of mind which will attract riches. I spent twenty-five years in research, analyzing more than 25,000 people, because I, too, wanted to know "how wealthy men become that way."

Without that research, this book could not have been written.

Here take notice of a very significant truth, viz: The business depression started in 1929, and continued on to an all-time record of destruction, until sometime after President Roosevelt entered office. Then the depression began to fade into nothingness. Just as an electrician in a theatre raises the lights so gradually that darkness is transmuted into light before you realize it, so did the spell of fear in the minds of the people gradually fade away and become faith.

Observe very closely: As soon as you master the principles of this philosophy, and begin to follow the instructions for applying those principles, your financial status will begin to improve, and everything you touch will begin to transmute itself into an asset for your benefit. Impossible? Not at all!

One of the main weaknesses of mankind is the average man's familiarity with the word "impossible." He knows all the rules which will not work. He knows all the things which cannot be done. This book was written for those who seek the rules which have made others successful, and are willing to *stake everything* on those rules.

A great many years ago I purchased a fine dictionary. The first thing I did with it was to turn to the word "impossible," and neatly clip it out of the book. That would not be an unwise thing for you to do.

Success comes to those who become success conscious.

Failure comes to those who indifferently allow themselves to become failure conscious.

The object of this book is to help all who seek it, to learn the art of changing their minds from failure consciousness to success consciousness.

Another weakness found in altogether too many people is the habit of measuring everything, and everyone, by *their own* impressions and beliefs. Some

Say with deep, earnest feeling: "I CAN succeed! All that is possible to anyone is possible to me. I AM successful. I do succeed, for I am full of the Power of Success."
—Wallace D. Wattles

One sound idea is all that one needs to achieve success.

Everything that happens to you, happens for you.

      —August Gold

who will read this will believe that no one can think and grow rich. They cannot think in terms of riches, because their thought habits have been steeped in poverty, want, misery, failure, and defeat.

These unfortunate people remind me of a prominent Chinese man, who came to America to be educated in American ways. He attended the University of Chicago. One day President Harper met this young man on the campus, stopped to chat with him for a few minutes, and asked what had impressed him as being the most noticeable characteristic of the American people.

"Why," the man exclaimed, "the queer slant of your eyes. Your eyes are off slant!"

What do we say about the Chinese?

We refuse to believe that which we do not understand. We foolishly believe that our own limitations are the proper measure of limitations. Sure, the other fellow's eyes are "off slant," because they are not the same as our own.

Millions of people look at the achievements of Henry Ford, after he has arrived, and envy him, because of his good fortune, or luck, or genius, or whatever it is that they credit for Ford's fortune. Perhaps one person in every hundred thousand knows the secret of Ford's success, and those who do know are too modest, or too reluctant, to speak of it, *because of its simplicity.* A single transaction will illustrate the "secret" perfectly.

A few years back, Ford decided to produce his now famous V-8 motor. He chose to build an engine with the entire eight cylinders cast in one block, and instructed his engineers to produce a design for the engine. The design was placed on paper, but the engineers agreed, to a man, that it was simply *impossible* to cast an eight cylinder gas engine block in one piece.

Ford said, "Produce it anyway."

"But," they replied, "it's impossible!"

"Go ahead," Ford commanded, "and stay on the job until you succeed no matter how much time is required."

The engineers went ahead. There was nothing else for them to do, if they were to remain on the Ford staff. Six months went by; nothing happened. Another six months passed, and still nothing happened. The engineers tried every conceivable plan to carry out the orders, but the thing seemed out of the question: *"Impossible!"*

When riches begin to come, they come so quickly, in such great abundance, that one wonders where they have been hiding during all those lean years.

At the end of the year Ford checked with his engineers, and again they informed him they had found no way to carry out his orders.

"Go right ahead," said Ford, "I want it, and I'll have it."

They went ahead, and then, as if by a stroke of magic, the secret was discovered.

The Ford determination had won once more!

This story may not be described with minute accuracy, but the sum and substance of it is correct. Deduce from it, you who wish to think and grow rich, the secret of the Ford millions, if you can. You'll not have to look very far.

Henry Ford is a success, because he understands, and *applies* the principles of success. One of these is desire: knowing what one wants. Remember this Ford story as you read, and pick out the lines in which the secret of his stupendous achievement have been described. If you can do this, if you can lay your finger on the particular group of principles which made Henry Ford rich, you can equal his achievements in almost any calling for which you are suited.

Success is getting what you want.
Happiness is wanting what you get.
—Dale Carnegie

YOU ARE "THE MASTER OF YOUR FATE, THE CAPTAIN OF YOUR SOUL," BECAUSE . . .

When Henley wrote the prophetic lines "I am the Master of my Fate, I am the Captain of my Soul," he should have informed us that we are the Masters of our Fate, the Captains of our Souls, *because* we have the power to control our thoughts.

He should have told us that the ether in which this little earth floats, in which we move and have our being, is a form of energy moving at an inconceivably high rate of vibration, and that the ether is filled with a form of universal power which adapts itself to the nature of the thoughts we hold in our minds; and influences us, in natural ways, to transmute our thoughts into their physical equivalent.

If the poet had told us of this great truth, we would know why it is that we are the Masters of our Fate, the Captains of our Souls. He should have told us, with great emphasis, that this power makes no attempt to discriminate between destructive thoughts and constructive thoughts, that it will urge us to translate

When you begin to think and grow rich, you will observe that riches begin with a state of mind, with definiteness of purpose, with little or no hard work.

into physical reality thoughts of poverty just as quickly as it will influence us to act upon thoughts of riches.

He should have told us, too, that our brains become magnetized with the dominating thoughts which we hold in our minds, and, by means with which no man is familiar, these "magnets" attract to us the forces, the people, the circumstances of life which harmonize with the nature of our *dominating* thoughts.

He should have told us that before we can accumulate riches in great abundance, we must magnetize our minds with intense desire for riches, that we must become "money conscious" until the desire for money drives us to create definite plans for acquiring it.

But, being a poet, and not a philosopher, Henley contented himself by stating a great truth in poetic form, leaving those who followed him to interpret the philosophical meaning of his lines.

Little by little, the truth has unfolded itself, until it now appears certain that the principles described in this book hold the secret of mastery over our economic fate.

We are now ready to examine the first of these principles. Maintain a spirit of open-mindedness, and remember as you read, they are the invention of no one man. The principles were gathered from the life experiences of more than five hundred men who actually accumulated riches in huge amounts; men who began in poverty, with but little education, without influence. The principles worked for these men. You can put them to work for your own enduring benefit.

You will find it easy, not hard, to do.

Before you read the next chapter, I want you to know that it conveys factual information which might easily change your entire financial destiny, as it has so definitely brought changes of stupendous proportions to two people described.

I want you to know, also, that the relationship between these two men and myself is such that I could have taken no liberties with the facts, even if I had wished to do so. One of them has been my closest personal friend for almost twenty-five years, the other is my own son. The unusual success of these two men, success which they generously accredit to the principle described in the next chapter, more than justifies this personal reference as a means of emphasizing the far-flung power of this principle.

So many of our dreams seem impossible, then improbable, then inevitable.

—Christopher Reeve

Success comes to those who become success conscious. Failure comes to those who indifferently allow themselves to become failure conscious. The object of this book is to help all who seek it, to learn the art of changing their minds from failure consciousness to success consciousness.

Almost fifteen years ago, I delivered the Commencement Address at Salem College, Salem, West Virginia. I emphasized the principle described in the next chapter, with so much intensity that one of the members of the graduating class definitely appropriated it, and made it a part of his own philosophy. The young man is now a Member of Congress, and an important factor in the present administration. Just before this book went to the publisher, he wrote me a letter in which he so clearly stated his opinion of the principle outlined in the next chapter that I have chosen to publish his letter as an introduction to that chapter. It gives you an idea of the rewards to come.

That which makes you want more money is the same as that which makes the plant grow; it is Life, seeing fuller expression.
—Wallace D. Wattles

My dear Napoleon:

My service as a Member of Congress having given me an insight into the problems of men and women, I am writing to offer a suggestion which may become helpful to thousands of worthy people.

With apologies, I must state that the suggestion, if acted upon, will mean several years of labor and responsibility for you, but I am enheartened to make the suggestion, because I know your great love for rendering useful service.

In 1922, you delivered the Commencement Address at Salem College, when I was a member of the graduating class. In that address, you planted in my mind an idea which has been responsible for the opportunity I now have to serve the people of my State, and will be responsible, in a very large measure, for whatever success I may have in the future.

The suggestion I have in mind is that you put into a book the sum and substance of the address you delivered at Salem College, and in that way give the people of America an opportunity to profit by your many years of experience and association with the men who, by their greatness, have made America the richest nation on earth.

I recall, as though it were yesterday, the marvelous description you gave of the method by which Henry Ford, with but little schooling, without a dollar, with no influential friends, rose to great heights. I made up my mind then, even before you had finished your speech, that I would make a place for myself, no matter how many difficulties I had to surmount.

Thousands of young people will finish their schooling this year, and within the next few years. Every one of them will be seeking just such a message of

We refuse to believe that which we do not understand. We foolishly believe that our own limitations are the proper measure of limitations.

The big secret in life is that there is no big secret. Whatever your goal, you can get there if you're willing to work.

—Oprah Winfrey

practical encouragement as the one I received from you. They will want to know where to turn, what to do, to get started in life. You can tell them, because you have helped to solve the problems of so many, many people.

If there is any possible way that you can afford to render so great a service, may I offer the suggestion that you include with every book one of your Personal Analysis Charts, in order that the purchaser of the book may have the benefit of a complete self-inventory, indicating, as you indicated to me years ago, exactly what is standing in the way of success.

Such a service as this, providing the readers of your book with a complete, unbiased picture of their faults and their virtues, would mean to them the difference between success and failure. The service would be priceless.

Millions of people are now facing the problem of staging a come-back, because of the depression, and I speak from personal experience when I say, I know these earnest people would welcome the opportunity to tell you their problems, and to receive your suggestions for the solution.

You know the problems of those who face the necessity of beginning all over again. There are thousands of people in America today who would like to know how they can convert ideas into money, people who must start at scratch, without finances, and recoup their losses. If anyone can help them, you can.

If you publish the book, I would like to own the first copy that comes from the press, personally autographed by you.

> With best wishes, believe me,
> Cordially yours,
> Jennings Randolph

Before we can accumulate riches in great abundance, we must magnetize our minds with intense desire for riches . . . we must become "money conscious" until the desire for money drives us to create definite plans for acquiring it.

QUESTIONS FOR SUCCESS

- *What is the most helpful idea from this chapter for you?*

- *How does the story of Edwin C. Barnes (pages 21–24) inspire you?*

- *When have you stopped "three feet from gold" in your life?*

- *Can you think of examples of when a "temporary defeat" turned into a victory in your life?*

- *Napoleon Hill writes, "This book was written for those who seek the rules which have made others successful, and are willing to stake everything on those rules." Are you willing to stake everything to move toward your burning desire?*

- *Would you categorize yourself as being "success conscious" or "failure conscious" up until now?*

- *What does the phrase "I am the Master of my Fate, I am the Captain of my Soul" mean to you?*

YOUR SUCCESS STEPS

- ☐ _____
- ☐ _____
- ☐ _____
- ☐ _____
- ☐ _____
- ☐ _____

CHAPTER 2

DESIRE

The Starting Point of All Achievement

The First Step Toward Riches

When Edwin C. Barnes climbed down from the freight train in Orange, New Jersey, more than thirty years ago, he may have resembled a tramp, but his *thoughts* were those of a king!

As he made his way from the railroad tracks to Thomas A. Edison's office, his mind was at work. He saw himself *standing in Edison's presence.* He heard himself asking Mr. Edison for an opportunity to carry out the one consuming obsession of his life, a burning desire to become the business associate of the great inventor.

Barnes' desire was not a *hope!* It was not a *wish!* It was a keen, pulsating desire, which transcended everything else. It was definite.

The desire was not new when he approached Edison. It had been Barnes' *dominating desire* for a long time. In the beginning, when the desire first appeared in his mind, it may have been, probably was, only a wish, but it was no mere wish when he appeared before Edison with it.

A few years later, Edwin C. Barnes again stood before Edison, in the same office where he first met the inventor. This time his desire had been translated into reality. *He was in business with Edison.* The dominating dream of his life had become a reality. Today, people who know Barnes envy him, because of the "break" life yielded him. They see him in the days of his triumph, without taking the trouble to investigate the *cause* of his success.

Your heart's desires are your great assets. They indicate the experiences you can have when you make your decisions to have them. They are mighty potentials awaiting your attention. They should never be ignored.

—Raymond Charles Barker

"You see the boats going up in smoke. That means that we cannot leave these shores alive unless we win! We now have no choice—we win—or we perish!" They won.

The happiest person is the person who thinks the most interesting thoughts.

—Timothy Dwight

Barnes succeeded because he chose a definite goal, placed all his energy, all his will-power, all his effort, everything back of that goal. He did not become the partner of Edison the day he arrived. He was content to start in the most menial work, as long as it provided an opportunity to take even one step toward his cherished goal.

Five years passed before the chance he had been seeking made its appearance. During all those years not one ray of hope, not one promise of attainment of his desire had been held out to him. To everyone, except himself, he appeared only another cog in the Edison business wheel, but in his own mind, he was the partner of Edison every minute of the time, from the very day that he first went to work there.

It is a remarkable illustration of the power of a definite desire. Barnes won his goal, because he wanted to be a business associate of Mr. Edison, more than he wanted anything else. He created a plan by which to attain that purpose. But he burned all bridges behind him. He stood by his desire until it became the dominating obsession of his life—and—finally, a fact.

When he went to Orange, he did not say to himself, "I will try to induce Edison to give me a job of some sort." He said, "I will see Edison, and put him on notice that I have come to go into business with him."

He did not say, "I will work there for a few months, and if I get no encouragement, I will quit and get a job somewhere else." He did say, "I will start anywhere. I will do anything Edison tells me to do, but *before I am through,* I will be his associate."

He did not say, "I will keep my eyes open for another opportunity, in case I fail to get what I want in the Edison organization." He said, "There is but one thing in this world that I am determined to have, and that is a business association with Thomas A. Edison. I will burn all bridges behind me, and stake my entire future on my ability to get what I want."

He left himself no possible way of retreat. He had to win or perish!

That is all there is to the Barnes story of success!

A long while ago, a great warrior faced a situation which made it necessary for him to make a decision which insured his success on the battlefield. He was about to send his armies against a powerful foe, whose men outnumbered his

Every person who wins in any undertaking must be willing to burn his ships and cut all sources of retreat. Only by so doing can one be sure of maintaining that state of mind known as a burning desire to win, essential to success.

own. He loaded his soldiers into boats, sailed to the enemy's country, unloaded soldiers and equipment, then gave the order to burn the ships that had carried them. Addressing his men before the first battle, he said, "You see the boats going up in smoke. That means that we cannot leave these shores alive unless we win! We now have no choice—*we win—or we perish!*" They won.

Every person who wins in any undertaking must be willing to burn his ships and cut all sources of retreat. Only by so doing can one be sure of maintaining that state of mind known as a burning desire to win, essential to success.

The morning after the great Chicago fire, a group of merchants stood on State Street, looking at the smoking remains of what had been their stores. They went into a conference to decide if they would try to rebuild, or leave Chicago and start over in a more promising section of the country. They reached a decision—all except one—to leave Chicago.

The merchant who decided to stay and rebuild pointed a finger at the remains of his store, and said, "Gentlemen, on that very spot I will build the world's greatest store, no matter how many times it may burn down."

That was more than fifty years ago. The store was built. It stands there today, a towering monument to the power of that state of mind known as a burning desire. The easy thing for Marshall Field to have done, would have been exactly what his fellow merchants did. When the going was hard, and the future looked dismal, they pulled up and went where the going seemed easier.

Mark well this difference between Marshall Field and the other merchants, because it is the same difference which distinguishes Edwin C. Barnes from thousands of other young men who have worked in the Edison organization. It is the same difference which distinguishes practically all who succeed from those who fail.

Every human being who reaches the age of understanding of the purpose of money wishes for it. *Wishing* will not bring riches. But *desiring* riches with a state of mind that becomes an obsession, then planning definite ways and means to acquire riches, and backing those plans with persistence which *does not recognize failure,* will bring riches.

The method by which desire for riches can be transmuted into its financial equivalent consists of six definite, practical steps, viz:

> *No man is born into the world whose work is not born with him.*
> —James Russell Lowell

> Wishing *will not bring riches. But* desiring *riches with a state of mind that becomes an obsession, then planning definite ways and means to acquire riches, and backing those plans with persistence which* does not recognize *failure, will bring riches.*

FIRST. Fix in your mind the exact amount of money you desire. It is not sufficient merely to say, "I want plenty of money." Be definite as to the amount. (There is a psychological reason for definiteness which will be described in a subsequent chapter.)

SECOND. Determine exactly what you intend to give in return for the money you desire. (There is no such reality as "something for nothing.")

THIRD. Establish a definite date when you intend to *possess* the money you desire.

FOURTH. Create a definite plan for carrying out your desire, and begin *at once,* whether you are ready or not, to put this plan into *action.*

FIFTH. Write out a clear, concise statement of the amount of money you intend to acquire, name the time limit for its acquisition, state what you intend to give in return for the money, and describe clearly the plan through which you intend to accumulate it.

SIXTH. Read your written statement aloud, twice daily, once just before retiring at night, and once after arising in the morning. As you read—see and feel and believe yourself already in possession of the money.

It is important that you follow the instructions described in these six steps. It is especially important that you observe and follow the instructions in the sixth paragraph. You may complain that it is impossible for you to "see yourself in possession of money" before you actually have it. Here is where a burning desire will come to your aid. If you truly desire money so keenly that your desire is an obsession, you will have no difficulty in convincing yourself that you will acquire it. The object is to want money, and to become so determined to have it that you convince yourself you will have it.

Only those who become "money conscious" ever accumulate great riches. "Money consciousness" means that the mind has become so thoroughly satu-

You may complain that it is impossible for
you to "see yourself in possession of money"
before you actually have it. Here is where a
burning desire will come to your aid.

rated with the desire for money, that one can see one's self already in possession of it.

To the uninitiated, who has not been schooled in the working principles of the human mind, these instructions may appear impractical. It may be helpful, to all who fail to recognize the soundness of the six steps, to know that the information they convey was received from Andrew Carnegie, who began as an ordinary laborer in the steel mills, but managed, despite his humble beginning, to make these principles yield him a fortune of considerably more than $100 million dollars.

It may be of further help to know that the six steps here recommended were carefully scrutinized by the late Thomas A. Edison, who placed his stamp of approval upon them as being not only the steps essential for the accumulation of money, but necessary for the attainment of *any definite goal*.

The steps call for no "hard labor." They call for no sacrifice. They do not require one to become ridiculous, or credulous. To apply them calls for no great amount of education. But the successful application of these six steps does call for sufficient *imagination* to enable one to see, and to understand, that accumulation of money cannot be left to chance, good fortune, and luck. One must realize that all who have accumulated great fortunes first did a certain amount of dreaming, hoping, wishing, desiring, and planning *before* they acquired money.

You may as well know, right here, that you can never have riches in great quantities, unless you can work yourself into a white heat of desire for money, and actually believe you will possess it.

You may as well know, also, that every great leader, from the dawn of civilization down to the present, was a dreamer. Christianity is the greatest potential power in the world today, because its founder was an intense dreamer who had the vision and the imagination to see realities in their mental and spiritual form before they had been transmuted into physical form.

If you do not see great riches in your imagination, you will never see them in your bank balance.

Never in the history of America has there been so great an opportunity for practical dreamers as now exists. The six-year economic collapse has reduced all men, substantially, to the same level. A new race is about to be run. The

Perhaps the most valuable result of all education is the ability to make yourself do the thing you have to do, when it ought to be done, whether you like it or not. It is the first lesson that ought to be learned.

—Thomas Henry Huxley

If you truly desire money so keenly that your desire is an obsession, you will have no difficulty in convincing yourself that you will acquire it. The object is to want money, and to become so determined to have it that you convince yourself you will have it.

The halfhearted in any field accomplish little. Those whose enthusiasm wanes soon adjust again to their own complaints.

—Raymond Charles Barker

stakes represent huge fortunes which will be accumulated within the next ten years. The rules of the race have changed, because we now live in a changed world that definitely favors the masses, those who had but little or no opportunity to win under the conditions existing during the depression, when fear paralyzed growth and development.

We who are in this race for riches should be encouraged to know that this changed world in which we live is demanding new ideas, new ways of doing things, new leaders, new inventions, new methods of teaching, new methods of marketing, new books, new literature, new features for the radio, new ideas for moving pictures. Back of all this demand for new and better things, there is one quality which one must possess to win, and that is definiteness of purpose, the knowledge of what one wants, and a burning desire to possess it.

The business depression marked the death of one age, and the birth of another. This changed world requires practical dreamers who can *and will* put their dreams into action. The practical dreamers have always been and always will be the pattern-makers of civilization.

We who desire to accumulate riches should remember the real leaders of the world always have been men who harnessed, and put into practical use, the intangible, unseen forces of unborn opportunity, and have converted those forces (or impulses of thought), into skyscrapers, cities, factories, airplanes, automobiles, and every form of convenience that makes life more pleasant.

Tolerance and an open mind are practical necessities of the dreamer of today. Those who are afraid of new ideas are doomed before they start. Never has there been a time more favorable to pioneers than the present. True, there is no wild and woolly West to be conquered, as in the days of the Covered Wagon; but there is a vast business, financial, and industrial world to be remolded and redirected along new and better lines.

In planning to acquire your share of the riches, let no one influence you to scorn the dreamer. To win the big stakes in this changed world, you must catch the spirit of the great pioneers of the past, whose dreams have given to civilization all that it has of value, the spirit which serves as the life-blood of our own country—your opportunity, and mine, to develop and market our talents.

The steps call for no "hard labor." They call for no sacrifice. They do not require one to become ridiculous, or credulous. To apply them calls for no great amount of education.

Let us not forget, Columbus dreamed of an Unknown world, staked his life on the existence of such a world, and discovered it!

Copernicus, the great astronomer, dreamed of a multiplicity of worlds, and revealed them! No one denounced him as "impractical" *after* he had triumphed. Instead, the world worshipped at his shrine, thus proving once more that "success requires no apologies, failure permits no alibis."

If the thing you wish to do is right, and *you believe in it,* go ahead and do it! Put your dream across, and never mind what "they" say if you meet with temporary defeat, for "they," perhaps, do not know that every failure brings with it the seed of an equivalent success.

Henry Ford, poor and uneducated, dreamed of a horseless carriage, went to work with what tools he possessed, without waiting for opportunity to favor him, and now evidence of his dream belts the entire earth. He has put more wheels into operation than any man who ever lived, because he was not afraid to back his dreams.

Thomas Edison dreamed of a lamp that could be operated by electricity, began where he stood to put his dream into action, and despite more than *ten thousand failures,* he stood by that dream until he made it a physical reality. Practical dreamers do not quit!

Whelan dreamed of a chain of cigar stores, transformed his dream into action, and now the United Cigar Stores occupy the best corners in America.

Lincoln dreamed of freedom for the black slaves, put his dream into action, and barely missed living to see a united North and South translate his dream into reality.

The Wright brothers dreamed of a machine that would fly through the air. Now one may see evidence all over the world that they dreamed soundly.

Marconi dreamed of a system for harnessing the intangible forces of the ether. Evidence that he did not dream in vain may be found in every wireless and radio in the world. Moreover, Marconi's dream brought the humblest cabin and the most stately manor house side by side. It made the people of every nation on earth back-door neighbors. It gave the President of the United States a medium by which he may talk to all the people of America at one time, and on short notice. It may interest you to know that Marconi's "friends" had him

Today is a new day. You will get out of it just what you put into it. If you have made mistakes, even serious mistakes, there is always another chance for you. And supposing you have tried and failed again and again, you may have a fresh start any moment you choose, for this thing that we call "failure" is not the falling down, but the staying down.

—Mary Pickford

The successful application of these six steps does call for sufficient imagination to enable one to see, and to understand, that accumulation of money cannot be left to chance, good fortune, and luck.

taken into custody, and examined in a psychopathic hospital, when he announced he had discovered a principle through which he could send messages through the air, without the aid of wires, or other direct physical means of communication. The dreamers of today fare better.

The world has become accustomed to new discoveries. Nay, it has shown a willingness to reward the dreamer who gives the world a new idea.

"The greatest achievement was, at first, and for a time, but a dream."

"The oak sleeps in the acorn. The bird waits in the egg, and in the highest vision of the soul, a waking angel stirs. Dreams are the seedlings of reality."

Awake, arise, and assert yourself, you dreamers of the world. Your star is now in the ascendency. The world depression brought the opportunity you have been waiting for. It taught people humility, tolerance, and openmindedness.

The world is filled with an abundance of opportunity which the dreamers of the past never knew.

A burning desire to be and to do is the starting point from which the dreamer must take off. Dreams are not born of indifference, laziness, or lack of ambition.

The world no longer scoffs at the dreamer, nor calls him impractical. If you think it does, take a trip to Tennessee, and witness what a dreamer President has done in the way of harnessing and using the great water power of America. A score of years ago, such a dream would have seemed like madness.

You have been disappointed, you have undergone defeat during the depression, you have felt the great heart within you crushed until it bled. Take courage, for these experiences have tempered the spiritual metal of which you are made—they are assets of incomparable value.

Remember, too, that all who succeed in life get off to a bad start, and pass through many heartbreaking struggles before they "arrive." The turning point in the lives of those who succeed usually comes at the moment of some crisis, through which they are introduced to their "other selves."

John Bunyan wrote *The Pilgrim's Progress,* which is among the finest of all English literature, after he had been confined in prison and sorely punished, because of his views on the subject of religion.

O. Henry discovered the genius which slept within his brain after he had met with great misfortune, and was confined in a prison cell, in Columbus, Ohio. Being forced, through misfortune, to become acquainted with his "other self,"

There is nothing wrong in wanting to get rich. The desire for riches is really the desire for a richer, fuller, and more abundant life; and that desire is praiseworthy.

—Wallace D. Wattles

One must realize that all who have accumulated great fortunes first did a certain amount of dreaming, hoping, wishing, desiring, and planning before they acquired money.

and to use his imagination, he discovered himself to be a great author instead of a miserable criminal and outcast. Strange and varied are the ways of life, and stranger still are the ways of Infinite Intelligence, through which men are sometimes forced to undergo all sorts of punishment before discovering their own brains, and their own capacity to create useful ideas through imagination.

Edison, the world's greatest inventor and scientist, was a "tramp" telegraph operator; he failed innumerable times before he was driven, finally, to the discovery of the genius which slept within his brain.

Charles Dickens began by pasting labels on blacking pots. The tragedy of his first love penetrated the depths of his soul, and converted him into one of the world's truly great authors. That tragedy produced, first, *David Copperfield,* then a succession of other works that made this a richer and better world for all who read his books. Disappointment over love affairs generally has the effect of driving men to drink, and women to ruin; and this, because most people never learn the art of transmuting their strongest emotions into dreams of a constructive nature.

Helen Keller became deaf, dumb, and blind shortly after birth. Despite her greatest misfortune, she has written her name indelibly in the pages of the history of the great. Her entire life has served as evidence that *no one ever is defeated until defeat has been accepted as a reality.*

Robert Burns was an illiterate country lad; he was cursed by poverty, and grew up to be a drunkard in the bargain. The world was made better for his having lived, because he clothed beautiful thoughts in poetry, and thereby plucked a thorn and planted a rose in its place.

Booker T. Washington was born in slavery, handicapped by race and color. Because he was tolerant, had an open mind at all times, on all subjects, and was a dreamer, he left his impress for good on an entire race.

Beethoven was deaf, Milton was blind, but their names will last as long as time endures, because they dreamed and translated their dreams into organized thought.

Before passing to the next chapter, kindle anew in your mind the fire of hope, faith, courage, and tolerance. If you have these states of mind, and a working knowledge of the principles described, all else that you need will come to you, when you are ready for it. Let Emerson state the thought in these words: "Every

It's the man who waits for his ship to come in who's always missing the boat.

—Anonymous

You may as well know . . . that every great leader, from the dawn of civilization down to the present, was a dreamer.

proverb, every book, every byword that belongs to thee for aid and comfort shall surely come home through open or winding passages. Every friend whom not thy fantastic will, but the great and tender soul in thee craveth, shall lock thee in his embrace."

There is a difference between wishing for a thing and being ready to receive it. No one is *ready* for a thing until he *believes* he can acquire it. The state of mind must be belief, not mere hope or wish. Open-mindedness is essential for belief. Closed minds do not inspire faith, courage, and belief.

Remember, no more effort is required to aim high in life, to demand abundance and prosperity, than is required to accept misery and poverty. A great poet has correctly stated this universal truth through these lines:

> *I bargained with Life for a penny,*
> *And Life would pay no more,*
> *However I begged at evening*
> *When I counted my scanty store.*
>
> *For Life is a just employer,*
> *He gives you what you ask,*
> *But once you have set the wages,*
> *Why, you must bear the task.*
>
> *I worked for a menial's hire,*
> *Only to learn, dismayed,*
> *That any wage I had asked of Life,*
> *Life would have willingly paid.*

DESIRE OUTWITS MOTHER NATURE

As a fitting climax to this chapter, I wish to introduce one of the most unusual persons I have ever known. I first saw him twenty-four years ago, a few minutes after he was born. He came into the world without any physical sign of ears,

Desire is the key to motivation, but it's the determination and commitment to an unrelenting pursuit of your goal—a commitment to excellence—that will enable you to attain the success you seek.
—Mario Andretti

If you do not see great riches in your imagination, you will never see them in your bank balance.

and the doctor admitted, when pressed for an opinion, that the child might be deaf, and mute for life.

I challenged the doctor's opinion. I had the right to do so; I was the child's father. I, too, reached a decision, and rendered an opinion, but I expressed the opinion silently, in the secrecy of my own heart. I decided that my son would hear and speak. Nature could send me a child without ears, but Nature *could not induce me to accept* the reality of the affliction.

In my own mind I knew that my son would hear and speak. How? I was sure there must be a way, and I knew I would find it. I thought of the words of the immortal Emerson: "The whole course of things goes to teach us faith. We need only obey. There is guidance for each of us, and by lowly listening, we shall hear *the right word.*"

The right word? Desire! More than anything else, I desired that my son should not be a deaf mute. From that desire I never receded, not for a second.

Many years previously, I had written, "Our only limitations are those we set up in our own minds." For the first time, I wondered if that statement were true. Lying on the bed in front of me was a newly born child, without the natural equipment of hearing. Even though he might hear and speak, he was obviously disfigured for life. Surely, this was a limitation which that child had not set up in his own mind.

What could I do about it? Somehow I would find a way to transplant into that child's mind my own burning desire for ways and means of conveying sound to his brain without the aid of ears.

As soon as the child was old enough to cooperate, I would fill his mind so completely with a burning desire to hear, that Nature would, by methods of her own, translate it into physical reality.

All this thinking took place in my own mind, but I spoke of it to no one. Every day I renewed the pledge I had made to myself, not to accept a deaf mute for a son.

As he grew older, and began to take notice of things around him, we observed that he had a slight degree of hearing. When he reached the age when children usually begin talking, he made no attempt to speak, but we could tell by his actions that he could hear certain sounds slightly. That was all I wanted

You will become as great as your dominant aspiration. If you cherish a vision, a lofty ideal in you heart, you will realize it.

—James Allen

If the thing you wish to do is right, and you believe in it, *go ahead and do it!*

to know! I was convinced that if he could hear, even slightly, he might develop still greater hearing capacity. Then something happened which gave me hope. It came from an entirely unexpected source.

We bought a Victrola. When the child heard the music for the first time, he went into ecstasies, and promptly appropriated the machine. He soon showed a preference for certain records, among them, "It's a Long Way to Tipperary." On one occasion, he played that piece over and over, for almost two hours, standing in front of the Victrola, *with his teeth clamped on the edge of the case.* The significance of this self-formed habit of his did not become clear to us until years afterward, for we had never heard of the principle of "bone conduction" of sound at that time.

Shortly after he appropriated the Victrola, I discovered that he could hear me quite clearly when I spoke with my lips touching his mastoid bone, or at the base of the brain. These discoveries placed in my possession the necessary media by which I began to translate into reality my *Burning Desire* to help my son develop hearing and speech. By that time he was making stabs at speaking certain words. The outlook was far from encouraging, but desire backed by faith knows no such word as impossible.

Having determined that he could hear the sound of my voice plainly, I began, immediately, to transfer to his mind the desire to hear and speak. I soon discovered that the child enjoyed bedtime stories, so I went to work, creating stories designed to develop in him self-reliance, imagination, and a *keen desire to hear and to be normal.*

There was one story in particular which I emphasized by giving it some new and dramatic coloring each time it was told. It was designed to plant in his mind the thought that his affliction was not a liability, but an asset of great value. Despite the fact that all the philosophy I had examined clearly indicated that every adversity brings with it the seed of an equivalent advantage, I must confess that I had not the slightest idea *how* this affliction could ever become an asset. However, I continued my practice of wrapping that philosophy in bedtime stories, hoping the time would come when he would find some plan by which his handicap could be made to serve some useful purpose.

Reason told me plainly that there was no adequate compensation for the lack

Old ideas will not create new conditions.

—Raymond Charles Barker

Awake, arise, and assert yourself, you dreamers of the world. Your star is now in the ascendency. . . . The world is filled with an abundance of opportunity which the dreamers of the past never knew.

of ears and natural hearing equipment. Desire backed by faith pushed reason aside, and inspired me to carry on.

As I analyze the experience in retrospect, I can see now that my *son's faith in me* had much to do with the astounding results. He did not question anything I told him. I sold him the idea that he had a distinct *advantage* over his older brother, and that this advantage would reflect itself in many ways. For example, the teachers in school would observe that he had no ears, and, because of this, they would show him special attention and treat him with extraordinary kindness. They always did. His mother saw to that, by visiting the teachers and arranging with them to give the child the extra attention necessary. I sold him the idea, too, that when he became old enough to sell newspapers (his older brother had already become a newspaper merchant), he would have a big advantage over his brother, for the reason that people would pay him extra money for his wares, because they could see that he was a bright, industrious boy, despite the fact he had no ears.

We could notice that, gradually, the child's hearing was improving. Moreover, he had not the slightest tendency to be self-conscious because of his affliction. When he was about seven, he showed the first evidence that our method of servicing his mind was bearing fruit. For several months he begged for the privilege of selling newspapers, but his mother would not give her consent. She was afraid that his deafness made it unsafe for him to go on the street alone.

Finally, he took matters in his own hands. One afternoon, when he was left at home with the servants, he climbed through the kitchen window, shinnied to the ground, and set out on his own. He borrowed six cents in capital from the neighborhood shoemaker, invested it in papers, sold out, reinvested, and kept repeating until late in the evening. After balancing his accounts, and paying back the six cents he had borrowed from his banker, he had a net profit of forty-two cents. When we got home that night, we found him in bed asleep, with the money tightly clenched in his hand.

His mother opened his hand, removed the coins, and cried. Of all things! Crying over her son's first victory seemed so inappropriate. My reaction was the reverse. I laughed heartily, for I knew that my endeavor to plant in the child's mind an attitude of faith in himself had been successful.

That clear mental picture you must have continually in mind, as the sailor has in mind the port toward which he is sailing the ship; you must keep your face toward it all the time. You must no more lose sight of it than the steersman loses sight of the compass.

—Wallace D. Wattles

You have been disappointed, you have undergone defeat . . . you have felt the great heart within you crushed until it bled. Take courage, for these experiences have tempered the spiritual metal of which you are made— they are assets of incomparable value.

Everything in our lives is either a blessing, or a blessing in disguise.

—Joel Fotinos

His mother saw, in his first business venture, a little deaf boy who had gone out in the streets and risked his life to earn money. I saw a brave, ambitious, self-reliant little business man whose stock in himself had been increased a hundred percent, because he had gone into business on his own initiative, and had won. The transaction pleased me, because I knew that he had given evidence of a trait of resourcefulness that would go with him all through life. Later events proved this to be true. When his older brother wanted something, he would lie down on the floor, kick his feet in the air, cry for it—and get it. When the "little deaf boy" wanted something, he would plan a way to earn the money, then buy it for himself. He still follows that plan!

Truly, my own son has taught me that handicaps can be converted into stepping stones on which one may climb toward some worthy goal, unless they are accepted as obstacles, and used as alibis.

The little deaf boy went through the grades, high school, and college without being able to hear his teachers, excepting when they shouted loudly, at close range. He did not go to a school for the deaf. We would not permit him to learn the sign language. We were determined that he should live a normal life, and associate with normal children, and we stood by that decision, although it cost us many heated debates with school officials.

While he was in high school, he tried an electrical hearing aid, but it was of no value to him; due, we believed, to a condition that was disclosed when the child was six, by Dr. J. Gordon Wilson, of Chicago, when he operated on one side of the boy's head, and discovered that there was no sign of natural hearing equipment.

During his last week in college (eighteen years after the operation), something happened which marked the most important turning-point of his life. Through what seemed to be mere chance, he came into possession of another electrical hearing device, which was sent to him on trial. He was slow about testing it, due to his disappointment with a similar device. Finally he picked the instrument up, and more or less carelessly, placed it on his head, hooked up the battery, and lo! as if by a stroke of magic, his lifelong desire for normal hearing became a reality! For the first time in his life he heard practically as well as any person with normal hearing. "God moves in mysterious ways, His wonders to perform."

Overjoyed because of the Changed World which had been brought to him

Remember . . . that all who succeed in life get off to a bad start, and pass through many heartbreaking struggles before they "arrive."

through his hearing device, he rushed to the telephone, called his mother, and heard her voice perfectly. The next day he plainly heard the voices of his professors in class, for the first time in his life! Previously he could hear them only when they shouted, at short range. He heard the radio. He *heard* the talking pictures. For the first time in his life, he could converse freely with other people, without the necessity of their having to speak loudly. Truly, he had come into possession of a Changed World. We had refused to accept Nature's error, and, by persistent desire, we had induced Nature to correct that error, through the only practical means available.

Desire had commenced to pay dividends, but the victory was not yet complete. The boy still had to find a definite and practical way to convert his handicap into an *equivalent asset.*

Hardly realizing the significance of what had already been accomplished, but intoxicated with the joy of his newly discovered world of sound, he wrote a letter to the manufacturer of the hearing aid, enthusiastically describing his experience. Something in his letter; something, perhaps which was not written on the lines, but back of them; caused the company to invite him to New York. When he arrived, he was escorted through the factory, and while talking with the Chief Engineer, telling him about his Changed World, a hunch, an idea, or an inspiration—call it what you wish—flashed into his mind. It was *this impulse of thought* which converted his affliction into an asset, destined to pay dividends in both money and happiness to thousands for all time to come.

The sum and substance of that impulse of thought was this: It occurred to him that he might be of help to the millions of deafened people who go through life without the benefit of hearing devices, if he could find a way to tell them the story of his Changed World. Then and there, he reached a decision to devote the remainder of his life to rendering useful service to the hard of hearing.

For an entire month, he carried on an intensive research, during which he analyzed the entire marketing system of the manufacturer of the hearing device, and created ways and means of communicating with the hard of hearing all over the world for the purpose of sharing with them his newly discovered Changed World. When this was done, he put in writing a two-year plan, based upon his findings. When he presented the plan to the company, he was instantly given a position, for the purpose of carrying out his ambition.

If one advances confidently in the direction of his dreams, and endeavors to live the life which he has imagined, he will meet with success unexpected in common hours.

—Henry David Thoreau

The turning point in the lives of those who succeed usually comes at the moment of some crisis, through which they are introduced to their "other selves."

Little did he dream, when he went to work, that he was destined to bring hope and practical relief to thousands of deafened people who, without his help, would have been doomed forever to deaf mutism.

Shortly after he became associated with the manufacturer of his hearing aid, he invited me to attend a class conducted by his company, for the purpose of teaching deaf mutes to hear, and to speak. I had never heard of such a form of education, therefore I visited the class, skeptical but hopeful that my time would not be entirely wasted. Here I saw a demonstration which gave me a greatly enlarged vision of what I had done to arouse and keep alive in my son's mind the desire for normal hearing. I saw deaf mutes actually being taught to hear and to speak, through application of the self-same principle I had used, more than twenty years previously, in saving my son from deaf mutism.

Thus, through some strange turn of the Wheel of Fate, my son Blair and I have been destined to aid in correcting deaf mutism for those as yet unborn, because we are the only living human beings, as far as I know, who have established definitely the fact that deaf mutism can be corrected to the extent of restoring to normal life those who suffer with this affliction. It has been done for one; it will be done for others.

There is no doubt in my mind that Blair would have been a deaf mute all his life, if his mother and I had not managed to shape his mind as we did. The doctor who attended at his birth told us, confidentially, the child might never hear or speak. A few weeks ago, Dr. Irving Voorhees, a noted specialist on such cases, examined Blair very thoroughly. He was astounded when he learned how well my son now hears, and speaks, and said his examination indicated that "theoretically, the boy should not be able to hear at all." But the lad does hear, despite the fact that X-ray pictures show there is no opening in the skull, whatsoever, from where his ears should be to the brain.

When I planted in his mind the desire to hear and talk, and live as a normal person, there went with that impulse some strange influence which caused Nature to become bridge-builder, and span the gulf of silence between his brain and the outer world, by some means which the keenest medical specialists have not been able to interpret. It would be sacrilege for me to even conjecture as to how Nature performed this miracle. It would be unforgivable if I neglected to tell the world as much as I know of the humble part I assumed in

I can teach anybody how to get what they want out of life. The problem is that I can't find anybody who can tell me what they want.

—Mark Twain

There is a difference between wishing for a thing and being ready to receive it. No one is ready for a thing until he believes he can acquire it.

the strange experience. It is my duty, and a privilege to say I believe, and not without reason, that nothing is impossible to the person who backs desire with enduring faith.

Verily, a burning desire has devious ways of transmuting itself into its physical equivalent. Blair desired normal hearing; now he has it! He was born with a handicap which might easily have sent one with a less defined desire to the street with a bundle of pencils and a tin cup. That handicap now promises to serve as the medium by which he will render useful service to many millions of hard of hearing; also, to give him useful employment at adequate financial compensation the remainder of his life.

The little "white lie" I planted in his mind when he was a child, by leading him to believe his affliction would become a great asset, which he could capitalize, has justified itself. Verily, there is nothing, right or wrong, which belief, plus burning desire, cannot make real. These qualities are free to everyone.

In all my experience in dealing with men and women who had personal problems, I never handled a single case which more definitely demonstrates the power of desire. Authors sometimes make the mistake of writing of subjects of which they have but superficial, or very elementary, knowledge. It has been my good fortune to have had the privilege of testing the soundness of the power of desire, through the affliction of my own son. Perhaps it was providential that the experience came as it did, for surely no one is better prepared than he to serve as an example of what happens when desire is put to the test. *If Mother Nature bends to the will of desire, is it logical that mere men can defeat a burning desire?*

Strange and imponderable is the power of the human mind! We do not understand the method by which it uses every circumstance, every individual, every physical thing within its reach, as a means of transmuting desire into its physical counterpart. Perhaps science will uncover this secret.

I planted in my son's mind the desire to hear and to speak as any normal person hears and speaks. That desire has now become a reality. I planted in his mind the desire to convert his greatest handicap into his greatest asset. That desire has been realized. The modus operandi by which this astounding result was achieved is not hard to describe. It consisted of three very definite facts. First, I mixed faith with the desire for normal hearing, which I passed on to my son. Second, I communicated my desire to him in every conceivable way

Desires are not hopes nor are they dreams. They are potentials to be unearthed and brought to fruition.
—Raymond Charles Barker

The state of mind must be belief, not mere hope or wish. Open-mindedness is essential for belief. Closed minds do not inspire faith, courage, and belief.

available, through persistent, continuous effort, over a period of years. Third, he believed me!

As this chapter was being completed, news came of the death of Mme. Schuman-Heink. One short paragraph in the news dispatch gives the clue to this unusual woman's stupendous success as a singer. I quote the paragraph, because the clue it contains is none other than desire.

Early in her career, Mme. Schuman-Heink visited the director of the Vienna Court Opera, to have him test her voice. But, he did not test it. After taking one look at the awkward and poorly dressed girl, he exclaimed, none too gently: "With such a face, and with no personality at all, how can you ever expect to succeed in opera? My good child, give up the idea. Buy a sewing machine, and go to work. You can never be a singer."

Never is a long time! The director of the Vienna Court Opera knew much about the technique of singing. He knew little about the power of desire, when it assumes the proportion of an obsession. If he had known more of that power, he would not have made the mistake of condemning genius without giving it an opportunity.

Several years ago, one of my business associates became ill. He became worse as time went on, and finally was taken to the hospital for an operation. Just before he was wheeled into the operating room, I took a look at him, and wondered how anyone as thin and emaciated as he could possibly go through a major operation successfully. The doctor warned me that there was little if any chance of my ever seeing him alive again. But that was the doctor's opinion. It was not the opinion of the patient. Just before he was wheeled away, he whispered feebly, "Do not be disturbed, Chief. I will be out of here in a few days." The attending nurse looked at me with pity. But the patient did come through safely. After it was all over, his physician said, "Nothing but his own desire to live saved him. He never would have pulled through if he had not refused to accept the possibility of death."

I believe in the power of desire backed by faith, because I have seen this power lift men from lowly beginnings to places of power and wealth; I have seen it rob the grave of its victims; I have seen it serve as the medium by which men staged a comeback after having been defeated in a hundred different ways;

Do not wait for a change in environment before you act; get a change of environment by action.
—Wallace D. Wattles

Remember, no more effort is required to aim high in life, to demand abundance and prosperity, than is required to accept misery and poverty.

I have seen it provide my own son with a normal, happy, successful life, despite Nature's having sent him into the world without ears.

How can one harness and use the power of desire? This has been answered through this and the subsequent chapters of this book. This message is going out to the world at the end of the longest, and perhaps, the most devastating depression America has ever known. It is reasonable to presume that the message may come to the attention of many who have been wounded by the depression, those who have lost their fortunes, others who have lost their positions, and great numbers who must reorganize their plans and stage a comeback. To all these I wish to convey the thought that all achievement, no matter what may be its nature, or its purpose, must begin with an intense, burning desire for something definite.

Through some strange and powerful principle of "mental chemistry" which she has never divulged, Nature wraps up in the impulse of strong desire "that something" which recognizes no such word as impossible, and accepts no such reality as failure.

If you want to be happy, set a goal that commands your thoughts, liberates your energy, and inspires your hopes.

—Andrew Carnegie

I wish to convey the thought that all achievement, no matter what may be its nature, or its purpose, must begin with an intense, burning desire for something definite.

QUESTIONS FOR SUCCESS

- *What is the most helpful idea from this chapter for you?*

- *How can you apply the story of the burning ships (pages 38–39) to your life?*

- *Have you created your "Statement of Desire"? If not, please do so and record it on page 8.*

- *Does your "Statement of Desire" accurately reflect your burning desire?*

- *Napoleon Hill writes, "Remember, too, that all who succeed in life get off to a bad start, and pass through many heartbreaking struggles before they 'arrive.' The turning point in the lives of those who succeed usually comes at the moment of some crisis, through which they are introduced to their 'other selves.'" What is the turning point in your life?*

- *What does Napoleon Hill mean when he refers to "their 'other selves'"?*

- *What is the difference between "wishing for a thing" and "being ready to receive it"?*

- *Are you truly ready to receive what you desire?*

YOUR SUCCESS STEPS

☐ ....

☐ ....

☐ ....

☐ ....

☐ ....

☐ ....

CHAPTER 3

FAITH

Visualization of and Belief in
Attainment of Desire

The Second Step Toward Riches

Faith is the head chemist of the mind. When faith is blended with the vibration of thought, the subconscious mind instantly picks up the vibration, translates it into its spiritual equivalent, and transmits it to Infinite Intelligence, as in the case of prayer.

The emotions of faith, love, and sex are the most powerful of all the major positive emotions. When the three are blended, they have the effect of "coloring" the vibration of thought in such a way that it instantly reaches the subconscious mind, where it is changed into its spiritual equivalent, the only form that induces a response from Infinite Intelligence.

Love and faith are psychic, related to the spiritual side of man. Sex is purely biological, and related only to the physical. The mixing, or blending, of these three emotions has the effect of opening a direct line of communication between the finite, thinking mind of man, and Infinite Intelligence.

What lies behind us and what lies before us are small matters compared to what lies within us.
—Ralph Waldo Emerson

HOW TO DEVELOP FAITH

There comes, now, a statement which will give a better understanding of the importance the principle of auto-suggestion assumes in the transmutation of

Faith is a state of mind which may be induced, or created, by affirmation or repeated instructions to the subconscious mind, through the principle of auto-suggestion.

The key is to have a dream that inspires us to go beyond our limits.
—Robert Kriegel

desire into its physical, or monetary equivalent; namely, faith is a state of mind which may be induced, or created, by affirmation or repeated instructions to the subconscious mind, through the principle of auto-suggestion.

As an illustration, consider the purpose for which you are, presumably, reading this book. The object is, naturally, to acquire the ability to transmute the intangible thought impulse of desire into its physical counterpart, money. By following the instructions laid down in the chapters on auto-suggestion, and the subconscious mind, as summarized in the chapter on auto-suggestion, you may convince the subconscious mind that you *believe* you will receive that for which you ask, and it will act upon that belief, which your subconscious mind passes back to you in the form of "faith," followed by definite plans for procuring that which you desire.

The method by which one develops faith, where it does not already exist, is extremely difficult to describe, almost as difficult, in fact, as it would be to describe the color of red to a blind man who has never seen color, and has nothing with which to compare what you describe to him. Faith is a state of mind which you may develop at will, after you have mastered the thirteen principles, because it is a state of mind which develops voluntarily, through application and use of these principles.

Repetition of affirmation of orders to your subconscious mind is the only known method of voluntary development of the emotion of faith.

Perhaps the meaning may be made clearer through the following explanation as to the way men sometimes become criminals. Stated in the words of a famous criminologist, "When men first come into contact with crime, they abhor it. If they remain in contact with crime for a time, they become accustomed to it, and endure it. If they remain in contact with it long enough, they finally embrace it, and become influenced by it."

This is the equivalent of saying that any impulse of thought which is repeatedly passed on to the subconscious mind is, finally, accepted and acted upon by the subconscious mind, which proceeds to translate that impulse into its physical equivalent, by the most practical procedure available.

In connection with this, consider again the statement, all thoughts which have been emotionalized (given feeling) and mixed with faith begin immediately to translate themselves into their physical equivalent or counterpart.

Faith is a state of mind which you may develop at will, after you have mastered the thirteen principles, because it is a state of mind which develops voluntarily, through application and use of these principles.

The emotions, or the "feeling" portion of thoughts, are the factors which give thoughts vitality, life, and action. The emotions of faith, love, and sex, when mixed with any thought impulse, give it greater action than any of these emotions can do singly.

Not only thought impulses which have been mixed with faith, but those which have been mixed with any of the positive emotions, or any of the negative emotions, may reach and influence the subconscious mind.

From this statement, you will understand that the subconscious mind will translate into its physical equivalent a thought impulse of a negative or destructive nature, just as readily as it will act upon thought impulses of a positive or constructive nature. This accounts for the strange phenomenon which so many millions of people experience, referred to as "misfortune," or "bad luck."

There are millions of people who believe themselves "doomed" to poverty and failure, because of some strange force over which they believe they have no control. They are the creators of their own "misfortunes," because of this negative belief, which is picked up by the subconscious mind, and translated into its physical equivalent.

This is an appropriate place at which to suggest again that you may benefit by passing on to your subconscious mind any desire which you wish translated into its physical or monetary equivalent, in a state of expectancy or belief that the transmutation will actually take place. Your belief, or faith, is the element which determines the action of your subconscious mind. There is nothing to hinder you from "deceiving" your subconscious mind when giving it instructions through auto-suggestion, as I deceived my son's subconscious mind.

To make this "deceit" more realistic, conduct yourself just as you would if you were already in possession of the material thing which you are demanding when you call upon your subconscious mind.

The subconscious mind will transmute into its physical equivalent, by the most direct and practical media available, any order which is given to it in a state of belief, or faith that the order will be carried out.

Surely, enough has been stated to give a starting point from which one may, through experiment and practice, acquire the ability to mix faith with any order given to the subconscious mind. Perfection will come through practice. It *cannot* come by merely *reading* instructions.

The greatest danger for most of us is not that our aim is too high and we miss it, but that it is too low and we reach it.

—Michelangelo

Repetition of affirmation of orders to your subconscious mind is the only known method of voluntary development of the emotion of faith.

Most folks are about as happy as they make up their minds to be.
—Abraham Lincoln

If it be true that one may become a criminal by association with crime (and this is a known fact), it is equally true that one may develop faith by voluntarily suggesting to the subconscious mind that one has faith. The mind comes, finally, to take on the nature of the influences which dominate it. Understand this truth, and you will know why it is essential for you to encourage the *positive emotions* as dominating forces of your mind, and discourage—and *eliminate*—negative emotions.

A mind dominated by positive emotions becomes a favorable abode for the state of mind known as faith. A mind so dominated may, at will, give the subconscious mind instructions, which it will accept and act upon immediately.

FAITH IS A STATE OF MIND WHICH MAY BE INDUCED BY AUTO-SUGGESTION

All down the ages, the religionists have admonished struggling humanity to "have faith" in this, that, and the other dogma or creed, but they have failed to tell people how to have faith. They have not stated that "faith is a state of mind, and that it may be induced by self-suggestion."

In language which any normal human being can understand, we will describe all that is known about the principle through which faith may be developed, where it does not already exist.

Have faith in yourself; faith in the Infinite.

Before we begin, you should be reminded again that:

Faith is the "eternal elixir" which gives life, power, and action to the impulse of thought!

The foregoing sentence is worth reading a second time, and a third, and a fourth. It is worth reading aloud!

Faith is the starting point of all accumulation of riches!

Faith is the basis of all "miracles," and all mysteries which cannot be analyzed by the rules of science!

Faith is the only known antidote for failure!

Faith is the element, the "chemical" which, when mixed with prayer, gives one direct communication with Infinite Intelligence.

The subconscious mind will translate into its physical equivalent a thought impulse of a negative or destructive nature, just as readily as it will act upon thought impulses of a positive or constructive nature.

Faith is the element which transforms the ordinary vibration of thought, created by the finite mind of man, into the spiritual equivalent.

Faith is the only agency through which the cosmic force of Infinite Intelligence can be harnessed and used by man.

Every one of the foregoing statements is capable of proof!

The proof is simple and easily demonstrated. It is wrapped up in the principle of auto-suggestion. Let us center our attention, therefore, upon the subject of self-suggestion, and find out what it is, and what it is capable of achieving.

It is a well-known fact that one comes, finally, to believe whatever one repeats to one's self, *whether the statement be true or false.* If a man repeats a lie over and over, he will eventually accept the lie as truth. Moreover, he will believe it to be the truth. Every man is what he is because of the dominating thoughts which he permits to occupy his mind. Thoughts which a man deliberately places in his own mind, and encourages with sympathy, and with which he mixes any one or more of the emotions, constitute the motivating forces which direct and control his every movement, act, and deed!

Comes, now, a very significant statement of truth:

Thoughts which are mixed with any of the feelings of emotions constitute a "magnetic" force which attracts, from the vibrations of the ether, other similar or related thoughts. A thought thus "magnetized" with emotion may be compared to a seed which, when planted in fertile soil, germinates, grows, and multiplies itself over and over again, until that which was originally one small seed becomes countless millions of seeds of the same brand!

The ether is a great cosmic mass of eternal forces of vibration. It is made up of both destructive vibrations and constructive vibrations. It carries, at all times, vibrations of fear, poverty, disease, failure, misery; and vibrations of prosperity, health, success, and happiness, just as surely as it carries the sound of hundreds of orchestrations of music, and hundreds of human voices, all of which maintain their own individuality, and means of identification, through the medium of radio.

From the great storehouse of the ether, the human mind is constantly attracting vibrations which harmonize with that which dominates the human mind. Any thought, idea, plan, or purpose which one *holds* in one's mind attracts, from the vibrations of the ether, a host of its relatives, adds these "relatives" to its own

Better keep yourself clean and bright; you are the window through which you must see the world.

—George Bernard Shaw

There are millions of people who believe themselves "doomed" to poverty and failure, because of some strange force over which they believe they have no control.

The average person lets his mind run riot and then complains bitterly about his difficulties. Tell him that he needs new ideas and to think differently than he has been thinking and he will laugh at you. The truth is that you can direct your mind and change any situation for the better. This includes your happiness. I am not saying that thinking is happiness. I am saying that thinking, based on exciting new ideas, is the cause of happiness.

—Raymond Charles Barker

force, and grows until it becomes the dominating, motivating master of the individual in whose mind it has been housed.

Now, let us go back to the starting point, and become informed as to how the original seed of an idea, plan, or purpose may be planted in the mind. The information is easily conveyed: any idea, plan, or purpose may be placed in the mind *through repetition of thought*. This is why you are asked to write out a statement of your major purpose, or Definite Chief Aim, commit it to memory, and repeat it, in audible words, day after day, until these vibrations of sound have reached your subconscious mind.

We are what we are because of the vibrations of thought which we pick up and register, through the stimuli of our daily environment.

Resolve to throw off the influences of any unfortunate environment, and to build your own life to order. Taking inventory of mental assets and liabilities, you will discover that your greatest weakness is lack of self-confidence. This handicap can be surmounted, and timidity translated into courage, through the aid of the principle of auto-suggestion. The application of this principle may be made through a simple arrangement of positive thought impulses stated in writing, memorized, and repeated, until they become a part of the working equipment of the subconscious faculty of your mind.

SELF-CONFIDENCE FORMULA

FIRST. I know that I have the ability to achieve the object of my Definite Purpose in life, therefore, I demand of myself persistent, continuous action toward its attainment, and I here and now promise to render such action.

SECOND. I realize the dominating thoughts of my mind will eventually reproduce themselves in outward, physical action, and gradually transform themselves into physical reality; therefore, I will concentrate my thoughts for thirty minutes daily upon the task of thinking of the person I intend to become, thereby creating in my mind a clear mental picture of that person.

THIRD. I know through the principle of auto-suggestion any desire that I persistently hold in my mind will eventually seek expression through

They are the creators of their own "misfortunes," because of this negative belief, which is picked up by the subconscious mind, and translated into its physical equivalent.

some practical means of attaining the object back of it; therefore, I will devote ten minutes daily to demanding of myself the development of self-confidence.

FOURTH. I have clearly written down a description of my Definite Chief Aim in life, and I will never stop trying until I shall have developed sufficient self-confidence for its attainment.

FIFTH. I fully realize that no wealth or position can long endure unless built upon truth and justice; therefore, I will engage in no transaction which does not benefit all whom it affects. I will succeed by attracting to myself the forces I wish to use, and the cooperation of other people. I will induce others to serve me, because of my willingness to serve others. I will eliminate hatred, envy, jealousy, selfishness, and cynicism, by developing love for all humanity, because I know that a negative attitude toward others can never bring me success. I will cause others to believe in me, because I will believe in them, and in myself.

I will sign my name to this formula, commit it to memory, and repeat it aloud once a day, with full faith that it will gradually influence my thoughts and actions so that I will become a self-reliant and successful person.

Back of this formula is a law of Nature which no man has yet been able to explain. It has baffled the scientists of all ages. The psychologists have named this law "auto-suggestion," and let it go at that.

The name by which one calls this law is of little importance. The important fact about it is—it works for the glory and success of mankind, IF it is used constructively. On the other hand, if used destructively, it will destroy just as readily. In this statement may be found a very significant truth; namely, that those who go down in defeat, and end their lives in poverty, misery, and distress, do so because of negative application of the principle of auto-suggestion. The cause may be found in the fact that all impulses of thought have a tendency to clothe themselves in their physical equivalent.

The subconscious mind (the chemical laboratory in which all thought impulses

Things are not brought into being by thinking about their opposites.
—Wallace D. Wattles

Your belief, or faith, is the element which determines the action of your subconscious mind.

Take the first step in faith. You don't have to see the whole staircase. Just take the first step.

—Martin Luther King, Jr.

are combined, and made ready for translation into physical reality) makes no distinction between constructive and destructive thought impulses. It works with the material we feed it, through our thought impulses. The subconscious mind will translate into reality a thought driven by fear just as readily as it will translate into reality a thought driven by courage, or faith.

The pages of medical history are rich with illustrations of cases of "suggestive suicide." A man may commit suicide through negative suggestion, just as effectively as by any other means. In a Midwestern city, a man by the name of Joseph Grant, a bank official, "borrowed" a large sum of the bank's money, without the consent of the directors. He lost the money through gambling. One afternoon, the Bank Examiner came and began to check the accounts. Grant left the bank, took a room in a local hotel, and when they found him, three days later, he was lying in bed, wailing and moaning, repeating over and over these words, "My God, this will kill me! I cannot stand the disgrace." In a short time he was dead. The doctors pronounced the case one of "mental suicide."

Just as electricity will turn the wheels of industry, and render useful service if used constructively, or snuff out life if wrongly used, so will the law of auto-suggestion lead you to peace and prosperity, or down into the valley of misery, failure, and death, according to your degree of understanding and application of it.

If you fill your mind with fear, doubt, and unbelief in your ability to connect with and use the forces of Infinite Intelligence, the law of auto-suggestion will take this spirit of unbelief and use it as a pattern by which your subconscious mind will translate it into its physical equivalent.

This statement is as true as the statement that two and two are four!

Like the wind which carries one ship East, and another West, the law of auto-suggestion will lift you up or pull you down, according to the way you set your sails of thought.

The law of auto-suggestion, through which any person may rise to altitudes of achievement which stagger the imagination, is well described in the following verse:

> *If you* think *you are beaten, you are,*
> *If you* think *you dare not, you don't,*

The subconscious mind will transmute into its physical equivalent, by the most direct and practical media available, any order which is given to it in a state of belief, or faith that the order will be carried out.

If you like to win, but you think you can't,
It is almost certain you won't.

If you think you'll lose, you're lost,
For out of the world we find,
Success begins with a fellow's will—
It's all in the state of mind.

If you think you are outclassed, you are,
You've got to think high to rise,
You've got to be sure of yourself before
You can ever win a prize.

Life's battles don't always go
To the stronger or faster man,
But soon or late the man who wins
Is the man WHO THINKS HE CAN!

> *Faith can move mountains. Doubt can create them.*
>
> —Howard Wight

Observe the words which have been emphasized, and you will catch the deep meaning which the poet had in mind.

Somewhere in your make-up (perhaps in the cells of your brain) there lies *sleeping* the seed of achievement which, if aroused and put into action, would carry you to heights such as you may never have hoped to attain.

Just as a master musician may cause the most beautiful strains of music to pour forth from the strings of a violin, so may you arouse the genius which lies asleep in your brain, and cause it to drive you upward to whatever goal you may wish to achieve.

Abraham Lincoln was a failure at everything he tried, until he was well past the age of forty. He was a Mr. Nobody from Nowhere, until a great experience came into his life, aroused the sleeping genius within his heart and brain, and gave the world one of its really great men. That "experience" was mixed with the emotions of sorrow and love. It came to him through Anne Rutledge, the only woman whom he ever truly loved.

It is a known fact that the emotion of love is closely akin to the state of mind

Perfection will come through practice. It cannot come by merely reading instructions.

known as faith, and this for the reason that love comes very near to translating one's thought impulses into their spiritual equivalent. During his work of research, the author discovered, from the analysis of the lifework and achievements of hundreds of men of outstanding accomplishment, that there was the influence of a woman's love back of nearly every one of them. The emotion of love, in the human heart and brain, creates a favorable field of magnetic attraction, which causes an influx of the higher and finer vibrations which are afloat in the ether.

If you wish evidence of the power of faith, study the achievements of men and women who have employed it. At the head of the list comes the Nazarene. Christianity is the greatest single force which influences the minds of men. The basis of Christianity is faith, no matter how many people may have perverted or misinterpreted the meaning of this great force, and no matter how many dogmas and creeds have been created in its name, which do not reflect its tenets.

The sum and substance of the teachings and the achievements of Christ, which may have been interpreted as "miracles," were nothing more nor less than faith. If there are any such phenomena as "miracles" they are produced only through the state of mind known as faith! Some teachers of religion, and many who call themselves Christians, neither understand nor practice faith.

Let us consider the power of faith, as it is now being demonstrated, by a man who is well known to all of civilization, Mahatma Gandhi, of India. In this man the world has one of the most astounding examples known to civilization of the possibilities of faith. Gandhi wields more potential power than any man living at this time, and this, despite the fact that he has none of the orthodox tools of power, such as money, battle ships, soldiers, and materials of warfare. Gandhi has no money, he has no home, he does not own a suit of clothes, but he does have power. How does he come by that power?

He created it out of his understanding of the principle of faith, and through his ability to transplant that faith into the minds of two hundred million people.

Gandhi has accomplished, through the influence of faith, that which the strongest military power on earth could not, and never will accomplish through soldiers and military equipment. He has accomplished the astounding feat of influencing two hundred million minds to coalesce and move in unison, as a single mind.

What other force on earth, except faith, could do as much?

There will come a day when employees as well as employers will discover the possibilities of faith. That day is dawning. The whole world has had ample opportunity, during the recent business depression, to witness what the lack of faith will do to business.

Surely, civilization has produced a sufficient number of intelligent human beings to make use of this great lesson which the depression has taught the world. During this depression, the world had evidence in abundance that widespread fear will paralyze the wheels of industry and business. Out of this experience will arise leaders in business and industry who will profit by the example which Gandhi has set for the world, and they will apply to business the same tactics which he has used in building the greatest following known in the history of the world. These leaders will come from the rank and file of the unknown men, who now labor in the steel plants, the coal mines, the automobile factories, and in the small towns and cities of America.

Business is due for a reform, make no mistake about this! The methods of the past, based upon economic combinations of force and fear, will be supplanted by the better principles of faith and cooperation. Men who labor will receive more than daily wages; they will receive dividends from the business the same as those who supply the capital for business; but first they must give more to their employers, and stop this bickering and bargaining by force, at the expense of the public. *They must earn the right to dividends!*

Moreover, and this is the most important thing of all—they will be led by leaders who will understand and apply the principles employed by Mahatma Gandhi. Only in this way may leaders get from their followers the spirit of full cooperation which constitutes power in its highest and most enduring form.

This stupendous machine age in which we live, and from which we are just emerging, has taken the soul out of men. Its leaders have driven men as though they were pieces of cold machinery; they were forced to do so by the employees who have bargained, at the expense of all concerned, to *get* and not to *give*. The watchword of the future will be human happiness and contentment, and when this state of mind shall have been attained, the production will take care of itself, more effectively than anything that has ever been accomplished where men did not, and could not, mix faith and individual interest with their labor.

Everything can be taken from a man or a woman but one thing: the last of human freedoms—to choose one's attitude in any given set of circumstances, to choose one's own way.

—Viktor Frankl

Have faith in yourself; faith in the Infinite.

There is nothing either good or bad, but thinking makes it so.

—Shakespeare

Because of the need for faith and cooperation in operating business and industry, it will be both interesting and profitable to analyze an event which provides an excellent understanding of the method by which industrialists and business men accumulate great fortunes, by *giving* before they try to *get*.

The event chosen for this illustration dates back to 1900, when the United States Steel Corporation was being formed. As you read the story, keep in mind these fundamental facts and you will understand how ideas have been converted into huge fortunes.

First, the huge United States Steel Corporation was born in the mind of Charles M. Schwab, in the form of an idea he created through his imagination! Second, he mixed faith with his idea. Third, he formulated a plan for the transformation of his idea into physical and financial reality. Fourth, he put his plan into action with his famous speech at the University Club. Fifth, he applied, and followed through on his plan with persistence, and backed it with firm decision until it had been fully carried out. Sixth, he prepared the way for success by a burning desire for success.

If you are one of those who have often wondered how great fortunes are accumulated, this story of the creation of the United States Steel Corporation will be enlightening. If you have any doubt that men can think and grow rich, this story should dispel that doubt, because you can plainly see in the story of the United States Steel the application of a major portion of the thirteen principles described in this book.

This astounding description of the power of an idea was dramatically told by John Lowell, in the *New York World-Telegram,* with whose courtesy it is here reprinted.

A PRETTY AFTER-DINNER SPEECH
FOR A BILLION DOLLARS

"When, on the evening of December 12, 1900, some eighty of the nation's financial nobility gathered in the banquet hall of the University Club on Fifth Avenue to do honor to a young man from out of the West, not half a dozen of

Faith is the "eternal elixir" which gives life, power, and action to the impulse of thought! The foregoing sentence is worth reading a second time, and a third, and a fourth. It is worth reading aloud!

the guests realized they were to witness the most significant episode in American industrial history.

"J. Edward Simmons and Charles Stewart Smith, their hearts full of gratitude for the lavish hospitality bestowed on them by Charles M. Schwab during a recent visit to Pittsburgh, had arranged the dinner to introduce the thirty-eight-year-old steel man to eastern banking society. But they didn't expect him to stampede the convention. They warned him, in fact, that the bosoms within New York's stuffed shirts would not be responsive to oratory, and that, if he didn't want to bore the Stillmans and Harrimans and Vanderbilts, he had better limit himself to fifteen or twenty minutes of polite vaporings and let it go at that.

"Even John Pierpont Morgan, sitting on the right hand of Schwab as became his imperial dignity, intended to grace the banquet table with his presence only briefly. And so far as the press and public were concerned, the whole affair was of so little moment that no mention of it found its way into print the next day.

"So the two hosts and their distinguished guests ate their way through the usual seven or eight courses. There was little conversation and what there was of it was restrained. Few of the bankers and brokers had met Schwab, whose career had flowered along the banks of the Monongahela, and none knew him well. But before the evening was over, they—and with them Money Master Morgan—were to be swept off their feet, and a billion-dollar baby, the United States Steel Corporation, was to be conceived.

"It is perhaps unfortunate, for the sake of history, that no record of Charlie Schwab's speech at the dinner ever was made. He repeated some parts of it at a later date during a similar meeting of Chicago bankers. And still later, when the Government brought suit to dissolve the Steel Trust, he gave his own version, from the witness stand, of the remarks that stimulated Morgan into a frenzy of financial activity.

"It is probable, however, that it was a 'homely' speech, somewhat ungrammatical (for the niceties of language never bothered Schwab), full of epigram and threaded with wit. But aside from that it had a galvanic force and effect upon the five billions of estimated capital that was represented by the diners. After it was over and the gathering was still under its spell, although Schwab

Somehow I can't believe there are many heights that can't be scaled by a man who knows the secret of making dreams come true. This special secret can be summarized in four C's. They are: curiosity, confidence, courage, and constancy, and the greatest of these is confidence.

—Walt Disney

Faith is the starting point of all accumulation of riches!

When a man feels throbbing within him the power to do what he undertakes as well as it can possibly be done, this is happiness, this is success.

—Orison Swett Marden

had talked for ninety minutes, Morgan led the orator to a recessed window where, dangling their legs from the high, uncomfortable seat, they talked for an hour more.

"The magic of the Schwab personality had been turned on, full force, but what was more important and lasting was the full-fledged, clear-cut program he laid down for the aggrandizement of Steel. Many other men had tried to interest Morgan in slapping together a Steel Trust after the pattern of the biscuit, wire and hoop, sugar, rubber, whisky, oil, or chewing gum combinations. John W. Gates, the gambler, had urged it, but Morgan distrusted him. The Moore boys, Bill and Jim, Chicago stock jobbers who had glued together a match trust and a cracker corporation, had urged it and failed. Elbert H. Gary, the sanctimonious country lawyer, wanted to foster it, but he wasn't big enough to be impressive. Until Schwab's eloquence took J. P. Morgan to the heights from which he could visualize the solid results of the most daring financial undertaking ever conceived, the project was regarded as a delirious dream of easy-money crackpots.

"The financial magnetism that began, a generation ago, to attract thousands of small and sometimes inefficiently managed companies into large and competition-crushing combinations, had become operative in the steel world through the devices of that jovial business pirate John W. Gates. Gates already had formed the American Steel and Wire Company out of a chain of small concerns, and together with Morgan had created the Federal Steel Company. The National Tube and American Bridge companies were two more Morgan concerns, and the Moore Brothers had forsaken the match and cookie business to form the 'American' group—Tin Plate, Steel Hoop, Sheet Steel—and the National Steel Company.

"But by the side of Andrew Carnegie's gigantic vertical trust, a trust owned and operated by fifty-three partners, those other combinations were picayune. They might combine to their heart's content but the whole lot of them couldn't make a dent in the Carnegie organization, and Morgan knew it.

"The eccentric old Scot knew it, too. From the magnificent heights of Skibo Castle he had viewed, first with amusement and then with resentment, the attempts of Morgan's smaller companies to cut into his business. When the attempts became too bold, Carnegie's temper was translated into anger and re-

The subconscious mind . . . makes no distinction between constructive and destructive thought impulses. It works with the material we feed it, through our thought impulses.

taliation. He decided to duplicate every mill owned by his rivals. Hitherto, he hadn't been interested in wire, pipe, hoops, or sheet. Instead, he was content to sell such companies the raw steel and let them work it into whatever shape they wanted. Now, with Schwab as his chief and able lieutenant, he planned to drive his enemies to the wall.

"So it was that in the speech of Charles M. Schwab, Morgan saw the answer to his problem of combination. A trust without Carnegie—giant of them all—would be no trust at all, a plum pudding, as one writer said, without the plums.

"Schwab's speech on the night of December 12, 1900, undoubtedly carried the inference, though not the pledge, that the vast Carnegie enterprise could be brought under the Morgan tent. He talked of the world future for steel, of reorganization for efficiency, of specialization, of the scrapping of unsuccessful mills and concentration of effort on the flourishing properties, of economies in the ore traffic, of economies in overhead and administrative departments, of capturing foreign markets.

"More than that, he told the buccaneers among them wherein lay the errors of their customary piracy. Their purposes, he inferred, had been to create monopolies, raise prices, and pay themselves fat dividends out of privilege. Schwab condemned the system in his heartiest manner. The shortsightedness of such a policy, he told his hearers, lay in the fact that it restricted the market in an era when everything cried for expansion. By cheapening the cost of steel, he argued, an ever-expanding market would be created; more uses for steel would be devised, and a goodly portion of the world trade could be captured. Actually, though he did not know it, Schwab was an apostle of modern mass production.

"So, the dinner at the University Club came to an end. Morgan went home, to think about Schwab's rosy predictions. Schwab went back to Pittsburgh to run the steel business for 'Wee Andra Carnegie,' while Gary and the rest went back to their stock tickers, to fiddle around in anticipation of the next move.

"It was not long coming. It took Morgan about one week to digest the feast of reason Schwab had placed before him. When he had assured himself that no financial indigestion was to result, he sent for Schwab—and found that young man rather coy. Mr. Carnegie, Schwab indicated, might not like it if he found his trusted company president had been flirting with the Emperor of Wall Street, the Street upon which Carnegie was resolved never to tread. Then it

Success doesn't come to you, you go to it.

—Marva Collins

The subconscious mind will translate into reality a thought driven by fear just as readily as it will translate into a reality a thought driven by courage, or faith.

The measure of success is not whether you have a tough problem to deal with, but whether it is the same problem you had last year.

—John Foster Dulles

was suggested by John W. Gates, the go-between, that if Schwab 'happened' to be in the Bellevue Hotel in Philadelphia, J. P. Morgan might also 'happen' to be there. When Schwab arrived, however, Morgan was inconveniently ill at his New York home, and so, on the elder man's pressing invitation, Schwab went to New York and presented himself at the door of the financier's library.

"Now certain economic historians have professed the belief that from the beginning to the end of the drama, the stage was set by Andrew Carnegie— that the dinner to Schwab, the famous speech, the Sunday night conference between Schwab and the Money King, were events arranged by the canny Scot. The truth is exactly the opposite. When Schwab was called in to consummate the deal, he didn't even know whether 'the little boss,' as Andrew was called, would so much as listen to an offer to sell, particularly to a group of men whom Andrew regarded as being endowed with something less than holiness. But Schwab did take into the conference with him, in his own handwriting, six sheets of copper-plate figures, representing to his mind the physical worth and the potential earning capacity of every steel company he regarded as an essential star in the new metal firmament.

"Four men pondered over these figures all night. The chief, of course, was Morgan, steadfast in his belief in the Divine Right of Money. With him was his aristocratic partner, Robert Bacon, a scholar and a gentleman. The third was John W. Gates, whom Morgan scorned as a gambler and used as a tool. The fourth was Schwab, who knew more about the processes of making and selling steel than any whole group of men then living. Throughout that conference, the Pittsburgher's figures were never questioned. If he said a company was worth so much, then it was worth that much and no more. He was insistent, too, upon including in the combination only those concerns he nominated. He had conceived a corporation in which there would be no duplication, not even to satisfy the greed of friends who wanted to unload their companies upon the broad Morgan shoulders. Thus he left out, by design, a number of the larger concerns upon which the Walruses and Carpenters of Wall Street had cast hungry eyes.

"When dawn came, Morgan rose and straightened his back. Only one question remained.

Like the wind which carries one ship East, and another West, the law of auto-suggestion will lift you up or pull you down, according to the way you set your sails of thought.

"'Do you think you can persuade Andrew Carnegie to sell?' he asked.

"'I can try,' said Schwab.

"'If you can get him to sell, I will undertake the matter,' said Morgan.

"So far so good. But would Carnegie sell? How much would he demand? (Schwab thought about $320 million). What would he take payment in? Common or preferred stocks? Bonds? Cash? Nobody could raise a third of a billion dollars in cash.

"There was a golf game in January on the frost-cracking heath of the St. Andrews links in Westchester, with Andrew bundled up in sweaters against the cold, and Charlie talking volubly, as usual, to keep his spirits up. But no word of business was mentioned until the pair sat down in the cozy warmth of the Carnegie cottage hard by. Then, with the same persuasiveness that had hypnotized eighty millionaires at the University Club, Schwab poured out the glittering promises of retirement in comfort, of untold millions to satisfy the old man's social caprices. Carnegie capitulated, wrote a figure on a slip of paper, handed it to Schwab and said, 'All right, that's what we'll sell for.'

"The figure was approximately $400 million and was reached by taking the $320 million mentioned by Schwab as a basic figure, and adding to it $80 million to represent the increased capital value over the previous two years.

"Later, on the deck of a trans-Atlantic liner, the Scotsman said ruefully to Morgan, 'I wish I had asked you for $100 million more.'

"'If you had asked for it, you'd have gotten it,' Morgan told him cheerfully.

"There was an uproar, of course. A British correspondent cabled that the foreign steel world was 'appalled' by the gigantic combination. President Hadley, of Yale, declared that unless trusts were regulated the country might expect 'an emperor in Washington within the next twenty-five years.' But that able stock manipulator, Keene, went at his work of shoving the new stock at the public so vigorously that all the excess water—estimated by some at nearly $600 million—was absorbed in a twinkling. So Carnegie had his millions, and the Morgan syndicate had $62 million for all its 'trouble,' and all the 'boys,' from Gates to Gary, had their millions.

I learned to keep going, even in bad times. I learned not to despair, even when my world was falling apart. I learned that there are no free lunches. And I learned the value of hard work.

—Lee Iacocca

Riches begin in the form of thought! The amount is limited only by the person in whose mind the thought is put into motion. Faith removes limitations!

All negative states are self-created
and can be self-neutralized.
—Raymond Charles Barker

"The thirty-eight-year-old Schwab had his reward. He was made president of the new corporation and remained in control until 1930."

The dramatic story of "Big Business" which you have just finished was included in this book because it is a perfect illustration of the method by which *desire can be transmuted into its physical equivalent!*

I imagine some readers will question the statement that a mere, intangible desire can be converted into its physical equivalent. Doubtless some will say, "You cannot convert nothing into something!" The answer is in the story of United States Steel.

That giant organization was created in the mind of one man. The plan by which the organization was provided with the steel mills that gave it financial stability was created in the mind of the same man. His faith, his desire, his imagination, his persistence were the real ingredients that went into United States Steel. The steel mills and mechanical equipment acquired by the corporation, after it had been brought into legal existence, were incidental, but careful analysis will disclose the fact that the appraised value of the properties acquired by the corporation increased in value by an estimated $600 million by the mere transaction which consolidated them under one management.

In other words, Charles M. Schwab's idea, plus the faith with which he conveyed it to the minds of J. P. Morgan and the others, was marketed for a profit of approximately $600 million. Not an insignificant sum for a single idea!

What happened to some of the men who took their share of the millions of dollars of profit made by this transaction is a matter with which we are not now concerned. The important feature of the astounding achievement is that it serves as unquestionable evidence of the soundness of the philosophy described in this book, because this philosophy was the warp and the woof of the entire transaction. Moreover, the practicability of the philosophy has been established by the fact that the United States Steel Corporation prospered, and became one of the richest and most powerful corporations in America, employing thousands of people, developing new uses for steel, and opening new markets; thus proving that the $600 million in profit which the Schwab idea produced was earned.

There are no limitations to the mind
except those we acknowledge.

Riches begin in the form of thought!

The amount is limited only by the person in whose mind the thought is put into motion. Faith removes limitations! Remember this when you are ready to bargain with Life for whatever it is that you ask as your price for having passed this way.

Remember, also, that the man who created the United States Steel Corporation was practically unknown at the time. He was merely Andrew Carnegie's "Man Friday" until he gave birth to his famous IDEA. After that he quickly rose to a position of power, fame, and riches.

Whether you think you can or think you can't, you are right.

—Henry Ford

There are no limitations to the mind except those we *acknowledge.*

Both *poverty* and *riches* are the offspring of thought.

Both poverty *and* riches *are the offspring of thought.*

QUESTIONS FOR SUCCESS

- *What is the most helpful idea from this chapter for you?*

- *How does Napoleon Hill define "faith"?*

- *How can you develop more faith?*

- *What are affirmations?*

- *How can memorizing the "Self-Confidence Formula" (pages 62–63) positively affect your life?*

- *Napoleon Hill writes, "Both poverty and riches are the offspring of thought." How has this been true for you?*

YOUR SUCCESS STEPS

☐ _____

☐ _____

☐ _____

☐ _____

☐ _____

☐ _____

CHAPTER 4

AUTO-SUGGESTION

The Medium for Influencing
the Subconscious Mind

The Third Step Toward Riches

Auto-suggestion is a term which applies to all suggestions and all self-administered stimuli which reach one's mind through the five senses. Stated in another way, auto-suggestion is self-suggestion. It is the agency of communication between that part of the mind where conscious thought takes place and that which serves as the seat of action for the subconscious mind.

Through the dominating thoughts which one *permits* to remain in the conscious mind (whether these thoughts be negative or positive is immaterial), the principle of auto-suggestion voluntarily reaches the subconscious mind and influences it with these thoughts.

No thought, whether it be negative or positive, can enter the subconscious mind without the aid of the principle of auto-suggestion, with the exception of thoughts picked up from the ether. Stated differently, all sense impressions which are perceived through the five senses are stopped by the conscious thinking mind, and may be either passed on to the subconscious mind, or rejected, at will. The conscious faculty serves, therefore, as an outer-guard to the approach of the subconscious.

Nature has so built man that he has absolute control over the material which reaches his subconscious mind, through his five senses, although this is not

All truly wise thoughts have been thought already thousands of times; but to make them really ours we must think them over again honestly till they take root in our personal expression.

—Goethe

Auto-suggestion is a term which applies to all suggestions and all self-administered stimuli which reach one's mind through the five senses. Stated in another way, auto-suggestion is self-suggestion.

Let a man strive to purify his thoughts. What a man thinketh, that is he; this is the eternal mystery. Dwelling within his Self with thoughts serene, he will obtain imperishable happiness. Man becomes that of which he thinks.

—The Upanishads

meant to be construed as a statement that man always exercises this control. In the great majority of instances, he does not exercise it, which explains why so many people go through life in poverty.

Recall what has been said about the subconscious mind resembling a fertile garden spot, in which weeds will grow in abundance if the seeds of more desirable crops are not sown therein. Auto-suggestion is the agency of control through which an individual may voluntarily feed his subconscious mind on thoughts of a creative nature, or, by neglect, permit thoughts of a destructive nature to find their way into this rich garden of the mind.

You were instructed, in the last of the six steps described in the chapter on Desire, to read aloud twice daily the written statement of your desire for money, and to see and feel yourself already in possession of the money! By following these instructions, you communicate the object of your desire directly to your subconscious mind in a spirit of absolute faith. Through repetition of this procedure, you voluntarily create thought habits which are favorable to your efforts to transmute desire into its monetary equivalent.

Go back to these six steps described in chapter two, and read them again, very carefully, before you proceed further. Then (when you come to it), read very carefully the four instructions for the organization of your "Master Mind" group, described in the chapter on Organized Planning. By comparing these two sets of instructions with that which has been stated on auto-suggestion, you, of course, will see that the instructions involve the application of the principle of auto-suggestion.

Remember, therefore, when reading aloud the statement of your desire (through which you are endeavoring to develop a "money consciousness"), that the mere reading of the words is of no consequence—unless you mix emotion, or feeling, with your words. If you repeat a million times the famous Emil Coué formula, "Day by day, in every way, I am getting better and better," without mixing emotion and faith with your words, you will experience no desirable results. Your subconscious mind recognizes and acts upon only thoughts which have been well mixed with emotion or feeling.

This is a fact of such importance as to warrant repetition in practically every chapter, because the lack of understanding of this is the main reason the major-

Through the dominating thoughts which one permits to remain in the conscious mind (whether these thoughts be negative or positive is immaterial), the principle of auto-suggestion voluntarily reaches the subconscious mind and influences it with these thoughts.

ity of people who try to apply the principle of auto-suggestion get no desirable results.

Plain, unemotional words do not influence the subconscious mind. You will get no appreciable results until you learn to reach your subconscious mind with thoughts, or spoken words which have been well emotionalized with belief.

Do not become discouraged if you cannot control and direct your emotions the first time you try to do so. Remember, there is no such possibility as something for nothing. Ability to reach and influence your subconscious mind has its price, and you must pay that price. You cannot cheat, even if you desire to do so. The price of ability to influence your subconscious mind is everlasting persistence in applying the principles described here. You cannot develop the desired ability for a lower price. You, and you alone, must decide whether or not the reward for which you are striving (the "money consciousness") is worth the price you must pay for it in effort.

Wisdom and "cleverness" alone will not attract and retain money except in a few very rare instances, where the law of averages favors the attraction of money through these sources. The method of attracting money described here does not depend upon the law of averages. Moreover, the method plays no favorites. It will work for one person as effectively as it will for another. Where failure is experienced, it is the individual, *not the method,* which has failed. If you try and fail, make another effort, and still another, until you succeed.

Your ability to use the principle of auto-suggestion will depend, very largely, upon your capacity to concentrate upon a given desire until that desire becomes a burning obsession.

When you begin to carry out the instructions in connection with the six steps described in the second chapter, it will be necessary for you to make use of the principle of concentration.

Let us here offer suggestions for the effective use of concentration. When you begin to carry out the first of the six steps, which instructs you to "fix in your own mind the exact amount of money you desire," hold your thoughts on that amount of money by concentration, or fixation of attention, with your eyes closed, until you can actually see the physical appearance of the money. Do this at least once each day. As you go through these exercises, follow the

All that we are is the result of what we have thought. The mind is everything. What we think, we become.

—Buddha

Man has absolute control over the material which reaches his subconscious mind . . . although this is not meant that man always exercises this control. In the great majority of instances, he does not exercise it, which explains why so many people go through life in poverty.

instructions given in the chapter on faith, and see yourself actually in possession of the money!

Here is a most significant fact—the subconscious mind takes any orders given it in a spirit of absolute faith, and acts upon those orders, although the orders often have to be presented *over and over again,* through repetition, before they are interpreted by the subconscious mind. Following the preceding statement, consider the possibility of playing a perfectly legitimate "trick" on your subconscious mind, by making it believe, *because you believe it,* that you must have the amount of money you are visualizing, that this money is already awaiting your claim, that the subconscious mind must hand over to you practical plans for acquiring the money which is yours.

Hand over the thought suggested in the preceding paragraph to your imagination, and see what your imagination can or will do to create practical plans for the accumulation of money through transmutation of your desire.

Do not wait for a definite plan, through which you intend to exchange services or merchandise in return for the money you are visualizing, but begin at once to see yourself in possession of the money, demanding and expecting meanwhile that your subconscious mind will hand over the plan, or plans, you need. Be on the alert for these plans, and when they appear, put them into action immediately. When the plans appear, they will probably "flash" into your mind through the sixth sense, in the form of an "inspiration." This inspiration may be considered a direct "telegram," or message from Infinite Intelligence. Treat it with respect, and act upon it as soon as you receive it. Failure to do this will be fatal to your success.

In the fourth of the six steps, you were instructed to "create a definite plan for carrying out your desire, and begin at once to put this plan into action." You should follow this instruction in the manner described in the preceding paragraph. Do not trust to your "reason" when creating your plan for accumulating money through the transmutation of desire. Your reason is faulty. Moreover, your reasoning faculty may be lazy, and, if you depend entirely upon it to serve you, it may disappoint you.

When visualizing the money you intend to accumulate (with closed eyes), *see yourself rendering the service, or delivering the merchandise you intend to give in return for this money. This is important!*

Thoughts lead on to purposes; purposes go forth in action; actions form habits; habits decide character; and character fixes our destiny.

—Tryon Edwards

Remember, there is no such possibility as something for nothing. Ability to reach and influence your subconscious mind has its price, and you must pay that price. You cannot cheat, even if you desire to do so.

SUMMARY OF INSTRUCTIONS

The fact that you are reading this book is an indication that you earnestly seek knowledge. It is also an indication that you are a student of this subject. If you are only a student, there is a chance that you may learn much that you did not know, but you will learn only by assuming an attitude of humility. If you choose to follow some of the instructions but neglect or refuse to follow others—*you will fail!* To get satisfactory results, you must follow all instructions in a spirit of faith.

The instructions given in connection with the six steps in the second chapter will now be summarized, and blended with the principles covered by this chapter, as follows:

Nothing is easier than saying words. Nothing is harder than living them day after day.

—Arthur Gordon

FIRST. Go into some quiet spot (preferably in bed at night) where you will not be disturbed or interrupted, close your eyes, and repeat aloud (so you may hear your own words) the written statement of the amount of money you intend to accumulate, the time limit for its accumulation, and a description of the service or merchandise you intend to give in return for the money. As you carry out these instructions, see yourself already in possession of the money.

For example: Suppose that you intend to accumulate $50,000 by the first of January, five years hence, that you intend to give personal services in return for the money, in the capacity of a salesman. Your written statement of your purpose should be similar to the following:

"By the first day of January, 19. ., I will have in my possession $50,000, which will come to me in various amounts from time to time during the interim.

"In return for this money I will give the most efficient service of which I am capable, rendering the fullest possible quantity, and the best possible quality of service in the capacity of salesman of . . . (describe the service or merchandise you intend to sell).

"I believe that I will have this money in my possession. My faith is so strong that I can now see this money before my eyes. I can touch it with

The method of attracting money described here does not depend upon the law of averages. Moreover, the method plays no favorites. It will work for one person as effectively as it will for another.

my hands. It is now awaiting transfer to me at the time and in the proportion that I deliver the service I intend to render in return for it. I am awaiting a plan by which to accumulate this money, and I will follow that plan when it is received."

I know for sure that what we dwell on is who we will become.
—Oprah Winfrey

SECOND. Repeat this program night and morning until you can see (in your imagination) the money you intend to accumulate.

THIRD. Place a written copy of your statement where you can see it night and morning, and read it just before retiring and upon arising until it has been memorized.

Remember, as you carry out these instructions, that you are applying the principle of auto-suggestion, for the purpose of giving orders to your subconscious mind. Remember, also, that your subconscious mind will act only upon instructions which are emotionalized, and handed over to it with "feeling." Faith is the strongest and most productive of the emotions. Follow the instructions given in the chapter on faith.

These instructions may, at first, seem abstract. Do not let this disturb you. Follow the instructions, no matter how abstract or impractical they may, at first, appear to be. The time will soon come, if you do as you have been instructed, *in spirit as well as in act,* when a whole new universe of power will unfold to you.

Skepticism, in connection with all new ideas, is characteristic of all human beings. But if you follow the instructions outlined, your skepticism will soon be replaced by belief, and this, in turn, will soon become crystallized into absolute faith. Then you will have arrived at the point where you may truly say, "I am the Master of my Fate, I am the Captain of my Soul!"

Many philosophers have made the statement that man is the master of his own *earthly* destiny, but most of them have failed to say *why* he is the master. The reason that man may be the master of his own earthly status, and especially his financial status, is thoroughly explained in this chapter. Man may become the master of himself, and of his environment, because he has the power to

Your ability to use the principle of auto-suggestion will depend, very largely, upon your capacity to concentrate upon a given desire until that desire becomes a burning obsession.

influence his own subconscious mind, and through it, gain the cooperation of Infinite Intelligence.

You are now reading the chapter which represents the keystone to the arch of this philosophy. The instructions contained in this chapter must be understood and applied with persistence if you are to succeed in transmuting desire into money.

The actual performance of transmuting desire into money involves the use of auto-suggestion as an agency by which one may reach, and influence, the subconscious mind. The other principles are simply tools with which to apply auto-suggestion. Keep this thought in mind, and you will, at all times, be conscious of the important part the principle of auto-suggestion is to play in your efforts to accumulate money through the methods described in this book.

Carry out these instructions as though you were a small child. Inject into your efforts something of the faith of a child. The author has been most careful to see that no impractical instructions were included, because of his sincere desire to be helpful.

After you have read the entire book, come back to this chapter, and follow in spirit, and in action, this instruction:

Read the entire chapter aloud once every night, until you become thoroughly convinced that the principle of auto-suggestion is sound, that it will accomplish for you all that has been claimed for it. As you read, *underscore with a pencil* every sentence which impresses you favorably.

Follow the foregoing instruction to the letter and it will open the way for a complete understanding and mastery of the principles of success.

The mental attitude of gratitude draws the mind into closer touch with the source from which the blessings come.

—Wallace D. Wattles

Man may become the master of himself, and of his environment, because he has the power to influence his own subconscious mind, and through it, gain the cooperation of Infinite Intelligence.

QUESTIONS FOR SUCCESS

- *What is the most helpful idea from this chapter for you?*

- *How does Napoleon Hill define "auto-suggestion"?*

- *How much control do you have over the material that reaches your mind?*

- *How diligent are you in protecting the "garden of [your] mind" from negative thoughts?*

- *What do you need to add to the words (auto-suggestions) to make your subconscious mind recognize and act upon them?*

- *Napoleon Hill writes, "Be on the alert for the plans [that your subconscious mind will hand over to you], and when they appear, put them into action immediately." What is an example of taking action immediately on a plan or an idea that has come into your mind?*

- *What does Napoleon Hill say will happen if you follow some of the instructions of auto-suggestion (page 81) but not others?*

- *How can you become the master of yourself and your environment (page 82)?*

YOUR SUCCESS STEPS

- ☐ _____
- ☐ _____
- ☐ _____
- ☐ _____
- ☐ _____
- ☐ _____

CHAPTER 5

SPECIALIZED KNOWLEDGE

Personal Experiences or Observations

The Fourth Step Toward Riches

There are two kinds of knowledge. One is general, the other is specialized. General knowledge, no matter how great in quantity or variety it may be, is of but little use in the accumulation of money. The faculties of the great universities possess, in the aggregate, practically every form of general knowledge known to civilization. *Most of the professors have but little or no money.* They specialize on *teaching* knowledge, but they do not specialize on the organization or the use of knowledge.

Knowledge will not attract money, unless it is organized, and intelligently directed, through practical plans of action, to the definite end of accumulation of money. Lack of understanding of this fact has been the source of confusion to millions of people who falsely believe that "knowledge is power." It is nothing of the sort! Knowledge is only *potential* power. It becomes power only when, and if, it is organized into definite plans of action, and directed to a definite end.

This "missing link" in all systems of education known to civilization today may be found in the failure of educational institutions to teach their students how to organize and use knowledge after they acquire it.

Many people make the mistake of assuming that, because Henry Ford had but little "schooling," he is not a man of "education." Those who make this mistake do not know Henry Ford, nor do they understand the real meaning

He who stops being better stops being good.

—Oliver Cromwell

There are two kinds of knowledge. One is general, the other is specialized.

Every man comes into the world with a predisposition to grow along certain lines, and growth is easier for him along those lines than in any other way.

—Wallace D. Wattles

of the word "educate." That word is derived from the Latin word "educo," meaning to educe, to draw out, to develop from within.

An educated man is not, necessarily, one who has an abundance of general or specialized knowledge. An educated man is one who has so developed the faculties of his mind that he may acquire anything he wants, or its equivalent, without violating the rights of others. Henry Ford comes well within the meaning of this definition.

During the world war, a Chicago newspaper published certain editorials in which, among other statements, Henry Ford was called "an ignorant pacifist." Mr. Ford objected to the statements, and brought suit against the paper for libeling him. When the suit was tried in the Courts, the attorneys for the paper pleaded justification, and placed Mr. Ford, himself, on the witness stand, for the purpose of proving to the jury that he was ignorant. The attorneys asked Mr. Ford a great variety of questions, all of them intended to prove, by his own evidence, that, while he might possess considerable specialized knowledge pertaining to the manufacture of automobiles, he was, in the main, ignorant.

Mr. Ford was plied with such questions as the following:

"Who was Benedict Arnold?" and "How many soldiers did the British send over to America to put down the Rebellion of 1776?" In answer to the last question, Mr. Ford replied, "I do not know the exact number of soldiers the British sent over, but I have heard that it was a considerably larger number than ever went back."

Finally, Mr. Ford became tired of this line of questioning, and in reply to a particularly offensive question, he leaned over, pointed his finger at the lawyer who had asked the question, and said, "If I should really want to answer the foolish question you have just asked, or any of the other questions you have been asking me, let me remind you that I have a row of electric pushbuttons on my desk, and by pushing the right button, I can summon to my aid men who can answer any question I desire to ask concerning the business to which I am devoting most of my efforts. Now, will you kindly tell me, why I should clutter up my mind with general knowledge, for the purpose of being able to answer questions, when I have men around me who can supply any knowledge I require?"

There certainly was good logic to that reply.

That answer floored the lawyer. Every person in the courtroom realized it

Knowledge will not attract money, unless it is organized, and intelligently directed, through practical plans of action, to the definite end of accumulation of money.

was the answer not of an ignorant man but of a man of education. Any man is educated who knows where to get knowledge when he needs it, and how to organize that knowledge into definite plans of action. Through the assistance of his "Master Mind" group, Henry Ford had at his command all the specialized knowledge he needed to enable him to become one of the wealthiest men in America. *It was not essential that he have this knowledge in his own mind.* Surely no person who has sufficient inclination and intelligence to read a book of this nature can possibly miss the significance of this illustration.

Before you can be sure of your ability to transmute desire into its monetary equivalent, you will require specialized knowledge of the service, merchandise, or profession which you intend to offer in return for fortune. Perhaps you may need much more specialized knowledge than you have the ability or the inclination to acquire, and if this should be true, you may bridge your weakness through the aid of your "Master Mind" group.

Andrew Carnegie stated that he, personally, knew nothing about the technical end of the steel business; moreover, he did not particularly care to know anything about it. The specialized knowledge which he required for the manufacture and marketing of steel he found available through the individual units of his "Master Mind" group.

The accumulation of great fortunes calls for power, and power is acquired through highly organized and intelligently directed specialized knowledge, but that knowledge does not, necessarily, have to be in the possession of the man who accumulates the fortune.

The preceding paragraph should give hope and encouragement to the man with ambition to accumulate a fortune who has not possessed himself of the necessary "education" to supply such specialized knowledge as he may require. Men sometimes go through life suffering from "inferiority complexes" because they are not men of "education." The man who can organize and direct a "Master Mind" group of men who possess knowledge useful in the accumulation of money is just as much a man of education as any man in the group. Remember this if you suffer from a feeling of inferiority because your schooling has been limited.

Thomas A. Edison had only three months of "schooling" during his entire life. He did not lack education, neither did he die poor.

Few persons realize how much of their happiness is dependent upon their work, upon the fact that they are kept busy and not left to feed upon themselves.

—John Burroughs

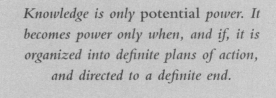

Knowledge is only potential power. It becomes power only when, and if, it is organized into definite plans of action, and directed to a definite end.

Henry Ford had less than a sixth-grade "schooling" but he has managed to do pretty well by himself, financially.

Specialized knowledge is among the most plentiful, and the cheapest, forms of service which may be had! If you doubt this, consult the payroll of any university.

IT PAYS TO KNOW HOW TO PURCHASE KNOWLEDGE

First of all, decide the sort of specialized knowledge you require, and the purpose for which it is needed. To a large extent your major purpose in life, the goal toward which you are working, will help determine what knowledge you need. With this question settled, your next move requires that you have accurate information concerning dependable sources of knowledge. The more important of these are:

a. One's own experience and education
b. Experience and education available through cooperation of others (Master Mind Alliance)
c. Colleges and universities
d. Public libraries (through books and periodicals in which may be found all the knowledge organized by civilization)
e. Special training courses (through night schools and home study schools in particular)

As knowledge is acquired it must be organized and put into use, for a definite purpose, through practical plans. Knowledge has no value except that which can be gained from its application toward some worthy end. This is one reason why college degrees are not valued more highly. They represent nothing but miscellaneous knowledge.

If you contemplate taking additional schooling, first determine the purpose for which you want the knowledge you are seeking, then learn where this particular sort of knowledge can be obtained, from reliable sources.

Successful men, in all callings, never stop acquiring specialized knowledge

The word [educate] is derived from the Latin word "educo," meaning to educe, to draw out, to develop from within.

related to their major purpose, business, or profession. Those who are not successful usually make the mistake of believing that the knowledge-acquiring period ends when one finishes school. The truth is that schooling does but little more than to put one in the way of learning how to acquire practical knowledge.

With this Changed World which began at the end of the economic collapse came also astounding changes in educational requirements. The order of the day is specialization! This truth was emphasized by Robert P. Moore, Secretary of Appointments of Columbia University.

New ideas have to have new vocabularies.
—Raymond Charles Barker

SPECIALISTS MOST SOUGHT

"Particularly sought after by employing companies are candidates who have specialized in some field—business-school graduates with training in accounting and statistics, engineers of all varieties, journalists, architects, chemists, and also outstanding leaders and activity men of the senior class.

"The man who has been active on the campus, whose personality is such that he gets along with all kinds of people and who has done an adequate job with his studies, has a most decided edge over the strictly academic student. Some of these, because of their all-around qualifications, have received several offers of positions, a few of them as many as six.

"In departing from the conception that the 'straight A' student was invariably the one to get the choice of the better jobs, Mr. Moore said that most companies look not only to academic records but to activity records and personalities of the students.

"One of the largest industrial companies, the leader in its field, in writing to Mr. Moore concerning prospective seniors at the college, said:

"'We are interested primarily in finding men who can make exceptional progress in management work. For this reason we emphasize qualities of character, intelligence and personality far more than specific educational background.'"

The accumulation of great fortunes calls for power, and power is acquired through highly organized and intelligently directed specialized knowledge, but that knowledge does not, necessarily, have to be in the possession of the man who accumulates the fortune.

"APPRENTICESHIP" PROPOSED

Not being able to do everything is no excuse for not doing everything you can.

—Ashleigh Brilliant

"Proposing a system of 'apprenticing' students in offices, stores and industrial occupations during the summer vacation, Mr. Moore asserts that after the first two or three years of college, every student should be asked 'to choose a definite future course and to call a halt if he has been merely pleasantly drifting without purpose through an unspecialized academic curriculum.

"'Colleges and universities must face the practical consideration that all professions and occupations now demand specialists,' he said, urging that educational institutions accept more direct responsibility for vocational guidance."

One of the most reliable and practical sources of knowledge available to those who need specialized schooling is the night schools operated in most large cities. The correspondence schools give specialized training anywhere the U.S. mails go, on all subjects that can be taught by the extension method. One advantage of home study training is the flexibility of the study programme which permits one to study during spare time. Another stupendous advantage of home study training (if the school is carefully chosen) is the fact that most courses offered by home study schools carry with them generous privileges of consultation which can be of priceless value to those needing specialized knowledge. No matter where you live, you can share the benefits.

Anything acquired without effort and without cost is generally unappreciated, often discredited; perhaps this is why we get so little from our marvelous opportunity in public schools. The self-discipline one receives from a definite programme of specialized study makes up, to some extent, for the wasted opportunity when knowledge was available without cost. Correspondence schools are highly organized business institutions. Their tuition fees are so low that they are forced to insist upon prompt payments. Being asked to pay, whether the student makes good grades or poor, has the effect of causing one to follow through with the course when he would otherwise drop it. The correspondence schools have not stressed this point sufficiently, for the truth is that their collection departments constitute the very finest sort of training on decision, promptness, action, and the habit of finishing that which one begins.

I learned this from experience, more than twenty-five years ago. I enrolled

First of all, decide the sort of specialized knowledge you require, and the purpose for which it is needed.

for a home study course in advertising. After completing eight or ten lessons I stopped studying, but the school did not stop sending me bills. Moreover, it insisted upon payment, whether I kept up my studies or not. I decided that if I had to pay for the course (which I had legally obligated myself to do), I should complete the lessons and get my money's worth. I felt, at the time, that the collection system of the school was somewhat too well organized, but I learned later in life that it was a valuable part of my training for which no charge had been made. Being forced to pay, I went ahead and completed the course. Later in life I discovered that the efficient collection system of that school had been worth much in the form of money earned, because of the training in advertising I had so reluctantly taken.

We have in this country what is said to be the greatest public school system in the world. We have invested fabulous sums for fine buildings, we have provided convenient transportation for children living in the rural districts so they may attend the best schools, but there is one astounding weakness to this marvelous system—it is free! One of the strange things about human beings is that they value only that which has a price. The free schools of America, and the free public libraries, do not impress people *because they are free*. This is the major reason why so many people find it necessary to acquire additional training after they quit school and go to work. It is also one of the major reasons why employers give greater consideration to employees who take home study courses. They have learned, from experience, that any person who has the ambition to give up a part of his spare time to studying at home has in him those qualities which make for leadership. This recognition is not a charitable gesture—it is sound business judgment upon the part of the employers.

There is one weakness in people for which there is no remedy. It is the universal weakness of lack of ambition! Persons, especially salaried people, who schedule their spare time to provide for home study, seldom remain at the bottom very long. Their action opens the way for the upward climb, removes many obstacles from their path, and gains the friendly interest of those who have the power to put them in the way of opportunity.

The home study method of training is especially suited to the needs of employed people who find, after leaving school, that they must acquire additional specialized knowledge but cannot spare the time to go back to school.

Formal education will make you a living; self-education will make you a fortune.

—Jim Rohn

Successful men, in all callings, never stop acquiring specialized knowledge related to their major purpose, business, or profession.

There are three ingredients in the good life: learning, earning, and yearning.

—Christopher Morley

The changed economic conditions prevailing since the depression have made it necessary for thousands of people to find additional or new sources of income. For the majority of these, the solution to their problem may be found only by acquiring specialized knowledge. Many will be forced to change their occupations entirely. When a merchant finds that a certain line of merchandise is not selling, he usually supplants it with another that is in demand. The person whose business is that of marketing personal services must also be an efficient merchant. If his services do not bring adequate returns in one occupation, he must change to another, where broader opportunities are available.

Stuart Austin Wier prepared himself as a Construction Engineer and followed this line of work until the depression limited his market to where it did not give him the income he required. He took inventory of himself, decided to change his profession to law, went back to school, and took special courses by which he prepared himself as a corporation lawyer. Despite the fact the depression had not ended, he completed his training, passed the Bar Examination, and quickly built a lucrative law practice, in Dallas, Texas; in fact, he is turning away clients.

Just to keep the record straight, and to anticipate the alibis of those who will say, "I couldn't go to school because I have a family to support," or "I'm too old," I will add the information that Mr. Wier was past forty and married when he went back to school. Moreover, by carefully selecting highly specialized courses in colleges best prepared to teach the subjects chosen, Mr. Wier completed in two years the work for which the majority of law students require four years. It pays to know how to purchase knowledge!

The person who stops studying merely because he has finished school is forever hopelessly doomed to mediocrity, no matter what may be his calling. The way of success is the way of continuous pursuit of knowledge.

Let us consider a specific instance.

During the depression a salesman in a grocery store found himself without a position. Having had some bookkeeping experience, he took a special course in accounting, familiarized himself with all the latest bookkeeping and office equipment, and went into business for himself. Starting with the grocer for whom he had formerly worked, he made contracts with more than a hundred small merchants to keep their books, at a very nominal monthly fee. His idea

Those who are not successful usually make the mistake of believing that the knowledge-acquiring period ends when one finishes school.

was so practical that he soon found it necessary to set up a portable office in a light delivery truck, which he equipped with modern bookkeeping machinery. He now has a fleet of these bookkeeping offices "on wheels" and employs a large staff of assistants, thus providing small merchants with accounting service equal to the best that money can buy, at very nominal cost.

Specialized knowledge plus imagination were the ingredients that went into this unique and successful business. Last year the owner of that business paid an income tax of almost ten times as much as was paid by the merchant for whom he worked when the depression forced upon him a temporary adversity which proved to be a blessing in disguise.

The beginning of this successful business was an idea!

Inasmuch as I had the privilege of supplying the unemployed salesman with that idea, I now assume the further privilege of suggesting another idea which has within it the possibility of even greater income. Also the possibility of rendering useful service to thousands of people who badly need that service.

The idea was suggested by the salesman who gave up selling and went into the business of keeping books on a wholesale basis. When the plan was suggested as a solution of his unemployment problem, he quickly exclaimed, "I like the idea, but I would not know how to turn it into cash." In other words, he complained he would not know how to market his bookkeeping knowledge *after he acquired it.*

So, that brought up another problem which had to be solved. With the aid of a young woman typist, clever at hand lettering, and who could put the story together, a very attractive book was prepared, describing the advantages of the new system of bookkeeping. The pages were neatly typed and pasted in an ordinary scrapbook, which was used as a silent salesman with which the story of this new business was so effectively told that its owner soon had more accounts than he could handle.

There are thousands of people, all over the country, who need the services of a merchandising specialist capable of preparing an attractive brief for use in marketing personal services. The aggregate annual income from such a service might easily exceed that received by the largest employment agency, and the benefits of the service might be made far greater to the purchaser than any to be obtained from an employment agency.

I was made to work. If you are equally industrious, you will be equally successful.

—Johann Sebastian Bach

One of the strange things about human beings is that they value only that which has a price.

My experience has shown me that the people who are exceptionally good in business aren't so because of what they know but because of their insatiable need to know more.

—Michael E. Gerber

The idea here described was born of necessity, to bridge an emergency which had to be covered, but it did not stop by merely serving one person. The woman who created the idea has a keen imagination. She saw in her newly born brainchild the making of a new profession, one that is destined to render valuable service to thousands of people who need practical guidance in marketing personal services.

Spurred to action by the instantaneous success of her first "prepared plan to market personal services," this energetic woman turned next to the solution of a similar problem for her son, who had just finished college but had been totally unable to find a market for his services. The plan she originated for his use was the finest specimen of merchandising of personal services I have ever seen.

When the plan book had been completed, it contained nearly fifty pages of beautifully typed, properly organized information, telling the story of her son's native ability, schooling, personal experiences, and a great variety of other information too extensive for description. The plan book also contained a complete description of the position her son desired, together with a marvelous word picture of the exact plan he would use in filling the position.

The preparation of the plan book required several weeks' labor, during which time its creator sent her son to the public library almost daily, to procure data needed in selling his services to best advantage. She sent him, also, to all the competitors of his prospective employer, and gathered from them vital information concerning their business methods which was of great value in the formation of the plan he intended to use in filling the position he sought. When the plan had been finished, it contained more than half a dozen very fine suggestions for the use and benefit of the prospective employer. (The suggestions were put into use by the company.)

One may be inclined to ask, "Why go to all this trouble to secure a job?" The answer is straight to the point, also it is dramatic, because it deals with a subject which assumes the proportion of a tragedy with millions of men and women whose sole source of income is personal services.

The answer is "Doing a thing well never is trouble! The plan prepared by this woman for the benefit of her son helped him get the job for which he applied, at the first interview, at a salary fixed by himself."

There is one weakness in people for which there is no remedy. It is the universal weakness of lack of ambition!

Moreover—and this, too, is important—the position did not require the young man to start at the bottom. He began as a junior executive, at an executive's salary.

"Why go to all this trouble?" do you ask.

Well, for one thing, the planned presentation of this young man's application for a position clipped off no less than ten years of time he would have required to get to where he began, had he "started at the bottom and worked his way up."

This idea of starting at the bottom and working one's way up may appear to be sound, but the major objection to it is this—too many of those who begin at the bottom never manage to lift their heads high enough to be seen by opportunity, so they remain at the bottom. It should be remembered, also, that the outlook from the bottom is not so very bright or encouraging. It has a tendency to kill off ambition. We call it "getting into a rut," which means that we accept our fate because we form the habit of daily routine, a habit that finally becomes so strong we cease to try to throw it off. And that is another reason why it pays to start one or two steps above the bottom. By so doing one forms the habit of looking around, of observing how others get ahead, of seeing opportunity, and of embracing it without hesitation.

Dan Halpin is a splendid example of what I mean. During his college days, he was manager of the famous 1930 National Championship Notre Dame football team, when it was under the direction of the late Knute Rockne.

Perhaps he was inspired by the great football coach to aim high, and not mistake temporary defeat for failure, just as Andrew Carnegie, the great industrial leader, inspired his young business lieutenants to set high goals for themselves. At any rate, young Halpin finished college at a mighty unfavorable time, when the depression had made jobs scarce, so, after a fling at investment banking and motion pictures, he took the first opening with a potential future he could find—selling electrical hearing aids on a commission basis. Anyone could start in that sort of job, and Halpin knew it, but it was enough to open the door of opportunity to him.

For almost two years, he continued in a job not to his liking, and he would never have risen above that job if he had not done something about his dissatisfaction. He aimed, first, at the job of Assistant Sales Manager of his com-

A human being is not attaining his full heights until he is educated.

—Horace Mann

The person who stops studying merely because he has finished school is forever hopelessly doomed to mediocrity, no matter what may be his calling. The way of success is the way of continuous pursuit of knowledge.

An education isn't how much you have committed to memory, or even how much you know. It's being able to differentiate between what you know and what you don't.

—Anatole France

pany, and got the job. That one step upward placed him high enough above the crowd to enable him to see still greater opportunity; also, it placed him where opportunity could see him.

He made such a fine record selling hearing aids that A. M. Andrews, Chairman of the Board of the Dictograph Products Company, a business competitor of the company for which Halpin worked, wanted to know something about that man Dan Halpin who was taking big sales away from the long established Dictograph Company. He sent for Halpin. When the interview was over, Halpin was the new Sales Manager, in charge of the Acousticon Division. Then, to test young Halpin's mettle, Mr. Andrews went away to Florida for three months, leaving him to sink or swim in his new job. He did not sink! Knute Rockne's spirit of "All the world loves a winner, and has no time for a loser," inspired him to put so much into his job that he was recently elected Vice-President of the company, and General Manager of the Acousticon and Silent Radio Division, a job which most men would be proud to earn through ten years of loyal effort. Halpin turned the trick in little more than six months.

It is difficult to say whether Mr. Andrews or Mr. Halpin is more deserving of eulogy, for the reason that both showed evidence of having an abundance of that very rare quality known as imagination. Mr. Andrews deserves credit for seeing in young Halpin a "go-getter" of the highest order. Halpin deserves credit for refusing to compromise with life by accepting and keeping a job he did not want, and that is one of the major points I am trying to emphasize through this entire philosophy—that we rise to high positions or remain at the bottom because of conditions we can control if we desire to control them.

I am also trying to emphasize another point, namely, that both success and failure are largely the results of habit! I have not the slightest doubt that Dan Halpin's close association with the greatest football coach America ever knew planted in his mind the same brand of desire to excel which made the Notre Dame football team world-famous. Truly, there is something to the idea that hero-worship is helpful, provided one worships a winner. Halpin tells me that Rockne was one of the world's greatest leaders of men in all history.

My belief in the theory that business associations are vital factors, both in failure and in success, was recently demonstrated, when my son Blair was negotiating with Dan Halpin for a position. Mr. Halpin offered him a beginning

One may be inclined to ask, "Why go to all this trouble to secure a job?" . . . The answer is "Doing a thing well never is trouble!"

salary of about one half what he could have gotten from a rival company. I brought parental pressure to bear, and induced him to accept the place with Mr. Halpin, because I believe that close association with one who refuses to compromise with circumstances he does not like is an asset that can never be measured in terms of money.

The bottom is a monotonous, dreary, unprofitable place for any person. That is why I have taken the time to describe how lowly beginnings may be circumvented by proper planning. Also, that is why so much space has been devoted to a description of this new profession, created by a woman who was inspired to do a fine job of planning because she wanted her son to have a favorable "break."

With the changed conditions ushered in by the world economic collapse came also the need for newer and better ways of marketing personal services. It is hard to determine why someone had not previously discovered this stupendous need, in view of the fact that more money changes hands in return for personal services than for any other purpose. The sum paid out monthly, to people who work for wages and salaries, is so huge that it runs into hundreds of millions, and the annual distribution amounts to billions.

Perhaps some will find, in the idea here briefly described, the nucleus of the riches they desire! Ideas with much less merit have been the seedlings from which great fortunes have grown. Woolworth's Five and Ten Cent Store idea, for example, had far less merit, but it piled up a fortune for its creator.

Those seeing opportunity lurking in this suggestion will find valuable aid in the chapter on Organized Planning. Incidentally, an efficient merchandiser of personal services would find a growing demand for his services wherever there are men and women who seek better markets for their services. By applying the Master Mind principle, a few people with suitable talent could form an alliance, and have a paying business very quickly. One would need to be a fair writer, with a flair for advertising and selling, one handy at typing and hand lettering, and one should be a first-class business getter who would let the world know about the service. If one person possessed all these abilities, he might carry on the business alone, until it outgrew him.

The woman who prepared the "Personal Service Sales Plan" for her son now receives requests from all parts of the country for her cooperation in preparing

Develop a passion for learning. If you do, you will never cease to grow.

—Anthony J. D'Angelo

Too many of those who begin at the bottom never manage to lift their heads high enough to be seen by opportunity, so they remain at the bottom.

Education is growth. Education is not a preparation for life; education is life itself.

—John Dewey

similar plans for others who desire to market their personal services for more money. She has a staff of expert typists, artists, and writers who have the ability to dramatize the case history so effectively that one's personal services can be marketed for much more money than the prevailing wages for similar services. She is so confident of her ability that she accepts, as the major portion of her fee, a percentage of the *increased* pay she helps her clients to earn.

It must not be supposed that her plan merely consists of clever salesmanship by which she helps men and women to demand and receive more money for the same services they formerly sold for less pay. She looks after the interests of the purchaser as well as the seller of personal services, and so prepares her plans that the employer receives full value for the additional money he pays. The method by which she accomplishes this astonishing result is a professional secret which she discloses to no one excepting her own clients.

If you have the imagination, and seek a more profitable outlet for your personal services, this suggestion may be the stimulus for which you have been searching. The idea is capable of yielding an income far greater than that of the "average" doctor, lawyer, or engineer whose education required several years in college. The idea is saleable to those seeking new positions, in practically all positions calling for managerial or executive ability, and those desiring re-arrangement of incomes in their present positions.

There is no fixed price for sound ideas!

Back of all ideas is specialized knowledge. Unfortunately, for those who do not find riches in abundance, specialized knowledge is more abundant and more easily acquired than ideas. Because of this very truth, there is a universal demand and an ever-increasing opportunity for the person capable of helping men and women to sell their personal services advantageously. Capability means imagination, the one quality needed to combine specialized knowledge with ideas, in the form of organized plans designed to yield riches.

If you have imagination this chapter may present you with an idea sufficient to serve as the beginning of the riches you desire. Remember, the idea is the main thing. Specialized knowledge may be found just around the corner—any corner!

Both success and failure are largely the results of habit!

QUESTIONS FOR SUCCESS

- *What is the most helpful idea from this chapter for you?*

- *What kinds of specialized knowledge do you have? What kinds of specialized knowledge would help you go to another level?*

- *How many kinds of specialized knowledge can you think of beyond those taught in school?*

- *How can a Master Mind Group contribute to your specialized knowledge?*

- *Napoleon Hill writes that those who are successful "never stop acquiring specialized knowledge related to their major purpose, business, or profession. Those who are not successful usually make the mistake of believing that the knowledge-acquiring period ends when one finishes school." How have you continued to acquire specialized knowledge?*

- *"Doing a thing well never is trouble!" Do you strive to do everything you do as well as you can?*

- *Both success and failure are largely the results of what (page 96)?*

YOUR SUCCESS STEPS

- [ ]
- [ ]
- [ ]
- [ ]
- [ ]
- [ ]

CHAPTER 6

IMAGINATION

The Workshop of the Mind

The Fifth Step Toward Riches

The imagination is literally the workshop wherein are fashioned all plans created by man. The impulse, the desire, is given shape, form, and action through the aid of the imaginative faculty of the mind.

It has been said that man can create anything which he can imagine.

Of all the ages of civilization, this is the most favorable for the development of the imagination, because it is an age of rapid change. On every hand one may contact stimuli which develop the imagination.

Through the aid of his imaginative faculty, man has discovered, and harnessed, more of Nature's forces during the past fifty years than during the entire history of the human race, previous to that time. He has conquered the air so completely that the birds are a poor match for him in flying. He has harnessed the ether, and made it serve as a means of instantaneous communication with any part of the world. He has analyzed and weighed the sun at a distance of millions of miles, and has determined, through the aid of imagination, the elements of which it consists. He has discovered that his own brain is both a broadcasting and a receiving station for the vibration of thought, and he is beginning now to learn how to make practical use of this discovery. He has increased the speed of locomotion, until he may now travel at a speed of more than three hundred miles an hour. The time will soon come when a man may breakfast in New York, and lunch in San Francisco.

It is better to light one small candle than to curse the darkness.

—Confucius

The imagination is literally the workshop wherein are fashioned all plans created by man.

Man's only limitation, within reason, lies in his development and use of his imagination. He has not yet reached the apex of development in the use of his imaginative faculty. He has merely discovered that he has an imagination, and has commenced to use it in a very elementary way.

TWO FORMS OF IMAGINATION

The imaginative faculty functions in two forms. One is known as "synthetic imagination," and the other as "creative imagination."

Synthetic Imagination:—Through this faculty, one may arrange old concepts, ideas, or plans into new combinations. This faculty *creates* nothing. It merely works with the material of experience, education, and observation with which it is fed. It is the faculty used most by the inventor, with the exception of the "genius" who draws upon the creative imagination when he cannot solve his problem through synthetic imagination.

Creative Imagination:—Through the faculty of creative imagination, the finite mind of man has direct communication with Infinite Intelligence. It is the faculty through which "hunches" and "inspirations" are received. It is by this faculty that all basic or new ideas are handed over to man. It is through this faculty that thought vibrations from the minds of others are received. It is through this faculty that one individual may "tune in," or communicate with the subconscious minds of other men.

The creative imagination works automatically, in the manner described in subsequent pages. This faculty functions only when the conscious mind is vibrating at an exceedingly rapid rate, as for example, when the conscious mind is stimulated through the emotion of a *strong desire*.

The creative faculty becomes more alert, more receptive to vibrations from the sources mentioned, in proportion to its development through use. This statement is significant! Ponder over it before passing on.

Keep in mind as you follow these principles that the entire story of how one may convert desire into money cannot be told in one statement. The story will be complete only when one has mastered, assimilated, and begun to make use of all the principles.

When the best things are not possible, the best may be made of those that are.

—Richard Hooker

It has been said that man can create anything which he can imagine.

The great leaders of business, industry, and finance, and the great artists, musicians, poets, and writers became great because they developed the faculty of creative imagination.

Both the synthetic and creative faculties of imagination become more alert with use, just as any muscle or organ of the body develops through use.

Desire is only a thought, an impulse. It is nebulous and ephemeral. It is abstract, and of no value, until it has been transformed into its physical counterpart. While the synthetic imagination is the one which will be used most frequently in the process of transforming the impulse of desire into money, you must keep in mind the fact that you may face circumstances and situations which demand use of the creative imagination as well.

Your mind is where you live. Your world, your body, and your situation react in exact accordance to your mind. Not someone else's mind, your *mind. An expanded consciousness expresses [itself] in an expanded experience.*

—Raymond Charles Barker

Your imaginative faculty may have become weak through inaction. It can be revived and made alert through use. This faculty does not die, though it may become quiescent through lack of use.

Center your attention, for the time being, on the development of the synthetic imagination, because this is the faculty which you will use more often in the process of converting desire into money.

Transformation of the intangible impulse, of desire, into the tangible reality, of money, calls for the use of a plan, or plans. These plans must be formed with the aid of the imagination, and mainly, with the synthetic faculty.

Read the entire book through, then come back to this chapter, and begin at once to put your imagination to work on the building of a plan, or plans, for the transformation of your desire into money. Detailed instructions for the building of plans have been given in almost every chapter. Carry out the instructions best suited to your needs; reduce your plan to writing, if you have not already done so. The moment you complete this, you will have definitely given concrete form to the intangible desire. Read the preceding sentence once more. Read it aloud, very slowly, and as you do so, remember that the moment you reduce the statement of your desire, and a plan for its realization, to writing, you have actually taken the first of a series of steps, which will enable you to convert the thought into its physical counterpart.

The earth on which you live, you, yourself, and every other material thing are the result of evolutionary change, through which microscopic bits of matter have been organized and arranged in an orderly fashion.

Man's only limitation, within reason, lies in his development and use of his imagination.

The great successful men of the world have used their imagination, they think ahead and create their mental picture in all its details, filling in here, adding a little there, altering this a bit and that a bit, but steadily building—steadily building.

—Robert Collier

Moreover—and this statement is of stupendous importance—this earth, every one of the billions of individual cells of your body, and every atom of matter, *began as an intangible form of energy.*

Desire is thought impulse! Thought impulses are forms of energy. When you begin with the thought impulse, desire, to accumulate money, you are drafting into your service the same "stuff" that Nature used in creating this earth, and every material form in the universe, including the body and brain in which the thought impulses function.

As far as science has been able to determine, the entire universe consists of but two elements—matter and energy.

Through the combination of energy and matter has been created everything perceptible to man, from the largest star which floats in the heavens down to, and including, man himself.

You are now engaged in the task of trying to profit by Nature's method. You are (sincerely and earnestly, we hope) trying to adapt yourself to Nature's laws, by endeavoring to convert desire into its physical or monetary equivalent. You can do it! It has been done before!

You can build a fortune through the aid of laws which are immutable. But, first, you must become familiar with these laws, and learn to use them. Through repetition, and by approaching the description of these principles from every conceivable angle, the author hopes to reveal to you the secret through which every great fortune has been accumulated. Strange and paradoxical as it may seem, the "secret" is not a secret. Nature, herself, advertises it in the earth on which we live, the stars, the planets suspended within our view, in the elements above and around us, in every blade of grass, and every form of life within our vision.

Nature advertises this "secret" in the terms of biology, in the conversion of a tiny cell, so small that it may be lost on the point of a pin, into the human being now reading this line. The conversion of desire into its physical equivalent is, certainly, no more miraculous!

Do not become discouraged if you do not fully comprehend all that has been stated. Unless you have long been a student of the mind, it is not to be expected that you will assimilate all that is in this chapter upon a first reading.

But you will, in time, make good progress.

The imaginative faculty functions in two forms. One is known as "synthetic imagination," and the other as "creative imagination."

The principles which follow will open the way for understanding of imagination. Assimilate that which you understand, as you read this philosophy for the first time; then, when you reread and study it, you will discover that something has happened to clarify it, and give you a broader understanding of the whole. Above all, do not stop, nor hesitate in your study of these principles until you have read the book at least three times, for then you will not want to stop.

You cannot depend on your eyes when your imagination is out of focus.

—Mark Twain

HOW TO MAKE PRACTICAL USE OF IMAGINATION

Ideas are the beginning points of all fortunes. Ideas are products of the imagination. Let us examine a few well-known ideas which have yielded huge fortunes, with the hope that these illustrations will convey definite information concerning the method by which imagination may be used in accumulating riches.

The Enchanted Kettle

Fifty years ago, an old country doctor drove to town, hitched his horse, quietly slipped into a drug store by the back door, and began "dickering" with the young drug clerk.

His mission was destined to yield great wealth to many people. It was destined to bring to the South the most far-flung benefit since the Civil War.

For more than an hour, behind the prescription counter, the old doctor and the clerk talked in low tones. Then the doctor left. He went out to the buggy and brought back a large, old-fashioned kettle, and a big wooden paddle (used for stirring the contents of the kettle), and deposited them in the back of the store.

The clerk inspected the kettle, reached into his inside pocket, took out a roll of bills, and handed it over to the doctor. The roll contained exactly $500—the clerk's entire savings!

The doctor handed over a small slip of paper on which was written a secret formula. The words on that small slip of paper were worth a king's ransom! *But not to the doctor!* Those magic words were needed to start the kettle to boil-

The creative faculty becomes more alert, more receptive to vibrations from the sources mentioned, in proportion to its development through use.

ing, but neither the doctor nor the young clerk knew what fabulous fortunes were destined to flow from that kettle.

The old doctor was glad to sell the outfit for $500. The money would pay off his debts, and give him freedom of mind. The clerk was taking a big chance by staking his entire life's savings on a mere scrap of paper and an old kettle! He never dreamed his investment would start a kettle to overflowing with gold that would surpass the miraculous performance of Aladdin's lamp.

What the clerk *really purchased* was an idea!

The old kettle and the wooden paddle and the secret message on a slip of paper were incidental. The strange performance of that kettle began to take place after the new owner mixed with the secret instructions an ingredient of which the doctor knew nothing.

Read this story carefully; give your imagination a test! See if you can discover what it was that the young man added to the secret message which caused the kettle to overflow with gold. Remember, as you read, that this is not a story from *Arabian Nights*. Here you have a story of facts, stranger than fiction, facts which began in the form of an idea.

Let us take a look at the vast fortunes of gold this idea has produced. It has paid, and still pays, huge fortunes to men and women all over the world who distribute the contents of the kettle to millions of people.

The Old Kettle is now one of the world's largest consumers of sugar, thus providing jobs of a permanent nature to thousands of men and women engaged in growing sugar cane, and in refining and marketing sugar.

The Old Kettle consumes, annually, millions of glass bottles, providing jobs to huge numbers of glass workers.

The Old Kettle gives employment to an army of clerks, stenographers, copy writers, and advertising experts throughout the nation. It has brought fame and fortune to scores of artists who have created magnificent pictures describing the product.

The Old Kettle has converted a small Southern city into the business capital of the South, where it now benefits, directly, or indirectly, every business and practically every resident of the city.

The influence of this idea now benefits every civilized country in the world, pouring out a continuous stream of gold to all who touch it.

The secret of success in life is for a man to be ready for his opportunity when it comes.

—Benjamin Disraeli

Keep in mind as you follow these principles that the entire story of how one may convert desire into money cannot be told in one statement. The story will be complete only when one has mastered, assimilated, and begun to make use of all the principles.

Gold from the kettle built and maintains one of the most prominent colleges of the South, where thousands of young people receive the training essential for success.

The Old Kettle has done other marvelous things.

All through the world depression, when factories, banks, and business houses were folding up and quitting by the thousands, the owner of this Enchanted Kettle went marching on, *giving continuous employment* to an army of men and women all over the world, and paying out extra portions of gold to those who, long ago, *had faith in the idea.*

If the product of that old brass kettle could talk, it would tell thrilling tales of romance in every language. Romances of love, romances of business, romances of professional men and women who are daily being stimulated by it.

The author is sure of at least one such romance, for he was a part of it, and it all began not far from the very spot on which the drug clerk purchased the Old Kettle. It was here that the author met his wife, and it was she who first told him of the Enchanted Kettle. It was the product of that kettle they were drinking when he asked her to accept him "for better or worse."

Now that you know the content of the Enchanted Kettle is a world-famous drink, it is fitting that the author confess that the home city of the drink supplied him with a wife, also that the drink itself provides him with *stimulation of thought without intoxication,* and thereby it serves to give the refreshment of mind which an author must have to do his best work.

Whoever you are, wherever you may live, whatever occupation you may be engaged in, just remember in the future, every time you see the words "Coca-Cola," that its vast empire of wealth and influence grew out of a single idea, and that the mysterious ingredient the drug clerk—Asa Candler—mixed with the secret formula was . . . imagination!

Stop and think of that for a moment.

Remember, also, that the thirteen steps to riches, described in this book, were the media through which the influence of Coca-Cola has been extended to every city, town, village, and cross-roads of the world, and that any idea you may create, as *sound and meritorious* as Coca-Cola, has the possibility of duplicating the stupendous record of this world-wide thirst-killer.

Truly, thoughts are things, and their scope of operation is the world, itself.

Health, happiness, and success depend upon the fighting spirit of each person. The big thing is not what happens to us in life—but what we do about what happens to us.

—George Allen

Your imaginative faculty may have become weak through inaction. It can be revived and made alert through use. This faculty does not die, though it may become quiescent through lack of use.

Create your future from your future, not your past.

—Werner Erhard

What I Would Do If I Had a Million Dollars

This story proves the truth of that old saying "Where there's a will, there's a way." It was told to me by that beloved educator and clergyman, the late Frank W. Gunsaulus, who began his preaching career in the stockyards region of South Chicago.

While Dr. Gunsaulus was going through college, he observed many defects in our educational system, defects which he believed he could correct, if he were the head of a college. His *deepest desire* was to become the directing head of an educational institution in which young men and women would be taught to "learn by doing."

He made up his mind to organize a new college in which he could carry out his ideas, without being handicapped by orthodox methods of education.

He needed a million dollars to put the project across! Where was he to lay his hands on so large a sum of money? That was the question that absorbed most of this ambitious young preacher's thought.

But he couldn't seem to make any progress.

Every night he took that thought to bed with him. He got up with it in the morning. He took it with him everywhere he went. He turned it over and over in his mind until it became a consuming *obsession* with him. A million dollars is a lot of money. He recognized that fact, but he also recognized the truth that *the only limitation is that which one sets up in one's own mind.*

Being a philosopher as well as a preacher, Dr. Gunsaulus recognized, as do all who succeed in life, that definiteness of purpose is the starting point from which one must begin. He recognized, too, that definiteness of purpose takes on animation, life, and power when backed by a burning desire to translate that purpose into its material equivalent.

He knew all these great truths, yet he did not know where, or how to lay his hands on a million dollars. The natural procedure would have been to give up and quit, by saying, "Ah well, my idea is a good one, but I cannot do anything with it, because I never can procure the necessary million dollars." That is exactly what the majority of people would have said, but it is not what Dr. Gunsaulus said. What he said, and what he did, are so important that I now introduce him, and let him speak for himself.

You are . . . trying to adapt yourself to Nature's laws, by endeavoring to convert desire into its physical or monetary equivalent. You can do it! It has been done before!

"One Saturday afternoon I sat in my room thinking of ways and means of raising the money to carry out my plans. For nearly two years, I had been thinking, but I *had done nothing but think!*

"The time had come for action!

"I made up my mind, then and there, that I would get the necessary million dollars within a week. How? I was not concerned about that. The main thing of importance was the *decision* to get the money within a specified time, and I want to tell you that the moment I reached a definite decision to get the money within a specified time, a strange feeling of assurance came over me, such as I had never before experienced. Something inside me seemed to say, 'Why didn't you reach that decision a long time ago? The money was waiting for you all the time!'

"Things began to happen in a hurry. I called the newspapers and announced I would preach a sermon the following morning, entitled 'What I Would Do If I Had a Million Dollars.'

"I went to work on the sermon immediately, but I must tell you, frankly, the task was not difficult, because I had been preparing that sermon for almost two years. The spirit back of it was a part of me!

"Long before midnight I had finished writing the sermon. I went to bed and slept with a feeling of confidence, for *I could see myself already in possession of the million dollars.*

"Next morning I arose early, went into the bathroom, read the sermon, then knelt on my knees and asked that my sermon might come to the attention of someone who would supply the needed money.

"While I was praying I again had that feeling of assurance that the money would be forthcoming. In my excitement, I walked out without my sermon, and did not discover the oversight until I was in my pulpit and about ready to begin delivering it.

"It was too late to go back for my notes, and what a blessing that I couldn't go back! Instead, my own subconscious mind yielded the material I needed. When I arose to begin my sermon, I closed my eyes, and spoke with all my heart and soul of my dreams. I not only talked to my audience, but I fancy I talked also to God. I told what I would do with a million dollars if that amount were placed in my hands. I described the plan I had in mind for organizing a

No matter how dark things seem to be or actually are, raise your sights and see the possibilities—always see them, for they're always there.
—Norman Vincent Peale

You can build a fortune through the aid of laws which are immutable. But, first, you must become familiar with these laws, and learn to use them.

great educational institution, where young people would learn to do practical things, and at the same time develop their minds.

"When I had finished and sat down, a man slowly arose from his seat, about three rows from the rear, and made his way toward the pulpit. I wondered what he was going to do. He came into the pulpit, extended his hand, and said, 'Reverend, I liked your sermon. I believe you can do everything you said you would, if you had a million dollars. To prove that I believe in you and your sermon, if you will come to my office tomorrow morning, I will give you the million dollars. My name is Phillip D. Armour.'"

Young Gunsaulus went to Mr. Armour's office and the million dollars was presented to him. With the money, he founded the Armour Institute of Technology.

That is more money than the majority of preachers ever see in an entire lifetime, yet the thought impulse back of the money was created in the young preacher's mind in a fraction of a minute. The necessary million dollars came as a result of an idea. Back of the idea was a DESIRE which young Gunsaulus had been nursing in his mind for almost two years.

Observe this important fact . . . he got the money within thirty-six hours after he reached a definite decision in his own mind to get it, and decided upon a definite plan for getting it!

There was nothing new or unique about young Gunsaulus' vague thinking about a million dollars, and weakly hoping for it. Others before him, and many since his time, have had similar thoughts. But there was something very unique and different about the decision he reached on that memorable Saturday, when he put vagueness into the background, and definitely said, "I will get that money within a week!"

God seems to throw Himself on the side of the man who knows *exactly* what he wants, *if he is determined* to get just that!

Moreover, the principle through which Dr. Gunsaulus got his million dollars is still alive! It is available to you! This universal law is as workable today as it was when the young preacher made use of it so successfully. This book describes, step by step, the thirteen elements of this great law, and suggests how they may be put to use.

Observe that Asa Candler and Dr. Frank Gunsaulus had one characteristic

You've got to think about big things while you're doing small things, so that all the small things go in the right direction.

—Alvin Toffler

Ideas are the beginning points of all fortunes. Ideas are products of the imagination.

in common. Both knew the astounding truth that ideas can be transmuted into cash through the power of definite purpose, plus definite plans.

If you are one of those who believe that hard work and honesty, alone, will bring riches, perish the thought! It is not true! Riches, when they come in huge quantities, are never the result of hard work! Riches come, if they come at all, in response to definite demands, based upon the application of definite principles, and not by chance or luck.

Generally speaking, an idea is an impulse of thought that impels action, by an appeal to the imagination. All master salesmen know that ideas can be sold where merchandise cannot. Ordinary salesmen do not know this—that is why they are "ordinary."

A publisher of books, which sell for a nickel, made a discovery that should be worth much to publishers generally. He learned that many people buy titles, and not contents of books. By merely changing the name of one book that was not moving, his sales on that book jumped upward more than a million copies. The inside of the book was not changed in any way. He merely ripped off the cover bearing the title that did not sell, and put on a new cover with a title that had "box-office" value.

That, as simple as it may seem, was an idea! It was imagination.

There is no standard price on ideas. The creator of ideas makes his own price, and, if he is smart, gets it.

The moving picture industry created a whole flock of millionaires. Most of them were men who couldn't create ideas—but—they had the imagination to recognize ideas when they saw them.

The next flock of millionaires will grow out of the radio business, which is new and not overburdened with men of keen imagination. The money will be made by those who discover or create new and more meritorious radio programmes and have the imagination to recognize merit, and to give the radio listeners a chance to profit by it.

The sponsor! That unfortunate victim who now pays the cost of all radio "entertainment" soon will become idea conscious, and demand something for his money. The man who beats the sponsor to the draw, and supplies programmes that render useful service, is the man who will become rich in this new industry.

The greatest discovery of my generation is that human beings can alter their lives by altering their attitude of mind.

—William James

"Something inside me seemed to say, 'Why didn't you reach that decision a long time ago? The money was waiting for you all the time!'"

All improvement is dependent upon you seeing yourself as being greater than you are. Then your potentials stir within you and your creative capacities unfold. By your own inner self, you are led aright, and you glimpse the you that you *are going to be.*

—Raymond Charles Barker

Crooners and light chatter artists who now pollute the air with wisecracks and silly giggles will go the way of all light timbers, and their places will be taken by real artists who interpret carefully planned programmes which have been designed to service the minds of men, as well as provide entertainment.

Here is a wide-open field of opportunity screaming its protest at the way it is being butchered, because of lack of imagination, and begging for rescue at any price. Above all, the thing that radio needs is new ideas!

If this new field of opportunity intrigues you, perhaps you might profit by the suggestion that the successful radio programmes of the future will give more attention to creating "buyer" audiences, and less attention to "listener" audiences. Stated more plainly, the builder of radio programmes who succeeds in the future must find practical ways to convert "listeners" into "buyers." Moreover, the successful producer of radio programmes in the future must key his features so that he can definitely show its effect upon the audience.

Sponsors are becoming a bit weary of buying glib selling talks, based upon statements grabbed out of thin air. They want, and in the future will demand, indisputable proof that the Whoosit programme not only gives millions of people the silliest giggle ever, but that the silly giggler can sell merchandise!

Another thing that might as well be understood by those who contemplate entering this new field of opportunity, radio advertising is going to be handled by an entirely new group of advertising experts, separate and distinct from the old-time newspaper and magazine advertising agency men. The old-timers in the advertising game *cannot read* the modern radio scripts, because they have been schooled to see ideas. The new radio technique demands men who can interpret ideas from a *written* manuscript in terms of *sound!* It cost the author a year of hard labor, and many thousands of dollars to learn this.

Radio, right now, is about where the moving pictures were when Mary Pickford and her curls first appeared on the screen. There is plenty of room in radio for those who can *produce or recognize* ideas.

If the foregoing comment on the opportunities of radio has not started your idea factory to work, you had better forget it. Your opportunity is in some other field. If the comment intrigued you in the slightest degree, then go further into it, and you may find the one idea you need to round out your career.

Never let it discourage you if you have no experience in radio. Andrew

If you are one of those who believe that hard work and honesty, alone, will bring riches, perish the thought! It is not true! Riches, when they come in huge quantities, are never the result of hard work!

Carnegie knew very little about making steel—I have Carnegie's own word for this—but he made practical use of two of the principles described in this book, and made the steel business yield him a fortune.

The story of practically every great fortune starts with the day when a creator of ideas and a seller of ideas got together and worked in harmony. Carnegie surrounded himself with men who could do all that he could not do—men who created ideas, and men who put ideas into operation—and made himself and the others fabulously rich.

Millions of people go through life hoping for favorable "breaks." Perhaps a favorable break can get one an opportunity, but the safest plan is not to depend upon luck. It was a favorable "break" that gave me the biggest opportunity of my life—but—twenty-five years *of determined effort* had to be devoted to that opportunity before it became an asset.

The "break" consisted of my good fortune in meeting and gaining the cooperation of Andrew Carnegie. On that occasion Carnegie planted in my mind the *idea* of organizing the principles of achievement into a philosophy of success. Thousands of people have profited by the discoveries made in the twenty-five years of research, and several fortunes have been accumulated through the application of the philosophy. The beginning was simple. It was an idea which anyone might have developed.

The favorable "break" came through Carnegie, but what about the determination, definiteness of purpose, and the desire to attain the goal, and the persistent effort of twenty-five years? It was no ordinary desire that survived disappointment, discouragement, temporary defeat, criticism, and the constant reminding of "waste of time." It was a burning desire! An obsession!

When the idea was first planted in my mind by Mr. Carnegie, it was coaxed, nursed, and enticed to *remain alive.* Gradually, the idea became a giant under its own power, and it coaxed, nursed, and drove me. Ideas are like that. First you give life and action and guidance to ideas, then they take on power of their own and sweep aside all opposition.

Ideas are intangible forces, but they have more power than the physical brains that give birth to them. They have the power to live on, after the brain that creates them has returned to dust. For example, take the power of Christianity. That began with a simple idea, born in the brain of Christ. Its chief tenet was

You are to become a creator, not a competitor; you are going to get what you want, but in such a way that when you get it every other man will have more than he has now.

—Wallace D. Wattles

Riches come, if they come at all, in response to definite demands, based upon the application of definite principles, and not by chance or luck.

If a man write a better book, preach a better sermon, or make a better mouse-trap than his neighbor, tho' he build his house in the woods, the world will make a beaten path to his door.

—Ralph Waldo Emerson

"Do unto others as you would have others do unto you." Christ has gone back to the source from whence He came, but His idea goes marching on. Some day, it may grow up, and come into its own, then it will have fulfilled Christ's deepest desire. The idea has been developing for only two thousand years. Give it time!

Success Requires No Explanations

Failure Permits No Alibis

Success requires no explanations.
Failure permits no alibis.

QUESTIONS FOR SUCCESS

- *What is the most helpful idea from this chapter for you?*

- *What are the two forms of imagination, and how are they unique?*

- *Which form of imagination will you use to create your goal?*

- *What is the beginning point of all fortunes (page 105)?*

- *Napoleon Hill writes, "Success requires no explanations, failure permits no alibis." How can that statement inspire you in your life?*

YOUR SUCCESS STEPS

☐ _____

☐ _____

☐ _____

☐ _____

☐ _____

☐ _____

CHAPTER 7

ORGANIZED PLANNING

The Crystallization of Desire Into Action

The Sixth Step Toward Riches

You have learned that everything man creates or acquires begins in the form of desire, that desire is taken on the first lap of its journey, from the abstract to the concrete, into the workshop of the imagination, where plans for its transition are created and organized.

In chapter two, you were instructed to take six definite, practical steps as your first move in translating the desire for money into its monetary equivalent. One of these steps is the formation of a definite, practical plan, or plans, through which this transformation may be made.

You will now be instructed how to build plans which will be practical, viz:

a. Ally yourself with a group of as many people as you may need for the creation and carrying out of your plan, or plans, for the accumulation of money—making use of the "Master Mind" principle described in a later chapter. (Compliance with this instruction is *absolutely essential*. Do not neglect it.)

b. Before forming your "Master Mind" alliance, decide what advantages, and benefits, *you* may offer the individual members of your group, in return for their cooperation. No one will work indefinitely without some form of compensation. No intelligent person

I believe that the true road to preeminent success in any line is to make yourself master of that line.

—Andrew Carnegie

You are engaged in an undertaking of major importance to you. To be sure of success, you must have plans which are faultless.

will either request or expect another to work without adequate compensation, although this may not always be in the form of money.

c. Arrange to meet with the members of your "Master Mind" group at least twice a week, and more often if possible, until you have jointly perfected the necessary plan, or plans, for the accumulation of money.

d. Maintain perfect harmony between yourself and every member of your "Master Mind" group. If you fail to carry out this instruction to the letter, you may expect to meet with failure. The "Master Mind" principle *cannot* obtain where perfect harmony does not prevail.

Keep in mind these facts:—

FIRST. You are engaged in an undertaking of major importance to you. To be sure of success, you must have plans which are faultless.

SECOND. You must have the advantage of the experience, education, native ability, and imagination of other minds. This is in harmony with the methods followed by every person who has accumulated a great fortune.

No individual has sufficient experience, education, native ability, and knowledge to insure the accumulation of a great fortune without the cooperation of other people. Every plan you adopt, in your endeavor to accumulate wealth, should be the joint creation of yourself and every other member of your "Master Mind" group. You may originate your own plans, either in whole or in part, but see that those plans are checked and approved by the members of your "Master Mind" alliance.

If the first plan which you adopt does not work successfully, replace it with a new plan; if this new plan fails to work, replace it in turn with still another, and so on, until you find a plan which does work. Right here is the point at which the majority of men meet with failure, because of their lack of persistence in creating new plans to take the place of those which fail.

The most intelligent man living cannot succeed in accumulating money—

There are many ideas in your mind which you have outgrown, and which, from force of habit, you still permit to dictate the actions of your life. Cease all this; abandon everything you have outgrown.

—Wallace D. Wattles

You must have the advantage of the experience, education, native ability, and imagination of other minds. This is in harmony with the methods followed by every person who has accumulated a great fortune.

nor in any other undertaking—without plans which are practical and workable. Just keep this fact in mind, and remember when your plans fail that temporary defeat is not permanent failure. It may only mean that your plans have not been sound. Build other plans. Start all over again.

Thomas A. Edison "failed" ten thousand times before he perfected the incandescent electric light bulb. That is—he met with *temporary defeat* ten thousand times, before his efforts were crowned with success.

Temporary defeat should mean only one thing—the certain knowledge that there is something wrong with your plan. Millions of men go through life in misery and poverty, because they lack a sound plan through which to accumulate a fortune.

Henry Ford accumulated a fortune, not because of his superior mind, but because he adopted and followed a plan which proved to be sound. A thousand men could be pointed out, each with a better education than Ford's, yet each of whom lives in poverty, because he does not possess the right plan for the accumulation of money.

Your achievement can be no greater than your plans are sound. That may seem to be an axiomatic statement, but it is true. Samuel Insull lost his fortune of over $100 million dollars. The Insull fortune was built on plans which were sound. The business depression forced Mr. Insull to change his plans; and the change brought "temporary defeat," because his new plans were not sound. Mr. Insull is now an old man; he may, consequently, accept "failure" instead of "temporary defeat," but if his experience turns out to be failure, it will be for the reason that he lacks the fire of persistence to rebuild his plans.

No man is ever whipped, until he quits—*in his own mind.*

This fact will be repeated many times, because it is so easy to "take the count" at the first sign of defeat.

James J. Hill met with temporary defeat when he first endeavored to raise the necessary capital to build a railroad from the East to the West, but he, too, turned defeat into victory *through new plans.*

Henry Ford met with temporary defeat, not only at the beginning of his automobile career, but after he had gone far toward the top. He created new plans, and went marching on to financial victory.

We see men who have accumulated great fortunes, but we often recognize

Clarity brings prosperity.

—Joel Fotinos

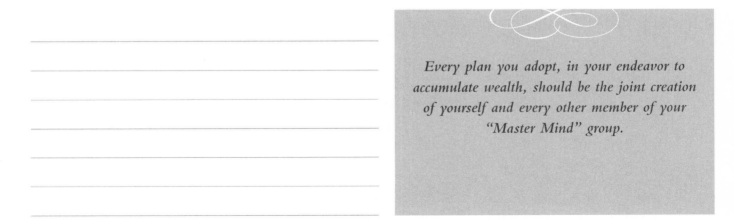

Every plan you adopt, in your endeavor to accumulate wealth, should be the joint creation of yourself and every other member of your "Master Mind" group.

Work and thou canst not escape the reward; whether thy work be fine or coarse, planting corn or writing epics, so only it be honest work, done to thine own approbation, it shall earn a reward to the senses as well as to the thought. No matter how often defeated, you are born to victory. The reward of a thing well done is to have done it.

—Ralph Waldo Emerson

only their triumph, overlooking the temporary defeats which they had to surmount before "arriving."

No follower of this philosophy can reasonably expect to accumulate a fortune without experiencing "temporary defeat." When defeat comes, accept it as a signal that your plans are not sound, rebuild those plans, and set sail once more toward your coveted goal. If you give up before your goal has been reached, you are a "quitter." A quitter never wins—and—a winner never quits. Lift this sentence out, write it on a piece of paper in letters an inch high, and place it where you will see it every night before you go to sleep, and every morning before you go to work.

When you begin to select members for your "Master Mind" group, endeavor to select those who do not take defeat seriously.

Some people foolishly believe that only money can make money. This is not true! Desire, transmuted into its monetary equivalent, through the principles laid down here, is the agency through which money is "made." Money, of itself, is nothing but inert matter. It cannot move, think, or talk, but it can "hear" when a man who desires it calls it to come!

PLANNING THE SALE OF SERVICES

The remainder of this chapter has been given over to a description of ways and means of marketing personal services. The information here conveyed will be of practical help to any person having any form of personal services to market, but it will be of priceless benefit to those who aspire to leadership in their chosen occupations.

Intelligent planning is essential for success in any undertaking designed to accumulate riches. Here will be found detailed instructions to those who must begin the accumulation of riches by selling personal services.

It should be encouraging to know that practically all the great fortunes began in the form of compensation for personal services, or from the sale of ideas. What else, except ideas and personal services, would one not possessed of property have to give in return for riches?

Broadly speaking, there are two types of people in the world. One type is

If the first plan which you adopt does not work successfully, replace it with a new plan; if this new plan fails to work, replace it in turn with still another, and so on, until you find a plan which does work.

known as leaders, and the other as followers. Decide at the outset whether you intend to become a leader in your chosen calling, or remain a follower. The difference in compensation is vast. The follower cannot reasonably expect the compensation to which a leader is entitled, although many followers make the mistake of expecting such pay.

It is no disgrace to be a follower. On the other hand, it is no credit to remain a follower. Most great leaders began in the capacity of followers. They became great leaders because they were intelligent followers. With few exceptions, the man who cannot follow a leader intelligently cannot become an efficient leader. The man who can follow a leader most efficiently is usually the man who develops into leadership most rapidly. An intelligent follower has many advantages, among them the opportunity to acquire knowledge from his leader.

> *A leader, once convinced that a particular course of action is the right one, must . . . be undaunted when the going gets tough.*
>
> —Ronald Reagan

THE MAJOR ATTRIBUTES OF LEADERSHIP

The following are important factors of leadership:—

1. Unwavering courage based upon knowledge of self, and of one's occupation. No follower wishes to be dominated by a leader who lacks self-confidence and courage. No intelligent follower will be dominated by such a leader very long.
2. Self-control. The man who cannot control himself can never control others. Self-control sets a mighty example for one's followers, which the more intelligent will emulate.
3. A keen sense of justice. Without a sense of fairness and justice, no leader can command and retain the respect of his followers.
4. Definiteness of decision. The man who wavers in his decisions shows that he is not sure of himself. He cannot lead others successfully.
5. Definiteness of plans. The successful leader must plan his work, and *work his plan*. A leader who moves by guesswork, without practical, definite plans, is comparable to a ship without a rudder. Sooner or later he will land on the rocks.
6. The habit of doing more than paid for. One of the penalties of lead-

> *Right here is the point at which the majority of people meet with failure, because of their lack of persistence in creating new plans to take the place of those which fail.*

A leader has the vision and conviction that a dream can be achieved. He inspires the power and energy to get it done.

—Ralph Lauren

ership is the necessity of willingness, upon the part of the leader, to do more than he requires of his followers.

7. A pleasing personality. No slovenly, careless person can become a successful leader. Leadership calls for respect. Followers will not respect a leader who does not grade high on all of the factors of a pleasing personality.

8. Sympathy and understanding. The successful leader must be in sympathy with his followers. Moreover, he must understand them and their problems.

9. Mastery of detail. Successful leadership calls for mastery of details of the leader's position.

10. Willingness to assume full responsibility. The successful leader must be willing to assume responsibility for the mistakes and the shortcomings of his followers. If he tries to shift this responsibility, he will not remain the leader. If one of his followers makes a mistake, and shows himself incompetent, the leader must consider that it is *he* who failed.

11. Cooperation. The successful leader must understand and *apply* the principle of cooperative effort and be able to induce his followers to do the same. Leadership calls for power, and power calls for co-operation.

There are two forms of Leadership. The first, and by far the most effective, is Leadership by Consent of, and with the sympathy of, the followers. The second is Leadership by Force, without the consent and sympathy of the followers.

History is filled with evidences that Leadership by Force cannot endure. The downfall and disappearance of dictators and kings is significant. It means that people will not follow forced leadership indefinitely.

The world has just entered a new era of relationship between leaders and followers, which very clearly calls for new leaders, and a new brand of leadership in business and industry. Those who belong to the old school of Leadership by Force, must acquire an understanding of the new brand of leadership (co-

The most intelligent man living cannot succeed in accumulating money—nor in any other undertaking—without plans which are practical and workable.

operation) or be relegated to the rank and file of the followers. There is no other way out for them.

The relationship of employer and employee, or of leader and follower, in the future, will be one of mutual cooperation, based upon an equitable division of the profits of business. In the future, the relationship of employer and employee will be more like a partnership than it has been in the past.

Napoleon, Kaiser Wilhelm of Germany, the Czar of Russia, and the King of Spain were examples of Leadership by Force. Their leadership passed. Without much difficulty, one might point to the prototypes of these ex-leaders among the business, financial, and labor leaders of America who have been dethroned or slated to go. *Leadership by Consent* of the followers is the only brand which can endure!

Men may follow the forced leadership temporarily, but they will not do so willingly.

The new brand of leadership will embrace the eleven factors of leadership, described in this chapter, as well as some other factors. The man who makes these the basis of his leadership will find abundant opportunity to lead in any walk of life. The depression was prolonged, largely, because the world lacked leadership of the new brand. At the end of the depression, the demand for leaders who are competent to apply the new methods of leadership has greatly exceeded the supply. Some of the old type of leaders will reform and adapt themselves to the new brand of leadership, but generally speaking, the world will have to look for new timber for its leadership.

This necessity may be your opportunity!

Show me a man who cannot bother to do little things and I'll show you a man who cannot be trusted to do big things.

—Lawrence D. Bell

THE TEN MAJOR CAUSES OF FAILURE IN LEADERSHIP

We come now to the major faults of leaders who fail, because it is just as essential to know what not to do as it is to know what to do.

1. **Inability to organize details.** Efficient leadership calls for ability to organize and to master details. No genuine leader is ever "too

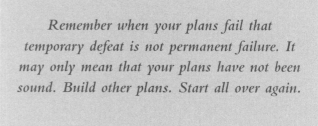

Remember when your plans fail that temporary defeat is not permanent failure. It may only mean that your plans have not been sound. Build other plans. Start all over again.

No one has ever done his best. The greatest creative minds, producing masterpieces in art, literature, dance, music, and the sciences, have never been satisfied with their works. Never judge yourself by what you have done. Judge yourself in terms of what you will do. You are not the past. You are the present becoming the future.

—Raymond Charles Barker

busy" to do anything which may be required of him in his capacity as leader. When a man, whether he is a leader or follower, admits that he is "too busy" to change his plans, or to give attention to any emergency, he admits his inefficiency. The successful leader must be the master of all details connected with his position. That means, of course, that he must acquire the habit of relegating details to capable lieutenants.

2. **Unwillingness to render humble service.** Truly great leaders are willing, when occasion demands, to perform any sort of labor which they would ask another to perform. "The greatest among ye shall be the servant of all" is a truth which all able leaders observe and respect.

3. **Expectation of pay for what they "know" instead of what they do with that which they know.** The world does not pay men for that which they "know." It pays them for what they DO, or induce others to do.

4. **Fear of competition from followers.** The leader who fears that one of his followers may take his position is practically sure to realize that fear sooner or later. The able leader trains understudies to whom he may delegate, at will, any of the details of his position. Only in this way may a leader multiply himself and prepare himself to be at many places, and give attention to many things at one time. It is an eternal truth that men receive more pay for their ability to get others to perform than they could possibly earn by their own efforts. An efficient leader may, through his knowledge of his job and the magnetism of his personality, greatly increase the efficiency of others, and induce them to render more service and better service than they could render without his aid.

5. **Lack of imagination.** Without imagination, the leader is incapable of meeting emergencies, and of creating plans by which to guide his followers efficiently.

6. **Selfishness.** The leader who claims all the honor for the work of his followers is sure to be met by resentment. The really great leader

Thomas A. Edison "failed" ten thousand times before he perfected the incandescent electric light bulb. That is—he met with temporary defeat ten thousand times, before his efforts were crowned with success.

claims none of the honors. He is contented to see the honors, when there are any, go to his followers, because he knows that most men will work harder for commendation and recognition than they will for money alone.

7. **Intemperance.** Followers do not respect an intemperate leader. Moreover, intemperance in any of its various forms destroys the endurance and the vitality of all who indulge in it.

8. **Disloyalty.** Perhaps this should have come at the head of the list. The leader who is not loyal to his trust, and to his associates, those above him, and those below him, cannot long maintain his leadership. Disloyalty marks one as being less than the dust of the earth, and brings down on one's head the contempt he deserves. Lack of loyalty is one of the major causes of failure in every walk of life.

9. **Emphasis of the "authority" of leadership.** The efficient leader leads by encouraging, and not by trying to instill fear in the hearts of his followers. The leader who tries to impress his followers with his "authority" comes within the category of Leadership by Force. If a leader is a real leader, he will have no need to advertise that fact except by his conduct—his sympathy, understanding, fairness, and a demonstration that he knows his job.

10. **Emphasis of title.** The competent leader requires no "title" to give him the respect of his followers. The man who makes too much over his title generally has little else to emphasize. The doors to the office of the real leader are open to all who wish to enter, and his working quarters are free from formality or ostentation.

These are among the more common of the causes of failure in leadership. Any one of these faults is sufficient to induce failure. Study the list carefully if you aspire to leadership, and make sure that you are free of these faults.

If we are ever to enjoy life, now is the time—not tomorrow, nor next year, nor in some future life after we have died. The best preparation for a better life next year is a full, complete, harmonious, joyous life this year.

—Thomas Dreier

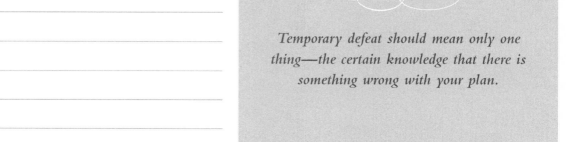

Temporary defeat should mean only one thing—the certain knowledge that there is something wrong with your plan.

SOME FERTILE FIELDS IN WHICH
"NEW LEADERSHIP" WILL BE REQUIRED

The way to have everything is to do one thing at a time, well.

—August Gold

Before leaving this chapter, your attention is called to a few of the fertile fields in which there has been a decline of leadership, and in which the new type of leader may find an abundance of opportunity.

FIRST. In the field of politics there is a most insistent demand for new leaders, a demand which indicates nothing less than an emergency. The majority of politicians have, seemingly, become high-grade, legalized racketeers. They have increased taxes and debauched the machinery of industry and business until the people can no longer stand the burden.

SECOND. The banking business is undergoing a reform. The leaders in this field have almost entirely lost the confidence of the public. Already the bankers have sensed the need of reform, and they have begun it.

THIRD. Industry calls for new leaders. The old type of leaders thought and moved in terms of dividends instead of thinking and moving in terms of human equations! The future leader in industry, to endure, must regard himself as a quasi-public official whose duty it is to manage his trust in such a way that it will work hardship on no individual, or group of individuals. Exploitation of working men is a thing of the past. Let the man who aspires to leadership in the field of business, industry, and labor remember this.

FOURTH. The religious leader of the future will be forced to give more attention to the temporal needs of his followers, in the solution of their economic and personal problems of the present, and less attention to the dead past, and the yet unborn future.

FIFTH. In the professions of law, medicine, and education, a new brand of leadership, and to some extent, new leaders will become a necessity. This is especially true in the field of education. The leader in that field

Your achievement can be no greater than your plans are sound.

must, in the future, find ways and means of teaching people how to apply the knowledge they receive in school. He must deal more with practice and less with theory.

SIXTH. New leaders will be required in the field of journalism. Newspapers of the future, to be conducted successfully, must be divorced from "special privilege" and relieved from the subsidy of advertising. They must cease to be organs of propaganda for the interests which patronize their advertising columns. The type of newspaper which publishes scandal and lewd pictures will eventually go the way of all forces which debauch the human mind.

Success is a science; if you have the conditions, you get the result.
—Oscar Wilde

These are but a few of the fields in which opportunities for new leaders and a new brand of leadership are now available. The world is undergoing a rapid change. This means that the media through which the changes in human habits are promoted must be adapted to the changes. The media here described are the ones which, more than any others, determine the trend of civilization.

WHEN AND HOW TO APPLY FOR A POSITION

The information described here is the net result of many years of experience during which thousands of men and women were helped to market their services effectively. It can, therefore, be relied upon as sound and practical.

MEDIA THROUGH WHICH SERVICES MAY BE MARKETED

Experience has proved that the following media offer the most direct and effective methods of bringing the buyer and seller of personal services together.

1. Employment bureaus. Care must be taken to select only reputable bureaus, the management of which can show adequate records of

No man is ever whipped, until he quits—in his own mind. This fact will be repeated many times, because it is so easy to "take the count" at the first sign of defeat.

Success isn't a result of spontaneous combustion. You must set yourself on fire.

—Arnold H. Glasow

achievement of satisfactory results. There are comparatively few such bureaus.

2. Advertising in newspapers, trade journals, magazines, and radio. Classified advertising may usually be relied upon to produce satisfactory results in the case of those who apply for clerical or ordinary salaried positions. Display advertising is more desirable in the case of those who seek executive connections, the copy to appear in the section of the paper which is most apt to come to the attention of the class of employer being sought. The copy should be prepared by an expert, who understands how to inject sufficient selling qualities to produce replies.

3. Personal letters of application, directed to particular firms or individuals most apt to need such services as are being offered. Letters should be *neatly typed,* always, and signed by hand. With the letter should be sent a complete "brief" or outline of the applicant's qualifications. Both the letter of application and the brief of experience or qualifications should be prepared by an expert. (See instructions as to information to be supplied.)

4. Application through personal acquaintances. When possible, the applicant should endeavor to approach prospective employers through some mutual acquaintance. This method of approach is particularly advantageous in the case of those who seek executive connections and do not wish to appear to be "peddling" themselves.

5. Application in person. In some instances, it may be more effective if the applicant offers personally his services to prospective employers, in which event a complete written statement of qualifications for the position should be presented, for the reason that prospective employers often wish to discuss with associates one's record.

We see men who have accumulated great fortunes, but we often recognize only their triumph, overlooking the temporary defeats which they had to surmount before "arriving."

INFORMATION TO BE SUPPLIED IN
A WRITTEN "BRIEF"

This brief should be prepared as carefully as a lawyer would prepare the brief of a case to be tried in court. Unless the applicant is experienced in the preparation of such briefs, an expert should be consulted, and his services enlisted for this purpose. Successful merchants employ men and women who understand the art and the psychology of advertising to present the merits of their merchandise. One who has personal services for sale should do the same. The following information should appear in the brief:

Do, every day, ALL that can be done that day. Every day is either a successful day or a day of failure; and it is the successful days which get you what you want.

—Wallace D. Wattles

1. *Education.* State briefly, but definitely, what schooling you have had, and in what subjects you specialized in school, giving the reasons for that specialization.
2. *Experience.* If you have had experience in connection with positions similar to the one you seek, describe it fully; state names and addresses of former employers. Be sure to bring out clearly any special experience you may have had which would equip you to fill the position you seek.
3. *References.* Practically every business firm desires to know all about the previous records, antecedents, etc., of prospective employees who seek positions of responsibility. Attach to your brief photostatic copies of letters from:
    a. Former employers
    b. Teachers under whom you studied
    c. Prominent people whose judgment may be relied upon
4. *Photograph of self.* Attach to your brief a recent, unmounted photograph of yourself.
5. *Apply for a specific position.* Avoid application for a position without describing exactly what particular position you seek. Never apply for "just a position." That indicates you lack specialized qualifications.
6. *State your qualifications* for the particular position for which you apply. Give full details as to the reason you believe you are qualified

No follower of this philosophy can reasonably expect to accumulate a fortune without experiencing "temporary defeat."

The successful always has a number of projects planned, to which he looks forward. Any one of them could change the course of his life overnight.

—Mark Caine

for the particular position you seek. This is the most important detail of your application. It will determine, more than anything else, what consideration you receive.

7. *Offer to go to work on probation.* In the majority of instances, if you are determined to have the position for which you apply, it will be most effective if you offer to work for a week, or a month, or for a sufficient length of time to enable your prospective employer to judge your value without pay. This may appear to be a radical suggestion, but experience has proved that it seldom fails to win at least a trial. If you are sure of your qualifications, a trial is all you need. Incidentally, such an offer indicates that you have confidence in your ability to fill the position you seek. It is most convincing. If your offer is accepted, and you make good, more than likely you will be paid for your "probation" period. Make clear the fact that your offer is based upon:

    a. Your confidence in your ability to fill the position

    b. Your confidence in your prospective employer's decision to employ you after trial

    c. Your determination to have the position you seek

8. *Knowledge of your prospective employer's business.* Before applying for a position, do sufficient research in connection with the business to familiarize yourself thoroughly with that business, and indicate in your brief the knowledge you have acquired in this field. This will be impressive, as it will indicate that you have imagination, and a real interest in the position you seek.

Remember that it is not the lawyer who knows the most law but the one who best prepares his case who wins. If your "case" is properly prepared and presented, your victory will have been more than half won at the outset.

Do not be afraid of making your brief too long. Employers are just as much interested in purchasing the services of well-qualified applicants as you are in securing employment. In fact, the success of most successful employers is due, in the main, to their ability to select well-qualified lieutenants. They want all the information available.

When defeat comes, accept it as a signal that your plans are not sound, rebuild those plans, and set sail once more toward your coveted goal.

Remember another thing: Neatness in the preparation of your brief will indicate that you are a painstaking person. I have helped to prepare briefs for clients which were so striking and out of the ordinary that they resulted in the employment of the applicant without a personal interview.

When your brief has been completed, have it neatly bound by an experienced binder, and lettered by an artist, or printer, similar to the following:

One important key to success is self-confidence. An important key to self-confidence is preparation.
—Arthur Ashe

BRIEF OF THE QUALIFICATIONS OF
Robert K. Smith
APPLYING FOR THE POSITION OF
{ Private Secretary to
the President of
THE BLANK COMPANY, INC. }

Change names each time the brief is shown.

This personal touch is sure to command attention. Have your brief neatly typed or mimeographed on the finest paper you can obtain, and bound with a heavy paper of the book-cover variety; the binder to be changed, and the proper firm name to be inserted, if it is to be shown to more than one company. Your photograph should be pasted on one of the pages of your brief. Follow these instructions to the letter, improving upon them wherever your imagination suggests.

Successful salesmen groom themselves with care. They understand that first impressions are lasting. Your brief is your salesman. Give it a good suit of clothes, so it will stand out in bold contrast to anything your prospective employer ever saw, in the way of an application for a position. If the position you seek is worth having, it is worth going after with care. Moreover, if you sell yourself to an employer in a manner that impresses him with your individuality, you probably will receive more money for your services from the very start than you would if you applied for employment in the usual conventional way.

If you seek employment through an advertising agency or an employment agency, have the agent use copies of your brief in marketing your services. This will help to gain preference for you, both with the agent and the prospective employers.

If you give up before your goal has been reached, you are a "quitter." A quitter never wins—and—a winner never quits.

HOW TO GET THE EXACT POSITION YOU DESIRE

Every minute you spend in planning saves ten minutes in execution; this gives you a one-thousand-percent return on energy!

—Brian Tracy

Everyone enjoys doing the kind of work for which he is best suited. An artist loves to work with paints, a craftsman with his hands, a writer loves to write. Those with less definite talents have their preferences for certain fields of business and industry. If America does anything well, it offers a full range of occupations: tilling the soil, manufacturing, marketing, and the professions.

FIRST. Decide exactly what kind of a job you want. If the job doesn't already exist, perhaps you can create it.

SECOND. Choose the company, or individual, for whom you wish to work.

THIRD. Study your prospective employer as to policies, personnel, and chances of advancement.

FOURTH. By analysis of yourself, your talents, and capabilities, figure what you can offer, and plan ways and means of giving advantages, services, developments, ideas that *you believe* you can successfully deliver.

FIFTH. Forget about "a job." Forget whether or not there is an opening. Forget the usual routine of "Have you got a job for me?" Concentrate on what *you can give*.

SIXTH. Once you have your plan in mind, arrange with an experienced writer to put it on paper in neat form, and in full detail.

SEVENTH. Present it to the *proper person with authority* and he will do the rest. Every company is looking for men who can give something of value, whether it be ideas, services, or "connections." Every company has room for the man who has a definite plan of action which is to the advantage of that company.

When you begin to select members for your "Master Mind" group, endeavor to select those who do not take defeat seriously.

This line of procedure may take a few days or weeks of extra time, but the difference in income, in advancement, and in gaining recognition will save years of hard work at small pay. It has many advantages, the main one being that it will often save from one to five years of time in reaching a chosen goal.

Every person who starts or "gets in" half-way up the ladder does so by deliberate and careful planning (excepting, of course, the Boss' son).

Time is our most valuable asset, yet we tend to waste it, kill it, and spend it rather than invest it.

—Jim Rohn

THE NEW WAY OF MARKETING SERVICES

"Jobs" Are Now "Partnerships"

Men and women who market their services to best advantage in the future must recognize the stupendous change which has taken place in connection with the relationship between employer and employee.

In the future, the "Golden Rule," and not the "Rule of Gold," will be the dominating factor in the marketing of merchandise as well as personal services. The future relationship between employers and their employees will be more in the nature of a partnership consisting of:

a. The employer
b. The employee
c. The public they serve

This new way of marketing personal services is called new for many reasons; first, both the employer and the employee of the future will be considered as fellow-employees whose business it will be to serve the public efficiently. In times past, employers and employees have bartered among themselves, driving the best bargains they could with one another, not considering that in the final analysis they were, in reality, bargaining at the expense of the third party, the public they served.

The depression served as a mighty protest from an injured public, whose rights had been trampled upon in every direction by those who were clamoring for individual advantages and profits. When the debris of the depression

Some people foolishly believe that only money can make money. This is not true!

The cause of failure is doing too many things in an inefficient manner, and not doing enough things in an efficient manner.

—Wallace D. Wattles

shall have been cleared away, and business shall have been once again restored to balance, both employers and employees will recognize that they are no longer privileged to drive bargains at the expense of those whom they serve. The real employer of the future will be the public. This should be kept uppermost in mind by every person seeking to market personal services effectively.

Nearly every railroad in America is in financial difficulty. Who does not remember the day when, if a citizen enquired at the ticket office, the time of departure of a train, he was abruptly referred to the bulletin board instead of being politely given the information?

The street car companies have experienced a "change of times" also. There was a time not so very long ago when street car conductors took pride in giving argument to passengers. Many of the street car tracks have been removed and passengers ride on a bus, whose driver is "the last word in politeness."

All over the country street car tracks are rusting from abandonment, or have been taken up. Wherever street cars are still in operation, passengers may now ride without argument, and one may even hail the car in the middle of the block, and the motorman will obligingly pick him up.

How times have changed! That is just the point I am trying to emphasize. Times have changed! Moreover, the change is reflected not merely in railroad offices and on street cars, but in other walks of life as well. The "public-be-damned" policy is now passé. It has been supplanted by the "we-are-obligingly-at-your-service, sir" policy.

The bankers have learned a thing or two during this rapid change which has taken place during the past few years. Impoliteness on the part of a bank official or bank employee today is as rare as it was conspicuous a dozen years ago. In the years past, some bankers (not all of them, of course) carried an atmosphere of austerity which gave every would-be borrower a chill when he even thought of approaching his banker for a loan.

The thousands of bank failures during the depression had the effect of removing the mahogany doors behind which bankers formerly barricaded themselves. They now sit at desks in the open, where they may be seen and approached at will by any depositor, or by anyone who wishes to see them, and the whole atmosphere of the bank is one of courtesy and understanding.

It used to be customary for customers to have to stand and wait at the corner

Money, of itself, is nothing but inert matter. It cannot move, think, or talk, but it can "hear" when a man who desires it calls it to come!

grocery until the clerks were through passing the time of day with friends, and the proprietor had finished making up his bank deposit, before being waited upon. Chain stores, managed by courteous men who do everything in the way of service, short of shining the customer's shoes, have pushed the old-time merchants into the background. Time marches on!

"Courtesy" and "Service" are the watch-words of merchandising today, and apply to the person who is marketing personal services even more directly than to the employer whom he serves, because, in the final analysis, both the employer and his employee are employed by the public they serve. If they fail to serve well, they pay by the loss of their privilege of serving.

We can all remember the time when the gas-meter reader pounded on the door hard enough to break the panels. When the door was opened, he pushed his way in, uninvited, with a scowl on his face which plainly said, "What the hell did you keep me waiting for?" All that has undergone a change. The meter-man now conducts himself as a gentleman who is "delighted-to-be-at-your-service-sir." Before the gas companies learned that their scowling meter-men were accumulating liabilities never to be cleared away, the polite salesmen of oil burners came along and did a land-office business.

During the depression, I spent several months in the anthracite coal region of Pennsylvania, studying conditions which all but destroyed the coal industry. Among several very significant discoveries was the fact that greed on the part of operators and their employees was the chief cause of the loss of business for the operators, and loss of jobs for the miners.

Through the pressure of a group of overzealous labor leaders, representing the employees, and the greed for profits on the part of the operators, the anthracite business suddenly dwindled. The coal operators and their employees drove sharp bargains with one another, adding the cost of the "bargaining" to the price of the coal, until, finally, they discovered they had built up a wonderful business for the manufacturers of oil-burning outfits and the producers of crude oil.

"The wages of sin is death!" Many have read this in the Bible, but few have discovered its meaning. Now, and for several years, the entire world has been listening by force to a sermon which might well be called "Whatsoever a man soweth, that shall he also reap."

Success consists of going from failure to failure without loss of enthusiasm.

—Winston Churchill

Intelligent planning is essential for success in any undertaking designed to accumulate riches.

Even if you are on the right track, you will get run over if you just sit there.

—Will Rogers

Nothing as widespread and effective as the depression could possibly be "just a coincidence." Behind the depression was a cause. Nothing ever happens without a cause. In the main, the cause of the depression is traceable directly to the worldwide habit of trying to reap without sowing.

This should not be mistaken to mean that the depression represents a crop which the world is being forced to reap without having sown. The trouble is that the world *sowed the wrong sort of seed.* Any farmer knows he cannot sow the seed of thistles, and reap a harvest of grain. Beginning at the outbreak of the world war, the people of the world began to sow the seed of service inadequate in both quality and quantity. Nearly everyone was engaged in the pastime of trying to get without giving.

These illustrations are brought to the attention of those who have personal services to market, to show that we are where we are, and what we are, because of *our own conduct!* If there is a principle of cause and effect, which controls business, finance, and transportation, this same principle controls individuals and determines their economic status.

WHAT IS YOUR "QQS" RATING?

The causes of success in marketing services effectively and permanently have been clearly described. Unless those causes are studied, analyzed, understood, and applied, no man can market his services effectively and permanently. Every person must be his own salesman of personal services. The quality and the quantity of service rendered, and the spirit in which it is rendered, determine to a large extent the price and the duration of employment. To market personal services effectively (which means a permanent market, at a satisfactory price, under pleasant conditions), one must adopt and follow the "QQS" formula, which means that quality, plus quantity, plus the proper spirit of cooperation, equals perfect salesmanship of service. Remember the "QQS" formula, but do more— apply it as a habit!

Let us analyze the formula to make sure we understand exactly what it means.

It should be encouraging to know that practically all the great fortunes began in the form of compensation for personal services, or from the sale of ideas.

1. *Quality* of service shall be construed to mean the performance of every detail, in connection with your position, in the most efficient manner possible, with the object of greater efficiency always in mind.

2. *Quantity* of service shall be understood to mean the habit of rendering all the service of which you are capable, at all times, with the purpose of increasing the amount of service rendered as greater skill is developed through practice and experience. Emphasis is again placed on the word "habit."

3. *Spirit* of service shall be construed to mean the habit of agreeable, harmonious conduct which will induce cooperation from associates and fellow employees.

Destiny is not a matter of chance, but of choice. Not something to wish for, but to attain.

—William Jennings Bryan

Adequacy of quality and quantity of service is not sufficient to maintain a permanent market for your services. The conduct, or the spirit in which you deliver service, is a strong determining factor in connection with both the price you receive and the duration of employment.

Andrew Carnegie stressed this point more than others in connection with his description of the factors which lead to success in the marketing of personal services. He emphasized again, and again, the necessity for harmonious conduct. He stressed the fact that he would not retain any man, no matter how great a quantity, or how efficient the quality of his work, *unless* he worked in a spirit of harmony. Mr. Carnegie insisted upon men being agreeable. To prove that he placed a high value upon this quality, he permitted many men *who conformed to his standards* to become very wealthy. Those who did not conform had to make room for others.

The importance of a pleasing personality has been stressed because it is a factor which enables one to render service in the proper spirit. If one has a personality which pleases, and renders service in a spirit of harmony, these assets often make up for deficiencies in both the quality and the quantity of service one renders. Nothing, however, can be successfully substituted for pleasing conduct.

Broadly speaking, there are two types of people in the world. One type is known as leaders, and the other as followers.

THE CAPITAL VALUE OF YOUR SERVICES

Rebellion against your handicaps gets you nowhere. Self-pity gets you nowhere. One must have the adventurous daring to accept oneself as a bundle of possibilities and undertake the most interesting game in the world—making the most of one's best.

—Harry Emerson Fosdick

The person whose income is derived entirely from the sale of personal services is no less a merchant than the man who sells commodities, and it might well be added, such a person is subject to exactly the same rules of conduct as the merchant who sells merchandise.

This has been emphasized because the majority of people who live by the sale of personal services make the mistake of considering themselves free from the rules of conduct, and the responsibilities attached to those who are engaged in marketing commodities.

The new way of marketing services has practically forced both employer and employee into partnership alliances, through which both take into consideration the rights of the third party, the public they serve.

The day of the "go-getter" has passed. He has been supplanted by the "go-giver." High-pressure methods in business finally blew the lid off. There will never be the need to put the lid back on, because, in the future, business will be conducted by methods that will require no pressure.

The actual capital value of your brains may be determined by the amount of income you can produce (by marketing your services). A fair estimate of the capital value of your services may be made by multiplying your annual income by sixteen and two-thirds, as it is reasonable to estimate that your annual income represents 6 percent of your capital value. Money rents for 6 percent per annum. Money is worth no more than brains. It is often worth much less.

Competent "brains," if effectively marketed, represent a much more desirable form of capital than that which is required to conduct a business dealing in commodities, because "brains" are a form of capital which cannot be permanently depreciated through depressions, nor can this form of capital be stolen or spent. Moreover, the money which is essential for the conduct of business is as worthless as a sand dune, until it has been mixed with efficient "brains."

Decide at the outset whether you intend to become a leader in your chosen calling, or remain a follower. The difference in compensation is vast.

THE THIRTY MAJOR CAUSES OF FAILURE

How many of these are holding you back?
Life's greatest tragedy consists of men and women who earnestly try, and fail! The tragedy lies in the overwhelmingly large majority of people who fail, as compared to the few who succeed.

I have had the privilege of analyzing several thousand men and women, 98 percent of whom were classed as "failures." There is something radically wrong with a civilization, and a system of education, which permit 98 percent of the people to go through life as failures. But I did not write this book for the purpose of moralizing on the rights and wrongs of the world; that would require a book a hundred times the size of this one.

My analysis work proved that there are thirty major reasons for failure, and thirteen major principles through which people accumulate fortunes. In this chapter, a description of the thirty major causes of failure will be given. As you go over the list, check yourself by it, point by point, for the purpose of discovering how many of these causes-of-failure stand between you and success.

1. **Unfavorable hereditary background.** There is but little, if anything, which can be done for people who are born with a deficiency in brain power. This philosophy offers but one method of bridging this weakness—through the aid of the Master Mind. Observe with profit, however, that this is the only one of the thirty causes of failure which may not be *easily corrected* by any individual.

2. **Lack of a well-defined purpose in life.** There is no hope of success for the person who does not have a central purpose, or *definite goal*, at which to aim. Ninety-eight out of every hundred of those whom I have analyzed had no such aim. Perhaps this was the major cause of their failure.

3. **Lack of ambition to aim above mediocrity.** We offer no hope for the person who is so indifferent as not to want to get ahead in life, and who is not willing to pay the price.

4. **Insufficient education.** This is a handicap which may be overcome

What looks like the end of the road in our personal experience is only the turn in the road, the beginning of a new and more beautiful journey. I have always tried to live by that philosophy, and it has kept me happy.

—Mary Pickford

The follower cannot reasonably expect the compensation to which a leader is entitled, although many followers make the mistake of expecting such pay.

with comparative ease. Experience has proven that the best-educated people are often those who are known as "self-made," or self-educated. It takes more than a college degree to make one a person of education. Any person who is educated is one who has learned to get whatever he wants in life without violating the rights of others. Education consists not so much of knowledge, but of knowledge effectively and persistently applied. Men are paid not merely for what they know, but more particularly for what they do with that which they know.

5. Lack of self-discipline. Discipline comes through self-control. This means that one must control all negative qualities. Before you can control conditions, you must first control yourself. Self-mastery is the hardest job you will ever tackle. If you do not conquer self, you will be conquered by self. You may see at one and the same time both your best friend and your greatest enemy by stepping in front of a mirror.

6. Ill health. No person may enjoy outstanding success without good health. Many of the causes of ill health are subject to mastery and control. These, in the main are:
   a. Overeating of foods not conducive to health
   b. Wrong habits of thought; giving expression to negatives
   c. Wrong use of, and over-indulgence in, sex
   d. Lack of proper physical exercise
   e. An inadequate supply of fresh air, due to improper breathing

7. Unfavorable environmental influences during childhood. "As the twig is bent, so shall the tree grow." Most people who have criminal tendencies acquire them as the result of bad environment, and improper associates during childhood.

8. Procrastination. This is one of the most common causes of failure. "Old Man Procrastination" stands within the shadow of every human being, waiting his opportunity to spoil one's chances of success. Most of us go through life as failures, because we are waiting for the "time to be right" to start doing something worthwhile. Do not wait. The

It is no disgrace to start all over. It is usually an opportunity.
—George Matthew Adams

Most great leaders began in the capacity of followers. They became great leaders because they were intelligent followers. With few exceptions, the man who cannot follow a leader intelligently cannot become an efficient leader.

time will never be "just right." Start where you stand, and work with whatever tools you may have at your command, and better tools will be found as you go along.

9. Lack of persistence. Most of us are good "starters" but poor "finishers" of everything we begin. Moreover, people are prone to give up at the first signs of defeat. There is no substitute for persistence. The person who makes persistence his watch-word discovers that "Old Man Failure" finally becomes tired, and makes his departure. Failure cannot cope with persistence.

10. Negative personality. There is no hope of success for the person who repels people through a negative personality. Success comes through the application of power, and power is attained through the cooperative efforts of other people. A negative personality will not induce cooperation.

11. Lack of controlled sexual urge. Sex energy is the most powerful of all the stimuli which move people into action. Because it is the most powerful of the emotions, it must be controlled, through transmutation, and converted into other channels.

12. Uncontrolled desire for "something for nothing." The gambling instinct drives millions of people to failure. Evidence of this may be found in a study of the Wall Street crash of '29, during which millions of people tried to make money by gambling on stock margins.

13. Lack of a well-defined power of decision. Men who succeed reach decisions promptly, and change them, if at all, very slowly. Men who fail reach decisions, if at all, very slowly, and change them frequently, and quickly. Indecision and procrastination are twin brothers. Where one is found, the other may usually be found also. Kill off this pair before they completely "hog-tie" you to the treadmill of failure.

14. One or more of the six basic fears. These fears have been analyzed for you in a later chapter. They must be mastered before you can market your services effectively.

15. Wrong selection of a mate in marriage. This is a most common cause of failure. The relationship of marriage brings people intimately into

The successful man will profit from his mistakes and try again in a different way.

—Dale Carnegie

The world has just entered a new era of relationship between leaders and followers, which very clearly calls for new leaders, and a new brand of leadership in business and industry.

Every major accomplishment is the result of a well-planned course of action. Such a plan puts order into the mind, and the mind is unhampered by irrelevant thinking.

—Raymond Charles Barker

contact. Unless this relationship is harmonious, failure is likely to follow. Moreover, it will be a form of failure that is marked by misery and unhappiness, destroying all signs of ambition.

16. Over-caution. The person who takes no chances generally has to take whatever is left when others are through choosing. Over-caution is as bad as under-caution. Both are extremes to be guarded against. Life itself is filled with the element of chance.

17. Wrong selection of associates in business. This is one of the most common causes of failure in business. In marketing personal services, one should use great care to select an employer who will be an inspiration, and who is, himself, intelligent and successful. We emulate those with whom we associate most closely. Pick an employer who is worth emulating.

18. Superstition and prejudice. Superstition is a form of fear. It is also a sign of ignorance. Men who succeed keep open minds and are afraid of nothing.

19. Wrong selection of a vocation. No man can succeed in a line of endeavor which he does not like. The most essential step in the marketing of personal services is that of selecting an occupation into which you can throw yourself wholeheartedly.

20. Lack of concentration of effort. The "jack-of-all-trades" seldom is good at any. Concentrate all of your efforts on one definite chief aim.

21. The habit of indiscriminate spending. The spend-thrift cannot succeed, mainly because he stands eternally in fear of poverty. Form the habit of systematic saving by putting aside a definite percentage of your income. Money in the bank gives one a very safe foundation of courage when bargaining for the sale of personal services. Without money, one must take what one is offered, and be glad to get it.

22. Lack of enthusiasm. Without enthusiasm one cannot be convincing. Moreover, enthusiasm is contagious, and the person who has it, under control, is generally welcome in any group of people.

23. Intolerance. The person with a "closed" mind on any subject seldom gets ahead. Intolerance means that one has stopped acquiring knowl-

Remember that it is not the lawyer who knows the most law but the one who best prepares his case who wins. If your "case" is properly prepared and presented, your victory will have been more than half won at the outset.

edge. The most damaging forms of intolerance are those connected with religious, racial, and political differences of opinion.

24. Intemperance. The most damaging forms of intemperance are connected with eating, strong drink, and sexual activities. Over-indulgence in any of these is fatal to success.

25. Inability to cooperate with others. More people lose their positions and their big opportunities in life because of this fault than for all other reasons combined. It is a fault which no well-informed business man or leader will tolerate.

26. Possession of power that was not acquired through self-effort. (Sons and daughters of wealthy men, and others who inherit money which they did not earn.) Power in the hands of one who did not acquire it gradually is often fatal to success. Quick riches are more dangerous than poverty.

27. Intentional dishonesty. There is no substitute for honesty. One may be temporarily dishonest by force of circumstances over which one has no control, without permanent damage. But, there is no hope for the person who is dishonest by choice. Sooner or later, his deeds will catch up with him, and he will pay by loss of reputation, and perhaps even loss of liberty.

28. Egotism and vanity. These qualities serve as red lights which warn others to keep away. They are fatal to success.

29. Guessing instead of thinking. Most people are too indifferent or lazy to acquire facts with which to think accurately. They prefer to act on "opinions" created by guesswork or snap judgments.

30. Lack of capital. This is a common cause of failure among those who start out in business for the first time, without sufficient reserve of capital to absorb the shock of their mistakes, and to carry them over until they have established a reputation.

31. Under this, name any particular cause of failure from which you have suffered that has not been included in the foregoing list.

In these thirty major causes of failure is found a description of the tragedy of life, which obtains for practically every person who tries and fails. It will be

> *By thought, the thing you want is brought to you; by action you receive it.*
>
> —Wallace D. Wattles

> *The world is undergoing a rapid change. This means that the media through which the changes in human habits are promoted must be adapted to the changes.*

People rarely succeed unless they have fun in what they are doing.

—Dale Carnegie

helpful if you can induce someone who knows you well to go over this list with you, and help to analyze you by the thirty causes of failure. It may be beneficial if you try this alone. Most people cannot see themselves as others see them. You may be one who cannot.

The oldest of admonitions is "Man, know thyself!" If you market merchandise successfully, you must know the merchandise. The same is true in marketing personal services. You should know all of your weaknesses in order that you may either bridge them or eliminate them entirely. You should know your strength in order that you may call attention to it when selling your services. You can know yourself only through *accurate* analysis.

The folly of ignorance in connection with self was displayed by a young man who applied to the manager of a well-known business for a position. He made a very good impression until the manager asked him what salary he expected. He replied that he had no fixed sum in mind *(lack of a definite aim)*. The manager then said, "We will pay you all you are worth, after we try you out for a week."

"I will not accept it," the applicant replied, "because I am getting more than that where I am now employed."

Before you even start to negotiate for a readjustment of your salary in your present position, or to seek employment elsewhere, be sure that you are worth more than you now receive.

It is one thing to want money—everyone wants more—but it is something entirely different to be worth more! Many people mistake their wants for their just dues. Your financial requirements or wants have nothing whatever to do with your worth. Your value is established entirely by your ability to render useful service or your capacity to induce others to render such service.

TAKE INVENTORY OF YOURSELF

28 questions you should answer

Annual self-analysis is an essential in the effective marketing of personal services, as is annual inventory in merchandising. Moreover, the yearly analysis should disclose a decrease in faults, and an increase in virtues. One goes ahead,

Successful salesmen groom themselves with care. They understand that first impressions are lasting.

stands still, or goes backward in life. One's object should be, of course, to go ahead. Annual self-analysis will disclose whether advancement has been made, and if so, how much. It will also disclose any backward steps one may have made. The effective marketing of personal services requires one to move forward even if the progress is slow.

Your annual self-analysis should be made at the end of each year, so you can include in your New Year's Resolutions any improvements which the analysis indicates should be made. Take this inventory by asking yourself the following questions, and by checking your answers with the aid of someone who will not permit you to deceive yourself as to their accuracy.

Great minds discuss ideas, average minds discuss events, small minds discuss people.

—Hyman G. Rickover

Self-Analysis Questionnaire for Personal Inventory

1. Have I attained the goal which I established as my objective for this year? (You should work with a definite yearly objective to be attained as a part of your major life objective.)
2. Have I delivered service of the best possible quality of which I was capable, or could I have improved any part of this service?
3. Have I delivered service in the greatest possible quantity of which I was capable?
4. Has the spirit of my conduct been harmonious, and cooperative at all times?
5. Have I permitted the habit of procrastination to decrease my efficiency and if so, to what extent?
6. Have I improved my personality, and if so, in what ways?
7. Have I been persistent in following my plans through to completion?
8. Have I reached decisions promptly and definitely on all occasions?
9. Have I permitted any one or more of the six basic fears to decrease my efficiency?
10. Have I been either over-cautious, or under-cautious?
11. Has my relationship with my associates in work been pleasant, or unpleasant? If it has been unpleasant, has the fault been partly, or wholly, mine?
12. Have I dissipated any of my energy through lack of concentration of effort?

Everyone enjoys doing the kind of work for which he is best suited. An artist loves to work with paints, a craftsman with his hands, a writer loves to write.

A nail is driven out by another
nail. Habit is overcome by habit.

—Erasmus

13. Have I been open-minded and tolerant in connection with all subjects?

14. In what way have I improved my ability to render service?

15. Have I been intemperate in any of my habits?

16. Have I expressed, either openly or secretly, any form of egotism?

17. Has my conduct toward my associates been such that it has induced them to respect me?

18. Have my opinions and decisions been based upon guesswork, or accuracy of analysis and thought?

19. Have I followed the habit of budgeting my time, my expenses, and my income, and have I been conservative in these budgets?

20. How much time have I devoted to unprofitable effort which I might have used to better advantage?

21. How may I re-budget my time, and change my habits so I will be more efficient during the coming year?

22. Have I been guilty of any conduct which was not approved by my conscience?

23. In what ways have I rendered more service and better service than I was paid to render?

24. Have I been unfair to anyone, and if so, in what way?

25. If I had been the purchaser of my own services for the year, would I be satisfied with my purchase?

26. Am I in the right vocation, and if not, why not?

27. Has the purchaser of my services been satisfied with the service I have rendered, and if not, why not?

28. What is my present rating on the fundamental principles of success? (Make this rating fairly, and frankly, and have it checked by someone who is courageous enough to do it accurately.)

Having read and assimilated the information conveyed through this chapter, you are now ready to create a practical plan for marketing your personal services. In this chapter will be found an adequate description of every principle essential in planning the sale of personal services, including the major attributes of leadership; the most common causes of failure in leadership; a description of

The real employer of the future will be the public. This should be kept uppermost in the mind by every person seeking to market personal services effectively.

the fields of opportunity for leadership; the main causes of failure in all walks of life, and the important questions which should be used in self-analysis.

This extensive and detailed presentation of accurate information has been included, because it will be needed by all who must begin the accumulation of riches by marketing personal services. Those who have lost their fortunes, and those who are just beginning to earn money, have nothing but personal services to offer in return for riches, therefore it is essential that they have available the practical information needed to market services to best advantage.

I can be changed by what happens to me, but I refuse to be reduced by it.

—Maya Angelou

The information contained in this chapter will be of great value to all who aspire to attain leadership in any calling. It will be particularly helpful to those aiming to market their services as business or industrial executives.

Complete assimilation and understanding of the information here conveyed will be helpful in marketing one's own services, and it will also help one to become more analytical and capable of judging people. The information will be priceless to personnel directors, employment managers, and other executives charged with the selection of employees, and the maintenance of efficient organizations. If you doubt this statement, test its soundness by answering in writing the twenty-eight self-analysis questions. That might be both interesting and profitable, even though you do not doubt the soundness of the statement.

WHERE AND HOW ONE MAY FIND OPPORTUNITIES TO ACCUMULATE RICHES

Now that we have analyzed the principles by which riches may be accumulated, we naturally ask, "Where may one find favorable opportunities to apply these principles?" Very well, let us take inventory and see what the United States of America offer the person seeking riches, great or small.

To begin with, let us remember, *all of us,* that we live in a country where *every law-abiding citizen enjoys freedom of thought and freedom of deed unequaled anywhere in the world.* Most of us have never taken inventory of the advantages of this freedom. We have never compared our unlimited freedom with the curtailed freedom in other countries.

The "public-be-damned" policy is now passé. It has been supplanted by the "we-are-obligingly-at-your-service, sir" policy.

You are not here merely to make a living. You are here in order to enable the world to live more amply, with greater vision, with a finer spirit of hope and achievement. You are here to enrich the world, and you impoverish yourself if you forget the errand.

—Woodrow Wilson

Here we have freedom of thought, freedom in the choice and enjoyment of education, freedom in religion, freedom in politics, freedom in the choice of a business, profession or occupation, freedom to accumulate and own without molestation, *all the property we can accumulate,* freedom to choose our place of residence, freedom in marriage, freedom through equal opportunity to all races, freedom of travel from one state to another, freedom in our choice of foods, and freedom to *aim for any station in life for which we have prepared ourselves,* even for the presidency of the United States.

We have other forms of freedom, but this list will give a bird's-eye view of the most important, which constitute opportunity of the highest order. This advantage of freedom is all the more conspicuous because the United States is the only country guaranteeing to every citizen, whether native born or naturalized, so broad and varied a list of freedoms.

Next, let us recount some of the blessings which our widespread freedom has placed within our hands. Take the average American family for example (meaning, the family of average income) and sum up the benefits available to every member of the family, in this land of opportunity and plenty!

a. **Food.** Next to freedom of thought and deed come food, clothing, and shelter, the three basic necessities of life.

Because of our universal freedom the average American family has available, at its very door, the choicest selection of food to be found anywhere in the world, and at prices within its financial range.

A family of two, living in the heart of Times Square district of New York City, far removed from the source of production of foods, took careful inventory of the cost of a simple breakfast, with this astonishing result:

ARTICLES OF FOOD	COST AT THE BREAKFAST TABLE
Grape Fruit Juice (from Florida)	$.02
Rippled Wheat Breakfast Food (from Kansas Farm)	$.02
Tea (from China)	$.02
Bananas (from South America)	$.02½

Any farmer knows he cannot sow the seed of thistles, and reap a harvest of grain.

Toasted Bread (from Kansas Farm)	$.01
Fresh Country Eggs (from Utah)	$.07
Sugar (from Cuba, or Utah)	$.0½
Butter and Cream (from New England)	$.03
GRAND TOTAL	$.20

It is not very difficult to obtain food in a country where two people can have breakfast consisting of all they want or need for a dime apiece! Observe that this simple breakfast was gathered, by some strange form of magic(?) from China, South America, Utah, Kansas and the New England States, and delivered on the breakfast table, ready for consumption, in the very heart of the most crowded city in America, at a cost well within the means of the most humble laborer.

The cost included all federal, state and city taxes! (Here is a fact the politicians did not mention when they were crying out to the voters to throw their opponents out of office because the people were being taxed to death.)

> *Since most of us spend our lives doing ordinary tasks, the most important thing is to carry them out extraordinarily well.*
> —Henry David Thoreau

b. **Shelter.** This family lives in a comfortable apartment, heated by steam, lighted with electricity, with gas for cooking, all for $65 a month. In a smaller city, or a more sparsely settled part of New York City, the same apartment could be had for as low as $20 a month.

The toast they had for breakfast in the food estimate was toasted on an electric toaster, which cost but a few dollars; the apartment is cleaned with a vacuum sweeper that is run by electricity. Hot and cold water is available, at all times, in the kitchen and the bathroom. The food is kept cool in a refrigerator that is run by electricity. The wife curls her hair, and washes her clothes and irons them with easily operated electrical equipment, on power obtained by sticking a plug in the wall. The husband shaves with an electric shaver, and they receive entertainment from all over the world, twenty-four hours a day, if they want it, without cost, by merely turning the dial of their radio.

There are other conveniences in this apartment, but the foregoing list will

> *"QQS" . . . quality, plus quantity, plus the proper spirit of cooperation, equals perfect salesmanship of service.*

give a fair idea of some of the concrete evidences of the freedom we, of America, enjoy. *(And this is neither political nor economic propaganda.)*

Try not to become a man of success, but rather to become a man of value. He is considered successful in our day who gets more out of life than he puts in. But a man of value will give more than he receives.

—Albert Einstein

c. **Clothing.** Anywhere in the United States, the woman of average clothing requirements can dress very comfortably and neatly for less than $200 a year, and the average man can dress for the same, or less.

Only the three basic necessities of food, clothing, and shelter have been mentioned. The average American citizen has other privileges and advantages available in return for modest effort, not exceeding eight hours per day of labor. Among these is the privilege of automobile transportation, with which one can go and come at will, at very small cost.

The average American has security of property rights not found in any other country in the world. He can place his surplus money in a bank with the assurance that his government will protect it, and make good to him if the bank fails. If an American citizen wants to travel from one state to another he needs no passport, no one's permission. He may go when he pleases, and return at will. Moreover, he may travel by train, private automobile, bus, airplane, or ship, as his pocketbook permits. In Germany, Russia, Italy, and most of the other European and Oriental countries, the people cannot travel with so much freedom, and at so little cost.

THE "MIRACLE" THAT HAS PROVIDED THESE BLESSINGS

We often hear politicians proclaiming the freedom of America, when they solicit votes, but seldom do they take the time or devote sufficient effort to the analysis of the source or nature of this "freedom." Having no axe to grind, no grudge to express, no ulterior motives to be carried out, I have the privilege of going into a frank analysis of that mysterious, abstract, greatly misunderstood "something" which gives to every citizen of America more blessings, more opportunities to accumulate wealth, more freedom of every nature, than may be found in any other country.

The day of the "go-getter" has passed. He has been supplanted by the "go-giver."

I have the right to analyze the source and nature of this unseen power, because I know, and have known for more than a quarter of a century, many of the men who organized that power, and many who are now responsible for its maintenance.

The name of this mysterious benefactor of mankind is capital!

Capital consists not alone of money, but more particularly of highly organized, intelligent groups of men who plan ways and means of using money efficiently for the good of the public, and profitably to themselves.

These groups consist of scientists, educators, chemists, inventors, business analysts, publicity men, transportation experts, accountants, lawyers, doctors, and both men and women who have highly specialized knowledge in all fields of industry and business. They pioneer, experiment, and blaze trails in new fields of endeavor. They support colleges, hospitals, public schools, build good roads, publish newspapers, pay most of the cost of government, and take care of the multitudinous detail essential to human progress. Stated briefly, the capitalists are the brains of civilization, because they supply the entire fabric of which all education, enlightenment and human progress consists.

Money, without brains, always is dangerous. Properly used, it is the most important essential of civilization. The simple breakfast here described could not have been delivered to the New York family at a dime each, *or at any other price,* if organized capital had not provided the machinery, the ships, the railroads, and the huge armies of trained men to operate them.

Some slight idea of the importance of organized capital may be had by trying to imagine yourself burdened with the responsibility of collecting, without the aid of capital, and delivering to the New York City family, the simple breakfast described.

To supply the tea, you would have to make a trip to China or India, both a very long way from America. Unless you are an excellent swimmer, you would become rather tired before making the round trip. Then, too, another problem would confront you. What would you use for money, even if you had the physical endurance to swim the ocean?

To supply the sugar, you would have to take another long swim to Cuba, or a long walk to the sugar beet section of Utah. But even then, you might come back without the sugar, because organized effort and money are necessary to

You can advance only by being larger than your present place; and no man is larger than his present place who leaves undone any of the work pertaining to that place.

—Wallace D. Wattles

Discipline comes through self-control. This means that one must control all negative qualities. Before you can control conditions, you must first control yourself.

It is the man who carefully advances step by step, with his mind becoming wider and wider—and progressively better able to grasp any theme or situation—persevering in what he knows to be practical, and concentrating his thought upon it, who is bound to succeed in the greatest degree.

—Alexander Graham Bell

produce sugar, to say nothing of what is required to refine, transport, and deliver it to the breakfast table anywhere in the United States.

The eggs, you could deliver easily enough from the barn yards near New York City, but you would have a very long walk to Florida and return, before you could serve the two glasses of grapefruit juice.

You would have another long walk, to Kansas, or one of the other wheat growing states, when you went after the four slices of wheat bread.

The Rippled Wheat Biscuits would have to be omitted from the menu, because they would not be available except through the labor of a trained organization of men and suitable machinery, all of which call for capital.

While resting, you could take off for another little swim down to South America, where you would pick up a couple of bananas, and on your return, you could take a short walk to the nearest farm having a dairy and pick up some butter and cream. Then your New York City family would be ready to sit down and enjoy breakfast, and *you could collect your two dimes for your labor!*

Seems absurd, doesn't it? Well, the procedure described would be the only possible way these simple items of food could be delivered to the heart of New York City, if we had no capitalistic system.

The sum of money required for the building and maintenance of the railroads and steam ships used in the delivery of that simple breakfast is so huge that it staggers one's imagination. It runs into hundreds of millions of dollars, not to mention the armies of trained employees required to man the ships and trains. But, transportation is only a part of the requirements of modern civilization in capitalistic America. Before there can be anything to haul, something must be grown from the ground, or manufactured and prepared for market. This calls for more millions of dollars for equipment, machinery, boxing, marketing, and for the wages of millions of men and women.

Steam ships and railroads do not spring up from the earth and function automatically. They come in response to the call of civilization, through the labor and ingenuity and organizing ability of men who have imagination, faith, enthusiasm, decision, persistence! These men are known as capitalists. They are motivated by the desire to build, construct, achieve, render useful service, earn profits and accumulate riches. And, because they render service without which there would be no civilization, they put themselves in the way of great riches.

Most of us go through life as failures, because we are waiting for the "time to be right" to start doing something worthwhile. Do not wait. The time will never be "just right."

Just to keep the record simple and understandable, I will add that these capitalists are the selfsame men of whom most of us have heard soap-box orators speak. They are the same men to whom radicals, racketeers, dishonest politicians and grafting labor leaders refer as "the predatory interests," or "Wall Street."

I am not attempting to present a brief for or against any group of men or any system of economics. I am not attempting to condemn collective bargaining when I refer to "grafting labor leaders," nor do I aim to give a clean bill of health to all individuals known as capitalists.

The purpose of this book—*a purpose to which I have faithfully devoted over a quarter of a century*—is to present to all who want the knowledge, the most dependable philosophy through which individuals may accumulate riches in whatever amounts they desire.

I have here analyzed the economic advantages of the capitalistic system for the two-fold purpose of showing:

1. That all who seek riches must recognize and adapt themselves to the system that controls all approaches to fortunes, large or small, and
2. To present the side of the picture opposite to that being shown by politicians and demagogues who deliberately becloud the issues they bring up, by referring to organized capital as if it were something poisonous.

This is a capitalistic country, it was developed through the use of capital, and we who claim the right to partake of the blessings of freedom and opportunity, we who seek to accumulate riches here, may as well know that neither riches nor opportunity would be available to us if organized capital had not provided these benefits.

For more than twenty years it has been a somewhat popular and growing pastime for radicals, self-seeking politicians, racketeers, crooked labor leaders, and on occasion religious leaders, to take pot-shots at "Wall Street, the money changers, and big business."

The practice became so general that we witnessed during the business depression, the unbelievable sight of high government officials lining up with the

The ultimate is not to win, but to reach within the depths of your capabilities and to compete against yourself.

—Billy Mills

Start where you stand, and work with whatever tools you may have at your command, and better tools will be found as you go along.

Discipline is remembering what you want.

—David Campbell

cheap politicians, and labor leaders, with the openly avowed purpose of throttling the system which has made Industrial America the richest country on earth. The line-up was so general and so well organized that it prolonged the worst depression America has ever known. It cost millions of men their jobs, because those jobs were inseparably a part of the industrial and capitalistic system which form the very backbone of the nation.

During this unusual alliance of government officials and self-seeking individuals who were endeavoring to profit by declaring "open season" on the American system of industry, a certain type of labor leader joined forces with the politicians and offered to deliver voters in return for legislation designed to permit men to take riches away from industry by organized force of numbers, instead of the better method of giving a fair day's work for a fair day's pay.

Millions of men and women throughout the nation are still engaged in this popular pastime of trying to get without giving. Some of them are lined up with labor unions, where they demand shorter hours and more pay! Others do not take the trouble to work at all. They demand government relief and are getting it. Their idea of their rights of freedom was demonstrated in New York City, where violent complaint was registered with the Postmaster, by a group of "relief beneficiaries," because the Postmen awakened them at 7:30 a.m. to deliver government relief checks. They demanded that the time of delivery be set up to 10:00 o'clock.

If you are one of those who believe that riches can be accumulated by the mere act of men who organize themselves into groups and demand more pay for less service, if you are one of those who demand government relief without early morning disturbance when the money is delivered to you, if you are one of those who believe in trading their votes to politicians in return for the passing of laws which permit the raiding of the public treasury, you may rest securely on your belief, with certain knowledge that no one will disturb you, because this is a free country where every man may think as he pleases, where nearly everybody can live with but little effort, where many may live well without doing any work whatsoever.

However, you should know the full truth concerning this freedom of which so many people boast, and so few understand. As great as it is, as far as it reaches,

Most of us are good "starters" but poor "finishers" of everything we begin. Moreover, people are prone to give up at the first signs of defeat. There is no substitute for persistence.

as many privileges as it provides, it does not, and cannot bring riches without effort.

There is but one dependable method of accumulating, and legally holding riches, and that is by rendering useful service. No system has ever been created by which men can legally acquire riches through mere force of numbers, or without giving in return an equivalent value of one form or another.

There is a principle known as the law of economics! This is more than a theory. It is a law no man can beat.

Mark well the name of the principle, and remember it, because it is far more powerful than all the politicians and political machines. It is above and beyond the control of all the labor unions. It cannot be swayed, nor influenced nor bribed by racketeers or self-appointed leaders in any calling. Moreover, it has an all-seeing eye, and a perfect system of bookkeeping, in which it keeps an accurate account of the transactions of every human being engaged in the business of trying to get without giving. Sooner or later its auditors come around, look over the records of individuals both great and small, and demand an accounting.

"Wall Street, Big Business, Capital Predatory Interests," or whatever name you choose to give the system which has given us American Freedom, represents a group of men who understand, respect, and adapt themselves to this powerful law of economics! Their financial continuation depends upon their respecting the law.

Most people living in America like this country, its capitalistic system and all. I must confess I know of no better country, where one may find greater opportunities to accumulate riches. Judging by their acts and deeds, there are some in this country who do not like it. That, of course is their privilege; if they do not like this country, its capitalistic system, its boundless opportunities, *they have the privilege of clearing out!* Always there are other countries, such as Germany, Russia, and Italy, where one may try one's hand at enjoying freedom, and accumulating riches providing one is not too particular.

America provides all the freedom and all the opportunity to accumulate riches that any honest person may require. When one goes hunting for game, one selects hunting grounds where game is plentiful. When seeking riches, the same rule would naturally obtain.

Entrepreneurs are simply those who understand that there is little difference between obstacle and opportunity and are able to turn both to their advantage.

—Victor Kiam

Without enthusiasm one cannot be convincing. Moreover, enthusiasm is contagious, and the person who has it, under control, is generally welcome in any group of people.

There will come a time when you believe everything is finished. That will be the beginning.

—Peter Nivio Zarlenga

If it is riches you are seeking, do not overlook the possibilities of a country whose citizens are so rich that women, alone, spend over $200 million annually for lip-sticks, rouge, and cosmetics. Think twice, you who are seeking riches, before trying to destroy the Capitalistic System of a country whose citizens spend over $50 million a year for greeting cards, with which to express their appreciation of their freedom!

If it is money you are seeking, consider carefully a country that spends hundreds of millions of dollars annually for cigarettes, the bulk of the income from which goes to only four major companies engaged in supplying this national builder of "nonchalance" and "quiet nerves."

By all means give plenty of consideration to a country whose people spend annually more than $15 million for the privilege of seeing moving pictures, and toss in a few additional millions for liquor, narcotics, and other less potent soft drinks and giggle-waters.

Do not be in too big a hurry to get away from a country whose people willingly, even eagerly, hand over millions of dollars annually for football, baseball, and prize fights.

And, by all means, stick by a country whose inhabitants give up more than a million dollars a year for chewing gum, and another million for safety razor blades.

Remember, also, that this is but the beginning of the available sources for the accumulation of wealth. Only a few of the luxuries and non-essentials have been mentioned. But, remember that the business of producing, transporting, and marketing these few items of merchandise gives regular employment to many millions of men and women, who receive for their services many millions of dollars monthly, and spend it freely for both the luxuries and the necessities.

Especially remember, that back of all this exchange of merchandise and personal services may be found an abundance of opportunity to accumulate riches. Here our American Freedom comes to one's aid. There is nothing to stop you, or anyone, from engaging in any portion of the effort necessary to carry on these businesses. If one has superior talent, training, experience, one may accumulate riches in large amounts. Those not so fortunate may accumulate

It is one thing to want money—everyone wants more—but it is something entirely different to be worth more!

smaller amounts. Anyone may earn a living in return for a very nominal amount of labor.

So—there you are!

Opportunity has spread its wares before you. Step up to the front, select what you want, create your plan, put the plan into action, and follow through with persistence. "Capitalistic" America will do the rest. You can depend upon this much—capitalistic America insures every person the opportunity to render useful service, and to collect riches in proportion to the value of the service.

The "System" denies no one this right, but it does not, and cannot, promise something for nothing, because the system, itself, is irrevocably controlled by the law of economics which neither recognizes nor tolerates for long, getting without giving.

The law of economics was passed by Nature! There is no Supreme Court to which violators of this law may appeal. The law hands out both penalties for its violation, and appropriate rewards for its observance, *without interference or the possibility of interference by any human being.* The law cannot be repealed. It is as fixed as the stars in the heavens, and subject to, and a part of the same system that controls the stars.

May one refuse to adapt one's self to the law of economics?

Certainly! This is a free country, where all men are born with equal rights, including the privilege of ignoring the law of economics.

What happens then?

Well, nothing happens until large numbers of men join forces for the avowed purpose of ignoring the law, and taking what they want by force. *Then comes the dictator, with well-organized firing squads and machine guns!*

We have not yet reached that stage in America! But we have heard all we want to know about how the system works. Perhaps we shall be fortunate enough not to demand personal knowledge of so gruesome a reality. Doubtless we shall prefer to continue with our freedom of speech, freedom of deed, and freedom to render useful service in return for riches.

The practice, by government officials of extending to men and women the privilege of raiding the public treasury in return for votes, sometimes results in election, but as night follows day, the final payoff comes, when every penny

Failure is success if we learn from it.
—Malcolm Forbes

Many people mistake their wants for their just dues. Your financial requirements or wants have nothing whatever to do with your worth.

*Success is simple. Do what's right,
the right way, at the right time.*
—Arnold H. Glasow

wrongfully used must be repaid with compound interest on compound interest. If those who make the grab are not forced to repay, the burden falls on their children, and their children's children, "even unto the third and fourth generations." There is no way to avoid the debt.

Men can, and sometimes do, form themselves into groups for the purpose of crowding wages up, and working hours down. There is a point beyond which they cannot go. It is the point at which the law of economics steps in, and the sheriff gets both the employer and the employees.

For six years, from 1929 to 1935, the people of America, both rich and poor, barely missed seeing the Old Man Economics hand over to the sheriff all the businesses, and industries and banks. It was not a pretty sight! It did not increase our respect for mob psychology through which men cast reason to the winds and start trying to get without giving.

We who went through those six discouraging years, when fear was in the saddle, and faith was on the ground, cannot forget how ruthlessly the law of economics exacted its toll from both rich and poor, weak and strong, old and young. We shall not wish to go through another such experience.

These observations are not founded upon short-time experience. They are the result of twenty-five years of careful analysis of the methods of both the most successful and the most unsuccessful men America has known.

*Opportunity has spread its wares
before you. Step up to the front, select
what you want, create your plan, put the
plan into action, and follow through
with persistence.*

QUESTIONS FOR SUCCESS

- *What is the most helpful idea from this chapter for you?*

- *What is a Master Mind and why is forming one important?*

- *How have you experienced "temporary defeat" in your life? How have you overcome it?*

- *Review "The Major Attributes of Leadership" (pages 121–122). Which attributes come naturally to you? Which attributes are challenging for you?*

- *Review "The Ten Major Causes of Failure in Leadership" (pages 123–125). Which of these causes can you identify with?*

- *Review "The Thirty Major Causes of Failure" (pages 139–143). Which of these causes can you identify with?*

- *Review the twenty-eight questions titled "Take Inventory of Yourself" (pages 144–146). You may want to answer these questions with a Master Mind partner or a close friend.*

- *How has reviewing the above four lists given you more self-awareness? What did you learn about yourself? How can that knowledge help you?*

YOUR SUCCESS STEPS

☐ _____

☐ _____

☐ _____

☐ _____

☐ _____

☐ _____

CHAPTER 8

DECISION

The Mastery of Procrastination

The Seventh Step Toward Riches

Accurate analysis of over 25,000 men and women who had experienced failure disclosed the fact that lack of decision was near the head of the list of the thirty major causes of failure. This is no mere statement of a theory—*it is a fact.*

Procrastination, the opposite of decision, is a common enemy which practically every man must conquer.

You will have an opportunity to test your capacity to reach *quick* and *definite* decisions when you finish reading this book, and are ready to begin putting into action the principles which it describes.

Analysis of several hundred people who had accumulated fortunes well beyond the million dollar mark disclosed the fact that *every one of them* had the habit of reaching decisions promptly, and of changing these decisions slowly, if, and when they were changed. People who fail to accumulate money, *without exception,* have the habit of reaching decisions, if at all, very *slowly,* and *of changing these decisions quickly and often.*

One of Henry Ford's most outstanding qualities is his *habit* of reaching decisions quickly and definitely, and changing them slowly. This quality is so pronounced in Mr. Ford, that it has given him the reputation of being obstinate. It was this quality which prompted Mr. Ford to continue to manufacture his

All that is necessary to break the spell of inertia and frustration is this: Act as if it were impossible to fail. That is the talisman, the formula, the command of right-about-face which turns us from failure towards success.

—Dorothea Brande

Accurate analysis of over 25,000 men and women who had experienced failure disclosed the fact that lack of decision was near the head of the list of the thirty major causes of failure. This is no mere statement of a theory—it is a fact.

The great virtue of man lies in his ability to correct his mistakes and continually to make a new man of himself.

     —Wang Yang-ming

famous Model "T" (the world's ugliest car), when all of his advisors, and many of the purchasers of the car, were urging him to change it.

Perhaps, Mr. Ford delayed too long in making the change, but the other side of the story is, that Mr. Ford's firmness of decision yielded a huge fortune, before the change in model became *necessary*. There is but little doubt that Mr. Ford's habit of definiteness of decision assumes the proportion of obstinacy, but this quality is preferable to slowness in reaching decisions and quickness in changing them.

The majority of people who fail to accumulate money sufficient for their needs, are, generally, easily influenced by the "opinions" of others. They permit the newspapers and the "gossiping" neighbors to do their "thinking" for them. "Opinions" are the cheapest commodities on earth. Everyone has a flock of opinions ready to be wished upon anyone who will accept them. If you are influenced by "opinions" when you reach decisions, you will not succeed in any undertaking, much less in that of transmuting your own desire into money.

If you are influenced by the opinions of others, you will have no desire of your own.

Keep your own counsel, when you begin to put into practice the principles described here, by *reaching your own decisions* and following them. Take no one into your confidence, except the members of your "Master Mind" group, and be very sure in your selection of this group, that you choose only those who will be in complete sympathy and harmony with your purpose.

Close friends and relatives, while not meaning to do so, often handicap one through "opinions" and sometimes through ridicule, which is meant to be humorous. Thousands of men and women carry inferiority complexes with them all through life, because some well-meaning, but ignorant person destroyed their confidence through "opinions" or ridicule.

You have a brain and mind of your own. Use it, and reach your own decisions. If you need facts or information from other people, to enable you to reach decisions, as you probably will in many instances; acquire these facts or secure the information you need quietly, without disclosing your purpose.

It is characteristic of people who have but a smattering or a veneer of knowledge to try to give the impression that they have much knowledge. Such people generally do too much talking, and too little listening. Keep your eyes

Procrastination, the opposite of decision, is a common enemy which practically every man must conquer.

and ears wide open—and your mouth closed—if you wish to acquire the habit of prompt decision. Those who talk too much do little else. If you talk more than you listen, you not only deprive yourself of many opportunities to accumulate useful knowledge, but you also disclose your plans and purposes to people who will take great delight in defeating you, because they envy you.

Remember, also, that every time you open your mouth in the presence of a person who has an abundance of knowledge, you display to that person your exact stock of knowledge, or your lack of it! Genuine wisdom is usually conspicuous through *modesty and silence.*

Keep in mind the fact that every person with whom you associate is, like yourself, seeking the opportunity to accumulate money. If you talk about your plans too freely, you may be surprised when you learn that some other person has beaten you to your goal by putting into action ahead of you, the plans of which you talked unwisely.

Let one of your first decisions be to keep a closed mouth and open ears and eyes.

As a reminder to yourself to follow this advice, it will be helpful if you copy the following epigram in large letters and place it where you will see it daily.

"Tell the world what you intend to do, but first show it."

This is the equivalent of saying that "deeds, and not words, are what count most."

Success and failure are results of the use of mind. Every success-motivated mind has been a decisive mind. Every failure-motivated mind has been an indecisive mind.
—Raymond Charles Barker

FREEDOM OR DEATH ON A DECISION

The value of decisions depends upon the courage required to render them. The great decisions, which served as the foundation of civilization, were reached by assuming great risks, which often meant the possibility of death.

Lincoln's decision to issue his famous Proclamation of Emancipation, which gave freedom to the colored people of America, was rendered with full understanding that his act would turn thousands of friends and political supporters against him. He knew, too, that the carrying out of that proclamation would mean death to thousands of men on the battlefield. In the end, it cost Lincoln his life. That required courage.

Analysis of several hundred people who had accumulated fortunes well beyond the million dollar mark disclosed the fact that every one of them had the habit of reaching decisions promptly, and of changing these decisions slowly.

Indecision is actually the individual's decision to fail. Many people are indecisive all their lives.
—Raymond Charles Barker

Socrates' decision to drink the cup of poison, rather than compromise in his personal belief, was a decision of courage. It turned Time ahead a thousand years, and gave to people then unborn the right to freedom of thought and of speech.

The decision of Gen. Robert E. Lee, when he came to the parting of the way with the Union, and took up the cause of the South, was a decision of courage, for he well knew that it might cost him his own life, that it would surely cost the lives of others.

But, the greatest decision of all time, as far as any American citizen is concerned, was reached in Philadelphia, July 4, 1776, when fifty-six men signed their names to a document, which they well knew would bring freedom to all Americans, or *leave every one of the fifty-six hanging from a gallows!*

You have heard of this famous document, but you may not have drawn from it the great lesson in personal achievement it so plainly taught.

We all remember the date of this momentous decision, but few of us realize what courage that decision required. We remember our history, as it was taught; we remember dates, and the names of the men who fought; we remember Valley Forge, and Yorktown; we remember George Washington, and Lord Cornwallis. But we know little of the real forces back of these names, dates, and places. We know still less of that intangible power, which insured us freedom *long before Washington's armies reached Yorktown.*

We read the history of the Revolution, and falsely imagine that George Washington was the Father of our Country, that it was he who won our freedom, while the truth is—Washington was only an accessory after the fact, because victory for his armies had been insured long before Lord Cornwallis surrendered. This is not intended to rob Washington of any of the glory he so richly merited. Its purpose, rather, is to give greater attention to the astounding power that was the real cause of his victory.

It is nothing short of tragedy that the writers of history have missed, entirely, even the slightest reference to the irresistible power, which gave birth and freedom to the nation destined to set up new standards of independence for all the peoples of the earth. I say it is a tragedy, because it is the selfsame power which must be used by every individual who surmounts the difficulties of Life, and forces Life to pay the price asked.

People who fail to accumulate money, without exception, have the habit of reaching decisions, if at all, very slowly, and of changing these decisions quickly and often.

Let us briefly review the events which gave birth to this power. The story begins with an incident in Boston, March 5, 1770. British soldiers were patrolling the streets, by their presence, openly threatening the citizens. The colonists resented armed men marching in their midst. They began to express their resentment openly, hurling stones as well as epithets, at the marching soldiers, until the commanding officer gave orders, "Fix bayonets. . . . Charge!"

The battle was on. It resulted in the death and injury of many. The incident aroused such resentment that the Provincial Assembly (made up of prominent colonists) called a meeting for the purpose of taking definite action. Two of the members of that Assembly were John Hancock and Samuel Adams—long live their names! They spoke up courageously, and declared that a move must be made to eject all British soldiers from Boston.

Remember this—a decision, in the minds of two men, might properly be called the beginning of the freedom which we of the United States now enjoy. Remember, too, that the decision of these two men called for faith, and courage, because it was dangerous.

Before the Assembly adjourned, Samuel Adams was appointed to call on the Governor of the Province, Hutchinson, and demand the withdrawal of the British troops.

The request was granted, the troops were removed from Boston, but the incident was not closed. It had caused a situation destined to change the entire trend of civilization. Strange, is it not, how the great changes, such as the American Revolution, and the world war, often have their beginnings in circumstances which seem unimportant? It is interesting, also, to observe that these important changes usually begin in the form of a definite decision in the minds of a relatively small number of people. Few of us know the history of our country well enough to realize that John Hancock, Samuel Adams, and Richard Henry Lee (of the Province of Virginia) were the real Fathers of our Country.

Richard Henry Lee became an important factor in this story by reason of the fact that he and Samuel Adams communicated frequently (by correspondence), sharing freely their fears and their hopes concerning the welfare of the people of their Provinces. From this practice, Adams conceived the idea that a mutual exchange of letters between the thirteen Colonies might help to bring

Act now. There is never any time but now, and there never will be any time but now.

—Wallace D. Wattles

The majority of people who fail to accumulate money sufficient for their needs are, generally, easily influenced by the "opinions" of others. They permit the newspapers and the "gossiping" neighbors to do their "thinking" for them.

Decision is the most important function of the individual mind. No creative process can begin until a decision is made.

—Raymond Charles Barker

about the coordination of effort so badly needed in connection with the solution of their problems. Two years after the clash with the soldiers in Boston (March '72), Adams presented this idea to the Assembly, in the form of a motion that a Correspondence Committee be established among the Colonies, with definitely appointed correspondents in each Colony, "for the purpose of friendly cooperation for the betterment of the Colonies of British America."

Mark well this incident! It was the beginning of the organization of the far-flung power destined to give freedom to you, and to me. The Master Mind had already been organized. It consisted of Adams, Lee, and Hancock. "I tell you further, that if two of you agree upon the earth concerning anything for which you ask, it will come to you from My Father, who is in Heaven."

The Committee of Correspondence was organized. Observe that this move provided the way for increasing the power of the Master Mind by adding to it men from all the Colonies. Take notice that this procedure constituted the first organized planning of the disgruntled Colonists.

In union there is strength! The citizens of the Colonies had been waging disorganized warfare against the British soldiers, through incidents similar to the Boston riot, but nothing of benefit had been accomplished. Their individual grievances had not been consolidated under one Master Mind. No group of individuals had put their hearts, minds, souls, and bodies together in one definite decision to settle their difficulty with the British once and for all, until Adams, Hancock, and Lee got together.

Meanwhile, the British were not idle. They, too, were doing some planning and "Master-Minding" on their own account, with the advantage of having back of them money, and organized soldiery.

The Crown appointed Gage to supplant Hutchinson as the Governor of Massachusetts. One of the new Governor's first acts was to send a messenger to call on Samuel Adams, for the purpose of endeavoring to stop his opposition—by fear.

We can best understand the spirit of what happened by quoting the conversation between Col. Fenton (the messenger sent by Gage) and Adams.

Col. Fenton: "I have been authorized by Governor Gage, to assure you, Mr. Adams, that the Governor has been empowered to confer upon you such benefits as would be satisfactory [endeavor to win Adams by promise of bribes]

Keep your eyes and ears wide open— and your mouth closed—if you wish to acquire the habit of prompt decision.

upon the condition that you engage to cease in your opposition to the measures of the government. It is the Governor's advice to you, Sir, not to incur the further displeasure of his majesty. Your conduct has been such as makes you liable to penalties of an Act of Henry VIII, by which persons can be sent to England for trial for treason, or misprision of treason, at the discretion of a governor of a province. But, by changing your political course, you will not only receive great personal advantages, but you will make your peace with the King."

Samuel Adams had the choice of two decisions. He could cease his opposition, and receive personal bribes, or he could continue, and run the risk of being hanged!

Clearly, the time had come when Adams was *forced* to reach *instantly,* a decision which could have cost his life. The majority of men would have found it difficult to reach such a decision. The majority would have sent back an evasive reply, but not Adams! He insisted upon Col. Fenton's word of honor, that the Colonel would deliver to the Governor the answer exactly as Adams would give it to him.

Adams' answer: "Then you may tell Governor Gage that I trust I have long since made my peace with the King of Kings. No personal consideration shall induce me to abandon the righteous cause of my Country. And, tell Governor Gage it is the advice of Samuel Adams to him, no longer to insult the feelings of an exasperated people."

Comment as to the character of this man seems unnecessary. It must be obvious to all who read this astounding message that its sender possessed loyalty of the highest order. *This is important.* (Racketeers and dishonest politicians have prostituted the honor for which such men as Adams died.)

When Governor Gage received Adams' caustic reply, he flew into a rage, and issued a proclamation which read, "I do, hereby, in His Majesty's name, offer and promise his most gracious pardon to all persons who shall forthwith lay down their arms, and return to the duties of peaceable subjects, excepting only from the benefit of such pardon, Samuel Adams and John Hancock, whose offences are of too flagitious a nature to admit of any other consideration but that of condign punishment."

As one might say, in modern slang, Adams and Hancock were "on the spot!" The threat of the irate Governor forced the two men to reach another decision,

I found it easier to get rich than I did to make excuses.

—Jim Rohn

Those who talk too much do little else. If you talk more than you listen, you not only deprive yourself of many opportunities to accumulate useful knowledge, but you also disclose your plans and purposes to people who will take great delight in defeating you.

To say you do not know what to do, or you do not know what you want, is to negate the Infinite Intelligence which is individualized in you. What you are really saying is that you are too lazy to determine your own experience, or you think another person is better equipped to determine your good.

—Raymond Charles Barker

equally as dangerous. They hurriedly called a secret meeting of their staunchest followers. (Here the Master Mind began to take on momentum.) After the meeting had been called to order, Adams locked the door, placed the key in his pocket, and informed all present that it was imperative that a Congress of the Colonists be organized, and that no man should leave the room until the decision for such a congress had been reached.

Great excitement followed. Some weighed the possible consequences of such radicalism (Old Man Fear). Some expressed grave doubt as to the wisdom of so *definite a decision* in defiance of the Crown. Locked in that room were two men immune to Fear, blind to the possibility of Failure. Hancock and Adams. Through the influence of their minds, the others were induced to agree that, through the Correspondence Committee, arrangements should be made for a meeting of the First Continental Congress, to be held in Philadelphia, September 5, 1774.

Remember this date. It is more important than July 4, 1776. If there had been no DECISION to hold a Continental Congress, there could have been no signing of the Declaration of Independence.

Before the first meeting of the new Congress, another leader, in a different section of the country was deep in the throes of publishing a "Summary View of the Rights of British America." He was Thomas Jefferson, of the Province of Virginia, whose relationship to Lord Dunmore (representative of the Crown in Virginia) was as strained as that of Hancock and Adams with their Governor.

Shortly after his famous "Summary of Rights" was published, Jefferson was informed that he was subject to prosecution for high treason against His Majesty's government. Inspired by the threat, one of Jefferson's colleagues, Patrick Henry, boldly spoke his mind, concluding his remarks with a sentence which shall remain forever a classic, *"If this be treason, then make the most of it."*

It was such men as these who, without power, without authority, without military strength, without money, sat in solemn consideration of the destiny of the Colonies, beginning at the opening of the First Continental Congress, and continuing at intervals for two years—until on June 7, 1776, Richard Henry Lee arose, addressed the Chair, and to the startled Assembly made this motion:

"Gentlemen, I make the motion that these United Colonies are, and of right

Remember . . . that every time you open your mouth in the presence of a person who has an abundance of knowledge, you display to that person your exact stock of knowledge, or your lack of it!

ought to be free and independent states, that they be absolved from all allegiance to the British Crown, and that all political connection between them and the state of Great Britain is, and ought to be totally dissolved."

Lee's astounding motion was discussed fervently, and at such length that he began to lose patience. Finally, after days of argument, he again took the floor, and declared, in a clear, firm voice, "Mr. President, we have discussed this issue for days. It is the only course for us to follow. Why, then Sir, do we longer delay? Why still deliberate? Let this happy day give birth to an American Republic. Let her arise, not to devastate and to conquer, but to reestablish the reign of peace, and of law. The eyes of Europe are fixed upon us. She demands of us a living example of freedom, that may exhibit a contrast, in the felicity of the citizen, to the ever increasing tyranny."

Before his motion was finally voted upon, Lee was called back to Virginia, because of serious family illness, but before leaving, he placed his cause in the hands of his friend Thomas Jefferson, who promised to fight until favorable action was taken. Shortly thereafter, the President of the Congress (Hancock) appointed Jefferson as Chairman of a Committee to draw up a Declaration of Independence.

Long and hard the Committee labored, on a document which would mean, when accepted by the Congress, that every man who signed it, would be signing his own death warrant, should the Colonies lose in the fight with Great Britain, which was sure to follow.

The document was drawn, and on June 28, the original draft was read before the Congress. For several days it was discussed, altered, and made ready. On July 4, 1776, Thomas Jefferson stood before the Assembly, and fearlessly read the most momentous decision ever placed upon paper.

"When in the course of human events it is necessary for one people to dissolve the political bands which have connected them with another, and to assume, among the powers of the earth, the separate and equal station to which the laws of Nature, and of Nature's God entitle them, a decent respect to the opinions of mankind requires that they should declare the causes which impel them to the separation. . . ."

When Jefferson finished, the document was voted upon, accepted, and signed by the fifty-six men, every one staking his own life upon his decision to write

Change will not come if we wait for some other person or some other time. We are the ones we've been waiting for. We are the change that we seek.

—Barack Obama

"Tell the world what you intend to do, but first show it."

Any wrong decision you have ever made will become unimportant when your attention has shifted from it to a creative reason for living right here and now.

—Raymond Charles Barker

his name. By that decision came into existence a nation destined to bring to mankind forever, the privilege of making decisions.

By decisions made in a similar spirit of Faith, and only by such decisions, can men solve their personal problems, and win for themselves high estates of material and spiritual wealth. Let us not forget this!

Analyze the events which led to the Declaration of Independence, and be convinced that this nation, which now holds a position of commanding respect and power among all nations of the world, was born of a decision created by a Master Mind, consisting of fifty-six men. Note well, the fact that it was their decision which insured the success of Washington's armies, because the *spirit* of that decision was in the heart of every soldier who fought with him, and served as a spiritual power which recognizes no such thing as failure.

Note, also (with great personal benefit) that the power which gave this nation its freedom, is the selfsame power that must be used by every individual who becomes self-determining. This power is made up of the principles described in this book. It will not be difficult to detect, in the story of the Declaration of Independence, at least six of these principles: desire, decision, faith, persistence, the Master Mind, and organized planning.

Throughout this philosophy will be found the suggestion that thought, backed by strong desire, has a tendency to transmute itself into its physical equivalent. Before passing on, I wish to leave with you the suggestion that one may find in this story, and in the story of the organization of the United States Steel Corporation, a perfect description of the method by which thought makes this astounding transformation.

In your search for the secret of the method, do not look for a miracle, because you will not find it. You will find only the eternal laws of Nature. These laws are available to every person who has the faith and the courage to use them. They may be used to bring freedom to a nation, or to accumulate riches. There is no charge save the time necessary to understand and appropriate them.

Those who reach decisions promptly and definitely know what they want, and generally get it. The leaders in every walk of life decide quickly, and firmly. That is the major reason why they are leaders. The world has the habit of making room for the man whose words and actions show that he knows where he is going.

In your search for the secret of the method, do not look for a miracle, because you will not find it. You will find only the eternal laws of Nature. These laws are available to every person who has the faith and the courage to use them.

Indecision is a habit which usually begins in youth. The habit takes on permanency as the youth goes through graded school, high school, and even through college, without definiteness of purpose. The major weakness of all educational systems is that they neither teach nor encourage the habit of definite decision.

It would be beneficial if no college would permit the enrollment of any student, unless and until the student declared his major purpose in matriculating. It would be of still greater benefit, if every student who enters the graded schools were compelled to accept training in the habit of decision, and forced to pass a satisfactory examination on this subject before being permitted to advance in the grades.

The habit of indecision acquired because of the deficiencies of our school systems, goes with the student into the occupation he chooses . . . if . . . in fact, he chooses his occupation. Generally, the youth just out of school seeks any job that can be found. He takes the first place he finds, because he has fallen into the habit of indecision. Ninety-eight out of every hundred people working for wages today are in the positions they hold, because they lacked the definiteness of decision to plan a definite position, and the knowledge of how to choose an employer.

Definiteness of decision always requires courage, sometimes very great courage. The fifty-six men who signed the Declaration of Independence staked their lives on the decision to affix their signatures to that document. The person who reaches a definite decision to procure the particular job, and make life pay the price he asks, does not stake his life on that decision; he stakes his economic freedom. Financial independence, riches, desirable business, and professional positions are not within reach of the person who neglects or refuses to expect, plan, and demand these things. The person who desires riches in the same spirit that Samuel Adams desired freedom for the Colonies is sure to accumulate wealth.

In the chapter on Organized Planning, you will find complete instructions for marketing every type of personal services. You will find also detailed information on how to choose the employer you prefer, and the particular job you desire. These instructions will be of no value to you unless you definitely decide to organize them into a plan of action.

Our beliefs in a rich future life are of little importance unless we coin them into a rich present life. Today should always be our most wonderful day.

—Thomas Dreier

Those who reach decisions promptly and definitely know what they want, and generally get it.

QUESTIONS FOR SUCCESS

- *What is the most helpful idea from this chapter for you?*

- *What is the opposite of decision (page 161)?*

- *Are you someone who reaches decisions quickly and then changes your mind slowly? How does that impact your life?*

- *How influenced by the opinions of others are you?*

- *Napoleon Hill writes, "'Tell the world what you intend to do, but first show it.'" How can you apply this to your life and pursuit of your goal(s)?*

YOUR SUCCESS STEPS

- ☐ _____

- ☐ _____

- ☐ _____

- ☐ _____

- ☐ _____

- ☐ _____

CHAPTER 9

PERSISTENCE

The Sustained Effort Necessary to Induce Faith

The Eighth Step Toward Riches

Persistence is an essential factor in the procedure of transmuting desire into its monetary equivalent. The basis of persistence is the power of will.

Will-power and desire, when properly combined, make an irresistible pair. Men who accumulate great fortunes are generally known as cold-blooded, and sometimes ruthless. Often they are misunderstood. What they have is will-power, which they mix with persistence, and place back of their desires to *insure* the attainment of their objectives.

Henry Ford has been generally misunderstood to be ruthless and cold-blooded. This misconception grew out of Ford's habit of following through in all of his plans with persistence.

The majority of people are ready to throw their aims and purposes overboard, and give up at the first sign of opposition or misfortune. A few carry on despite all opposition, until they attain their goal. These few are the Fords, Carnegies, Rockefellers, and Edisons.

There may be no heroic connotation to the word "persistence," but the quality is to the character of man what carbon is to steel.

The building of a fortune, generally, involves the application of the entire thirteen factors of this philosophy. These principles must be understood; they must be applied with persistence by all who accumulate money.

Great works are performed not by strength but by perseverance.

—Samuel Johnson

The basis of persistence is the power of will.

No greater good can come to any man or woman than to become self-active.

—Wallace D. Wattles

If you are following this book with the intention of applying the knowledge it conveys, your first test as to your persistence will come when you begin to follow the six steps described in the second chapter. Unless you are one of the two out of every hundred who already have a definite goal at which you are aiming, and a definite plan for its attainment, you may read the instructions, and then pass on with your daily routine, and never comply with those instructions.

The author is checking you up at this point, because lack of persistence is one of the major causes of failure. Moreover, experience with thousands of people has proved that lack of persistence is a weakness common to the majority of men. It is a weakness which may be overcome by effort. The ease with which lack of persistence may be conquered will depend *entirely* upon the intensity of one's desire.

The starting point of all achievement is desire. Keep this constantly in mind. Weak desires bring weak results, just as a small amount of fire makes a small amount of heat. If you find yourself lacking in persistence, this weakness may be remedied by building a stronger fire under your desires.

Continue to read through to the end, then go back to chapter two, and start *immediately* to carry out the instructions given in connection with the six steps. The eagerness with which you follow these instructions will indicate clearly how much or how little you really desire to accumulate money. If you find that you are indifferent, you may be sure that you have not yet acquired the "money consciousness" which you must possess, before you can be sure of accumulating a fortune.

Fortunes gravitate to men whose minds have been prepared to "attract" them, just as surely as water gravitates to the ocean. In this book may be found all the stimuli necessary to "attune" any normal mind to the vibrations which will attract the object of one's desires.

If you find you are weak in persistence, center your attention upon the instructions contained in the chapter on power; surround yourself with a "Master Mind" group, and through the cooperative efforts of the members of this group, you can develop persistence. You will find additional instructions for the development of persistence in the chapters on auto-suggestion, and the subconscious mind. Follow the instructions outlined in these chapters until your habit nature hands over to your subconscious mind a clear picture of the

Will-power and desire, when properly combined, make an irresistible pair.

object of your desire. From that point on, you will not be handicapped by lack of persistence.

Your subconscious mind works continuously, while you are awake, and while you are asleep.

Spasmodic, or occasional, effort to apply the rules will be of no value to you. To get results, you must apply all of the rules until their application becomes a fixed habit with you. In no other way can you develop the necessary "money consciousness."

Poverty is attracted to the one whose mind is favorable to it, as money is attracted to him whose mind has been deliberately prepared to attract it, and through the same laws. Poverty consciousness will voluntarily seize the mind which is not occupied with the money consciousness. A poverty consciousness develops without *conscious* application of habits favorable to it. The money consciousness must be created to order, unless one is born with such a consciousness.

Catch the full significance of the statements in the preceding paragraph, and you will understand the importance of persistence in the accumulation of a fortune. Without persistence, you will be defeated, even before you start. With persistence you will win.

If you have ever experienced a nightmare, you will realize the value of persistence. You are lying in bed, half awake, with a feeling that you are about to smother. You are unable to turn over, or to move a muscle. You realize that you must begin to regain control over your muscles. Through persistent effort of will-power, you finally manage to move the fingers of one hand. By continuing to move your fingers, you extend your control to the muscles of one arm, until you can lift it. Then you gain control of the other arm in the same manner. You finally gain control over the muscles of one leg, and then extend it to the other leg. Then—with one supreme effort of will—you regain complete control over your muscular system, and "snap" out of your nightmare. The trick has been turned step by step.

You may find it necessary to "snap" out of your mental inertia, through a similar procedure, moving slowly at first, then increasing your speed, until you gain complete control over your will. Be persistent no matter how slowly you may, at first, have to move. With persistence will come success.

Courage and perseverance have a magical talisman, before which difficulties disappear and obstacles vanish into air.

—John Quincy Adams

The majority of people are ready to throw their aims and purposes overboard, and give up at the first sign of opposition or misfortune. A few carry on despite all opposition, until they attain their goal.

Perseverance is a great element of success. If you only knock long enough and loud enough at the gate, you are sure to wake up somebody.

—Henry Wadsworth Longfellow

If you select your "Master Mind" group with care, you will have in it, at least one person who will aid you in the development of persistence. Some men who have accumulated great fortunes did so because of necessity. They developed the habit of persistence, because they were so closely driven by circumstances, that they *had to become persistent.*

There is no substitute for persistence! It cannot be supplanted by any other quality! Remember this, and it will hearten you, in the beginning, when the going may seem difficult and slow.

Those who have cultivated the habit of persistence seem to enjoy insurance against failure. No matter how many times they are defeated, they finally arrive up toward the top of the ladder. Sometimes it appears that there is a hidden Guide whose duty is to test men through all sorts of discouraging experiences. Those who pick themselves up after defeat and keep on trying, arrive; and the world cries, "Bravo! I knew you could do it!" The hidden Guide lets no one enjoy great achievement without passing the persistence test. Those who can't take it, simply do not make the grade.

Those who can "take it" are bountifully rewarded for their persistence. They receive, as their compensation, whatever goal they are pursuing. That is not all! They receive something infinitely more important than material compensation—the knowledge that "every failure brings with it the seed of an equivalent advantage."

There are exceptions to this rule; a few people know from experience the soundness of persistence. They are the ones who have not accepted defeat as being anything more than temporary. They are the ones whose desires are so persistently applied that defeat is finally changed into victory. We who stand on the side-lines of Life see the overwhelmingly large number who go down in defeat, never to rise again. We see the few who take the punishment of defeat *as an urge to greater effort.* These, fortunately, never learn to accept Life's reverse gear. But what we do not see, what most of us never suspect of existing, is the silent but irresistible power which comes to the rescue of those who fight on in the face of discouragement. If we speak of this power at all we call it persistence, and let it go at that. One thing we all know, if one does not possess persistence, one does not achieve noteworthy success in any calling.

Lack of persistence is a weakness common to the majority of men. It is a weakness which may be overcome by effort. The ease with which lack of persistence may be conquered will depend entirely upon the intensity of one's desire.

As these lines are being written, I look up from my work, and see before me, less than a block away, the great mysterious Broadway, the "Graveyard of Dead Hopes" and the "Front Porch of Opportunity." From all over the world people have come to Broadway, seeking fame, fortune, power, love, or whatever it is that human beings call success. Once in a great while someone steps out from the long procession of seekers, and the world hears that another person has mastered Broadway. But Broadway is not easily nor quickly conquered. She acknowledges talent, recognizes genius, pays off in money, only *after* one has refused to quit.

Then we know he has discovered the secret of how to conquer Broadway. The secret is always inseparably attached to one word, "persistence"!

The secret is told in the struggle of Fannie Hurst, whose persistence conquered the Great White Way. She came to New York in 1915, to convert writing into riches. The conversion did not come quickly, but it came. For four years Miss Hurst learned about "the Sidewalks of New York" from firsthand experience. She spent her days laboring, and her nights hoping. When hope grew dim, she did not say, "All right, Broadway, you win!" She said, "Very well, Broadway, you may whip some, but not me. I'm going to force you to give up."

One publisher *(The Saturday Evening Post)* sent her *thirty-six* rejection slips, before she "broke the ice" and got a story across. The average writer, like the "average" in other walks of life, would have given up the job when the first rejection slip came. She pounded the pavements for four years to the tune of the publisher's "no," because she was determined to win.

Then came the "payoff." The spell had been broken, the unseen Guide had tested Fannie Hurst, and she could take it. From that time on publishers made a beaten path to her door. Money came so fast she hardly had time to count it. Then the moving-picture men discovered her, and money came not in small change, but in floods. The moving picture rights to her latest novel, *Great Laughter,* brought $100,000, said to be the highest price ever paid for a story before publication. Her royalties from the sale of the book probably will run much more.

Briefly, you have a description of what persistence is capable of achieving.

Know the true value of time! Snatch, seize, and enjoy every moment of it. No idleness, no laziness, no procrastination. Never put off till tomorrow what you can do today.

—Lord Chesterfield

Weak desires bring weak results, just as a small amount of fire makes a small amount of heat. If you find yourself lacking in persistence, this weakness may be remedied by building a stronger fire under your desires.

Fannie Hurst is no exception. Wherever men and women accumulate great riches, you may be sure they first acquired persistence. Broadway will give any beggar a cup of coffee and a sandwich, but it demands persistence of those who go after the big stakes.

Kate Smith will say "amen" when she reads this. For years she sang, without money, and without price, before any microphone she could reach. Broadway said to her, "Come and get it, if you can take it." She did take it until one happy day Broadway got tired and said, "Aw, what's the use? You don't know when you're whipped, so name your price, and go to work in earnest." Miss Smith named her price! It was plenty. Away up in figures so high that one week's salary is far more than most people make in a whole year.

Verily it pays to be persistent!

And here is an encouraging statement which carries with it a suggestion of great significance—thousands of singers who excel Kate Smith are walking up and down Broadway looking for a "break"—without success. Countless others have come and gone; many of them sang well enough, but they failed to make the grade because they lacked the courage to keep on keeping on, until Broadway became tired of turning them away.

Persistence is a state of mind, therefore it can be cultivated. Like all states of mind, persistence is based upon definite causes, among them these:—

a. **Definiteness of purpose.** Knowing what one wants is the first and, perhaps, the most important step toward the development of persistence. A strong motive forces one to surmount many difficulties.

b. **Desire.** It is comparatively easy to acquire and to maintain persistence in pursuing the object of intense desire.

c. **Self-reliance.** Belief in one's ability to carry out a plan encourages one to follow the plan through with persistence. (Self-reliance can be developed through the principle described in the chapter on auto-suggestion.)

d. **Definiteness of plans.** Organized plans, even though they may be weak and entirely impractical, encourage persistence.

e. **Accurate knowledge.** Knowing that one's plans are sound, based

Energy follows action.

—Joel Fotinos

The eagerness with which you follow these instructions will indicate clearly how much or how little you really desire to accumulate money.

upon experience or observation, encourages persistence; "guessing" instead of "knowing" destroys persistence.

f. **Co-operation.** Sympathy, understanding, and harmonious co-operation with others tend to develop persistence.

g. **Will-power.** The habit of concentrating one's thoughts upon the building of plans, for the attainment of a definite purpose, leads to persistence.

h. **Habit.** Persistence is the direct result of habit. The mind absorbs and becomes a part of the daily experiences upon which it feeds. Fear, the worst of all enemies, can be effectively cured *by forced repetition of acts of courage.* Everyone who has seen active service in war knows this.

Before leaving the subject of persistence, take inventory of yourself, and determine in what particular, if any, you are lacking in this essential quality. Measure yourself courageously, point by point, and see how many of the eight factors of persistence you lack. The analysis may lead to discoveries that will give you a new grip on yourself.

SYMPTOMS OF LACK OF PERSISTENCE

Here you will find the real enemies which stand between you and noteworthy achievement. Here you will find not only the "symptoms" indicating weakness of persistence, but also the deeply seated subconscious causes of this weakness. Study the list carefully, and face yourself squarely if you really wish to know who you are, and what you are capable of doing. These are the weaknesses which must be mastered by all who accumulate riches.

1. Failure to recognize and to clearly define exactly what one wants.
2. Procrastination, with or without cause. (Usually backed up with a formidable array of alibis and excuses.)
3. Lack of interest in acquiring specialized knowledge.

If you desire to advance, and you are not doing so, remember that it can be only because your thought is better than your practice. You must do as well as you think.

—Wallace D. Wattles

Fortunes gravitate to those whose minds have been prepared to "attract" them, just as surely as water gravitates to the ocean.

Our greatest glory is not in never falling, but in rising every time we fall.

—Oliver Goldsmith

4. Indecision, the habit of "passing the buck" on all occasions, instead of facing issues squarely. (Also backed by alibis.)

5. The habit of relying upon alibis instead of creating definite plans for the solution of problems.

6. Self-satisfaction. There is but little remedy for this affliction, and no hope for those who suffer from it.

7. Indifference, usually reflected in one's readiness to compromise on all occasions, rather than meet opposition and fight it.

8. The habit of blaming others for one's mistakes, and accepting unfavorable circumstances as being unavoidable.

9. Weakness of desire, due to neglect in the choice of motives that impel action.

10. Willingness, even eagerness, to quit at the first sign of defeat. (Based upon one or more of the six basic fears.)

11. Lack of organized plans, placed in writing where they may be analyzed.

12. The habit of neglecting to move on ideas, or to grasp opportunity when it presents itself.

13. Wishing instead of willing.

14. The habit of compromising with poverty instead of aiming at riches. General absence of ambition to *be,* to *do,* and to *own.*

15. Searching for all the short-cuts to riches, trying to get without giving a fair equivalent, usually reflected in the habit of gambling, endeavoring to drive "sharp" bargains.

16. Fear of criticism, failure to create plans and to put them into action, because of what other people will think, do, or say. This enemy belongs at the head of the list, because it generally exists in one's subconscious mind, where its presence is not recognized. (See the Six Basic Fears in a later chapter.)

Let us examine some of the symptoms of the Fear of Criticism. The majority of people permit relatives, friends, and the public at large to so influence them that they cannot live their own lives, because they fear criticism.

Huge numbers of people make mistakes in marriage, stand by the bargain,

Spasmodic, or occasional, effort to apply the rules will be of no value to you. To get results, you must apply all of the rules until their application becomes a fixed habit with you. In no other way can you develop the necessary "money consciousness."

and go through life miserable and unhappy, because they fear criticism which may follow if they correct the mistake. (Anyone who has submitted to this form of fear knows the irreparable damage it does, by destroying ambition, self-reliance, and the desire to achieve.)

Millions of people neglect to acquire belated educations, after having left school, because they fear criticism.

Countless numbers of men and women, both young and old, permit relatives to wreck their lives in the name of duty, because they fear criticism. (Duty does not require any person to submit to the destruction of his personal ambitions and the right to live his own life in his own way.)

People refuse to take chances in business, because they fear the criticism which may follow if they fail. *The fear of criticism in such cases is stronger than the desire for success.*

Too many people refuse to set high goals for themselves, or even neglect selecting a career, because they fear the criticism of relatives and "friends" who may say, "Don't aim so high, people will think you are crazy."

When Andrew Carnegie suggested that I devote twenty years to the organization of a philosophy of individual achievement my first impulse of thought was fear of what people might say. The suggestion set up a goal for me, far out of proportion to any I had ever conceived. As quick as a flash, my mind began to create alibis and excuses, all of them traceable to the inherent fear of criticism. Something inside of me said, "You can't do it—the job is too big, and requires too much time—what will your relatives think of you?—how will you earn a living?—no one has ever organized a philosophy of success, what right have you to believe you can do it?—who are you, anyway, to aim so high?—remember your humble birth—what do you know about philosophy—people will think you are crazy—(and they did)—why hasn't some other person done this before now?"

These and many other questions flashed into my mind, and demanded attention. It seemed as if the whole world had suddenly turned its attention to me with the purpose of ridiculing me into giving up all desire to carry out Mr. Carnegie's suggestion.

I had a fine opportunity, then and there, to kill off ambition before it gained control of me. Later in life, after having analyzed thousands of people, I dis-

Diligence is the mother of good fortune.

—Benjamin Disraeli

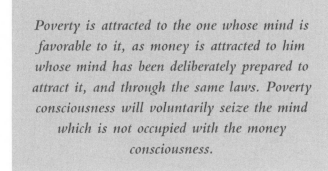

Poverty is attracted to the one whose mind is favorable to it, as money is attracted to him whose mind has been deliberately prepared to attract it, and through the same laws. Poverty consciousness will voluntarily seize the mind which is not occupied with the money consciousness.

I do not think there is any other quality so essential to success of any kind as the quality of perseverance. It overcomes almost everything, even nature.

—John D. Rockefeller

covered that most ideas are stillborn, and need the breath of life injected into them through definite plans of immediate action. The time to nurse an idea is at the time of its birth. Every minute it lives gives it a better chance of surviving. The fear of criticism is at the bottom of the destruction of most ideas which never reach the planning and action stage.

Many people believe that material success is the result of favorable "breaks." There is an element of ground for the belief, but those depending entirely upon luck are nearly always disappointed, because they overlook another important factor which must be present before one can be sure of success. It is the knowledge with which favorable "breaks" can be made to order.

During the depression, W. C. Fields, the comedian, lost all his money, and found himself without income, without a job, and his means of earning a living (vaudeville) no longer existed. Moreover, he was past sixty, when many men consider themselves "old." He was so eager to stage a comeback that he offered to work without pay, in a new field (movies). In addition to his other troubles, he fell and injured his neck. To many that would have been the place to give up and quit. But Fields was persistent. He knew that if he carried on he would get the "breaks" sooner or later, and he did get them, but not by chance.

Marie Dressler found herself down and out, with her money gone, with no job, when she was about sixty. She, too, went after the "breaks," and got them. Her persistence brought an astounding triumph late in life, long beyond the age when most men and women are done with ambition to achieve.

Eddie Cantor lost his money in the 1929 stock crash, but he still had his persistence and his courage. With these, plus two prominent eyes, he exploited himself back into an income of $10,000 a week! Verily, if one has persistence, one can get along very well without many other qualities.

The only "break" anyone can afford to rely upon is a self-made "break." These come through the application of persistence. The starting point is definiteness of purpose.

Examine the first hundred people you meet, ask them what they want most in life, and ninety-eight of them will not be able to tell you. If you press them for an answer, some will say—security, many will say—money, a few will say—

Without persistence, you will be defeated, even before you start. With persistence you will win.

happiness, others will say—fame and power, and still others will say—social recognition, ease in living, ability to sing, dance, or write, but none of them will be able to define these terms, or give the slightest indication of a plan by which they hope to attain these vaguely expressed wishes. Riches do not respond to wishes. They respond only to definite plans, backed by definite desires, through constant persistence.

We are what we repeatedly do. Excellence then, is not an act, but a habit.

—Aristotle

HOW TO DEVELOP PERSISTENCE

There are four simple steps which lead to the habit of persistence. They call for no great amount of intelligence, no particular amount of education, and but little time or effort. The necessary steps are:—

1. A definite purpose backed by burning desire for its fulfillment.
2. A definite plan, expressed in continuous action.
3. A mind closed tightly against all negative and discouraging influences, including negative suggestions of relatives, friends and acquaintances.
4. A friendly alliance with one or more persons who will encourage one to follow through with both plan and purpose.

These four steps are essential for success in all walks of life. The entire purpose of the thirteen principles of this philosophy is to enable one to take these four steps as a matter of *habit*.

These are the steps by which one may control one's economic destiny.
They are the steps that lead to freedom and independence of thought.
They are the steps that lead to riches, in small or great quantities.
They lead the way to power, fame, and worldly recognition.
They are the four steps which guarantee favorable "breaks."
They are the steps that convert dreams into physical realities.
They lead, also, to the mastery of fear, discouragement, indifference.

There is no substitute for persistence! It cannot be supplanted by any other quality! Remember this, and it will hearten you, in the beginning, when the going may seem difficult and slow.

In the confrontation between the stream and the rock, the stream always wins—not through strength but by perseverance.

—H. Jackson Brown, Jr.

There is a magnificent reward for all who learn to take these four steps. It is the privilege of writing one's own ticket, and of making Life yield whatever price is asked.

I have no way of knowing the facts, but I venture to conjecture that Mrs. Wallis Simpson's great love for a man was not accidental, nor the result of favorable "breaks" alone. There was a burning desire, and careful searching at every step of the way. Her first duty was to love. What is the greatest thing on earth? The Master called it love—not man-made rules, criticism, bitterness, slander, or political "marriages," but love.

She knew what she wanted, not after she met the Prince of Wales, but long before that. Twice when she had failed to find it, she had the courage to continue her search. "To thine own self be true, and it must follow, as the night the day, thou canst not then be false to any man."

Her rise from obscurity was of the slow, progressive, persistent order, but it was sure! She triumphed over unbelievably long odds; and, no matter who you are, or what you may think of Wallis Simpson, or the king who gave up his crown for her love, she is an astounding example of applied persistence, an instructor on the rules of self-determination, from whom the entire world might profitably take lessons.

When you think of Wallis Simpson, think of one who knew what she wanted, and shook the greatest empire on earth to get it. Women who complain that this is a man's world, that women do not have an equal chance to win, owe it to themselves to study carefully the life of this unusual woman, who, at an age which most women consider "old," captured the affections of the most desirable bachelor in the entire world.

And what of King Edward? What lesson may we learn from his part in the world's greatest drama of recent times? Did he pay too high a price for the affections of the woman of his choice?

Surely no one but he can give the correct answer.

The rest of us can only conjecture. This much we know, the king came into the world without his own consent. He was born to great riches, without requesting them. He was persistently sought in marriage; politicians and statesmen throughout Europe tossed dowagers and princesses at his feet. Because he

Those who have cultivated the habit of persistence seem to enjoy insurance against failure.

was the first born of his parents, he inherited a crown, which he did not seek, and perhaps did not desire. For more than forty years he was not a free agent, could not live his life in his own way, had but little privacy, and finally assumed duties inflicted upon him when he ascended the throne.

Some will say, "With all these blessings, King Edward should have found peace of mind, contentment, and joy of living."

The truth is that back of all the privileges of a crown, all the money, the fame, and the power inherited by King Edward, there was an emptiness which could be filled only by love.

His greatest desire was for love. Long before he met Wallis Simpson, he doubtless felt this great universal emotion tugging at the strings of his heart, beating upon the door of his soul, and crying out for expression.

And when he met a kindred spirit, crying out for this same holy privilege of expression, he recognized it, and without fear or apology, opened his heart and bade it enter. All the scandalmongers in the world cannot destroy the beauty of this international drama, through which two people found love, and had the courage to face open criticism, renounce all else to give it *holy* expression.

King Edward's decision to give up the Crown of the world's most powerful empire, for the privilege of going the remainder of the way through life with the woman of his choice, was a decision that required courage. The decision also had a price, but who has the right to say the price was too great? Surely not He who said, "He among you who is without sin, let him cast the first stone."

As a suggestion to any evil-minded person who chooses to find fault with the Duke of Windsor, because his desire was for love, and for openly declaring his love for Wallis Simpson, and giving up his throne for her, let it be remembered that the open declaration was not essential. He could have followed the custom of clandestine liaison which has prevailed in Europe for centuries, without giving up either his throne, or the woman of his choice, and there would have been no complaint from either church or laity. But this unusual man was built of sterner stuff. His love was clean. It was deep and sincere. It represented the one thing which above all else he truly desired, therefore, he took what he wanted, and paid the price demanded.

Never give up. Never, never give up! We shall go on to the end.
—Winston Churchill

"Every failure brings with it the seed of an equivalent advantage."

If Europe had been blessed with more rulers with the human heart and the traits of honesty of ex-king Edward, for the past century, that unfortunate hemisphere now seething with greed, hate, lust, political connivance, and threats of war, would have a different and a better story to tell. A story in which Love and not Hate would rule.

In the words of Stuart Austin Wier we raise our cup and drink this toast to ex-king Edward and Wallis Simpson:

Blessed is the man who has come to know that our muted thoughts are our sweetest thoughts.

Blessed is the man who, from the blackest depths, can see the luminous figure of love, and seeing, sing; and singing, say: "Sweeter far than uttered lays are the thoughts I have of you."

In these words would we pay tribute to the two people who, more than all others of modern times, have been the victims of criticism and the recipients of abuse, because they found Life's greatest treasure, and claimed it. (Mrs. Simpson read and approved this analysis.)

Most of the world will applaud the Duke of Windsor and Wallis Simpson, because of their persistence in searching until they found life's greatest reward. All of us can profit by following their example in our own search for that which we demand of life.

What mystical power gives to men of persistence the capacity to master difficulties? Does the quality of persistence set up in one's mind some form of spiritual, mental or chemical activity which gives one access to supernatural forces? Does Infinite Intelligence throw *itself* on the side of the person who still fights on, after the battle has been lost, with the whole world on the opposing side?

These and many other similar questions have arisen in my mind as I have observed men like Henry Ford, who started at scratch, and built an Industrial Empire of huge proportions, with little else in the way of a beginning but persistence. Or, Thomas A. Edison, who, with less than three months of schooling, became the world's leading inventor and converted persistence into the talking machine, the moving picture machine, and the incandescent light, to say nothing of half a hundred other useful inventions.

I had the happy privilege of analyzing both Mr. Edison and Mr. Ford, year by year, over a long period of years, and therefore, the opportunity to study them at close range, so I speak from actual knowledge when I say that I found no quality save persistence, in either of them, that even remotely suggested the major source of their stupendous achievements.

As one makes an impartial study of the prophets, philosophers, "miracle" men, and religious leaders of the past, one is drawn to the inevitable conclusion that persistence, concentration of effort, and definiteness of purpose were the major sources of their achievements.

Consider, for example, the strange and fascinating story of Mohammed; analyze his life, compare him with men of achievement in this modern age of industry and finance, and observe how they have one outstanding trait in common, persistence!

If you are keenly interested in studying the strange power which gives potency to persistence, read a biography of Mohammed, especially the one by Essad Bey. This brief review of that book, by Thomas Sugrue, in the *Herald-Tribune,* will provide a preview of the rare treat in store for those who take the time to read the entire story of one of the most astounding examples of the power of persistence known to civilization.

When you know what to think and do, then you must use your will to compel yourself to think and do the right things.

—Wallace D. Wattles

THE LAST GREAT PROPHET

Reviewed by Thomas Sugrue

"Mohammed was a prophet, but he never performed a miracle. He was not a mystic; he had no formal schooling; he did not begin his mission until he was forty. When he announced that he was the Messenger of God, bringing word of the true religion, he was ridiculed and labeled a lunatic. Children tripped him and women threw filth upon him. He was banished from his native city, Mecca, and his followers were stripped of their worldly goods and sent into the desert after him. When he had been preaching ten years he had nothing to

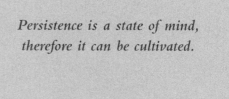

Persistence is a state of mind, therefore it can be cultivated.

Nothing in the world can take the place of persistence. . . . The slogan "Press on" has solved, and always will solve, the problems of the human race.

—Calvin Coolidge

show for it but banishment, poverty and ridicule. Yet before another ten years had passed, he was dictator of all Arabia, ruler of Mecca, and the head of a New World religion which was to sweep to the Danube and the Pyrenees before exhausting the impetus he gave it. That impetus was three-fold: the power of words, the efficacy of prayer, and man's kinship with God.

"His career never made sense. Mohammed was born to impoverished members of a leading family of Mecca. Because Mecca, the crossroads of the world, home of the magic stone called the Caaba, great city of trade, and the center of trade routes, was unsanitary, its children were sent to be raised in the desert by Bedouins. Mohammed was thus nurtured, drawing strength and health from the milk of nomad, vicarious mothers. He tended sheep and soon hired out to a rich widow as leader of her caravans. He traveled to all parts of the Eastern World, talked with many men of diverse beliefs and observed the decline of Christianity into warring sects. When he was twenty-eight, Khadija, the widow, looked upon him with favor, and married him. Her father would have objected to such a marriage, so she got him drunk and held him up while he gave the paternal blessing. For the next twelve years Mohammed lived as a rich and respected and very shrewd trader. Then he took to wandering in the desert, and one day he returned with the first verse of the Koran and told Khadija that the archangel Gabriel had appeared to him and said that he was to be the Messenger of God.

"The Koran, the revealed word of God, was the closest thing to a miracle in Mohammed's life. He had not been a poet; he had no gift of words. Yet the verses of the Koran, as he received them and recited them to the faithful, were better than any verses which the professional poets of the tribes could produce. This, to the Arabs, was a miracle. To them the gift of words was the greatest gift, the poet was all-powerful. In addition the Koran said that all men were equal before God, that the world should be a democratic state Islam. It was this political heresy, plus Mohammed's desire to destroy all the 360 idols in the courtyard of the Caaba, which brought about his banishment. The idols brought the desert tribes to Mecca, and that meant trade. So the business men of Mecca, the capitalists, of which he had been one, set upon Mohammed. Then he retreated to the desert and demanded sovereignty over the world.

"The rise of Islam began. Out of the desert came a flame which would not

Most ideas are stillborn, and need the breath of life injected into them through definite plans of immediate action. The time to nurse an idea is at the time of its birth.

be extinguished—a democratic army fighting as a unit and prepared to die without wincing. Mohammed had invited the Jews and Christians to join him; for he was not building a new religion. He was calling all who believed in one God to join in a single faith. If the Jews and Christians had accepted his invitation Islam would have conquered the world. They didn't. They would not even accept Mohammed's innovation of humane warfare. When the armies of the prophet entered Jerusalem not a single person was killed because of his faith. When the crusaders entered the city, centuries later, not a Moslem man, woman, or child was spared. But the Christians did accept one Moslem idea—the place of learning, the university."

The difference between a successful person and others is not a lack of strength, not a lack of knowledge, but rather a lack of will.

—Vincent T. Lombardi

Riches do not respond to wishes. They respond only to definite plans, backed by definite desires, through constant persistence.

QUESTIONS FOR SUCCESS

- *What is the most helpful idea from this chapter for you?*

- *What is the basis of persistence (page 173)?*

- *Napoleon Hill writes, "Weak desires bring weak results, just as a small amount of fire makes a small amount of heat. If you find yourself lacking in persistence, this weakness may be remedied by building a stronger fire under your desires." How can "building a stronger fire under your desires" help to overcome a lack of persistence?*

- *How can a Master Mind help you in building your persistence?*

- *Do you have a "poverty consciousness" or a "money consciousness"? Why?*

- *Review "Symptoms of Lack of Persistence." How many of those symptoms can you identify with?*

- *What are the four steps to developing persistence (page 183)?*

YOUR SUCCESS STEPS

- ☐ _____
- ☐ _____
- ☐ _____
- ☐ _____
- ☐ _____
- ☐ _____

CHAPTER 10

POWER OF THE MASTER MIND

The Driving Force

The Ninth Step Toward Riches

Power is essential for success in the accumulation of money. Plans are inert and useless, without sufficient power to translate them into action. This chapter will describe the method by which an individual may attain and apply power.

Power may be defined as "organized and intelligently directed knowledge." Power, as the term is here used, refers to organized effort, sufficient to enable an individual to transmute desire into its monetary equivalent. Organized effort is produced through the coordination of effort of two or more people, who work toward a definite end, in a spirit of harmony.

Power is required for the accumulation of money! Power is necessary for the retention of money after it has been accumulated!

Let us ascertain how power may be acquired. If power is "organized knowledge," let us examine the sources of knowledge:

a. **Infinite Intelligence.** This source of knowledge may be contacted through the procedure described in another chapter, with the aid of Creative Imagination.

b. **Accumulated experience.** The accumulated experience of man

> *We make a living by what we get,*
> *but we make a life by what we give.*
> —Winston Churchill

> *Power is essential for success in*
> *the accumulation of money.*

No great man ever complains of
want of opportunity.
        —Ralph Waldo Emerson

(or that portion of it which has been organized and recorded) may be found in any well-equipped public library. An important part of this accumulated experience is taught in public schools and colleges, where it has been classified and organized.

c. **Experiment and research.** In the field of science, and in practically every other walk of life, men are gathering, classifying, and organizing new facts daily. This is the source to which one must turn when knowledge is not available through "accumulated experience." Here, too, the Creative Imagination must often be used.

Knowledge may be acquired from any of the foregoing sources. It may be converted into power by organizing it into definite plans and by expressing those plans in terms of action.

Examination of the three major sources of knowledge will readily disclose the difficulty an individual would have, if he depended upon his efforts alone, in assembling knowledge and expressing it through definite plans in terms of action. If his plans are comprehensive, and if they contemplate large proportions, he must, generally, induce others to cooperate with him, before he can inject into them the necessary element of power.

GAINING POWER THROUGH THE "MASTER MIND"

The "Master Mind" may be defined as: "Coordination of knowledge and effort, in a spirit of harmony, between two or more people, for the attainment of a definite purpose."

No individual may have great power without availing himself of the "Master Mind." In a preceding chapter, instructions were given for the creation of plans for the purpose of translating desire into its monetary equivalent. If you carry out these instructions with persistence and intelligence, and use discrimination in the selection of your "Master Mind" group, your objective will have been half-way reached, even before you begin to recognize it.

So you may better understand the "intangible" potentialities of power available to you, through a properly chosen "Master Mind" group, we will here

The "Master Mind" may be defined as:
"Coordination of knowledge and effort, in a
spirit of harmony, between two or more people,
for the attainment of a definite purpose."

explain the two characteristics of the Master Mind principle, one of which is economic in nature, and the other psychic. The economic feature is obvious. Economic advantages may be created by any person who surrounds himself with the advice, counsel, and personal cooperation of a group of men who are willing to lend him wholehearted aid, in a spirit of perfect harmony. This form of cooperative alliance has been the basis of nearly every great fortune. Your understanding of this great truth may definitely determine your financial status.

The success you experience can never exceed your self-concept.
—Joel Fotinos

The psychic phase of the Master Mind principle is much more abstract, much more difficult to comprehend, because it has reference to the spiritual forces with which the human race, as a whole, is not well acquainted. You may catch a significant suggestion from this statement: "No two minds ever come together without, thereby, creating a third, invisible, intangible force which may be likened to a third mind."

Keep in mind the fact that there are only two known elements in the whole universe, energy and matter. It is a well-known fact that matter may be broken down into units of molecules, atoms, and electrons. There are units of matter which may be isolated, separated, and analyzed.

Likewise, there are units of energy.

The human mind is a form of energy, a part of it being spiritual in nature. When the minds of two people are coordinated in a spirit of harmony, the spiritual units of energy of each mind form an affinity, which constitutes the "psychic" phase of the Master Mind.

The Master Mind principle, or rather the economic feature of it, was first called to my attention by Andrew Carnegie, over twenty-five years ago. Discovery of this principle was responsible for the choice of my life's work.

Mr. Carnegie's Master Mind group consisted of a staff of approximately fifty men, with whom he surrounded himself, for the definite purpose of manufacturing and marketing steel. He attributed his entire fortune to the power he accumulated through this "Master Mind."

Analyze the record of any man who has accumulated a great fortune, and many of those who have accumulated modest fortunes, and you will find that they have either consciously, or unconsciously employed the "Master Mind" principle.

Great power can be accumulated through no other principle!

No individual may have great power without availing himself of the "Master Mind."

To think health when surrounded by the appearances of disease, or to think riches when in the midst of appearances of poverty, requires power; but he who acquires this power becomes a Master Mind. He can conquer fate; he can have what he wants.

—Wallace D. Wattles

Energy is Nature's universal set of building blocks, out of which she constructs every material thing in the universe, including man, and every form of animal and vegetable life. Through a process which only Nature completely understands, she translates energy into matter.

Nature's building blocks are available to man, in the energy involved in thinking! Man's brain may be compared to an electric battery. It absorbs energy from the ether, which permeates every atom of matter, and fills the entire universe.

It is a well-known fact that a group of electric batteries will provide more energy than a single battery. It is also a well-known fact that an individual battery will provide energy in proportion to the number and capacity of the cells it contains.

The brain functions in a similar fashion. This accounts for the fact that some brains are more efficient than others, and leads to this significant statement—a group of brains coordinated (or connected) in a spirit of harmony will provide more thought-energy than a single brain, just as a group of electric batteries will provide more energy than a single battery.

Through this metaphor it becomes immediately obvious that the Master Mind principle holds the secret of the power wielded by men who surround themselves with other men of brains.

There follows, now, another statement which will lead still nearer to an understanding of the psychic phase of the Master Mind principle: When a group of individual brains are coordinated and function in harmony, the increased energy created through that alliance becomes available to every individual brain in the group.

It is a well-known fact that Henry Ford began his business career under the handicap of poverty, illiteracy, and ignorance. It is an equally well-known fact that, within the inconceivably short period of ten years, Mr. Ford mastered these three handicaps, and that within twenty-five years he made himself one of the richest men in America. Connect with this fact the additional knowledge that Mr. Ford's most rapid strides became noticeable from the time he became a personal friend of Thomas A. Edison, and you will begin to understand what the influence of one mind upon another can accomplish. Go a step further, and consider the fact that Mr. Ford's most outstanding achievements began from the time that he formed the acquaintances of Harvey Firestone,

"No two minds ever come together without, thereby, creating a third, invisible, intangible force which may be likened to a third mind."

John Burroughs, and Luther Burbank (each a man of great brain capacity) and you will have further evidence that power may be produced through friendly alliance of minds.

There is little if any doubt that Henry Ford is one of the best-informed men in the business and industrial world. The question of his wealth needs no discussion. Analyze Mr. Ford's intimate personal friends, some of whom have already been mentioned, and you will be prepared to understand the following statement:—

"Men take on the nature and the habits and the power of thought of those with whom they associate in a spirit of sympathy and harmony."

Henry Ford whipped poverty, illiteracy, and ignorance by allying himself with great minds, whose vibrations of thought he absorbed into his own mind. Through his association with Edison, Burbank, Burroughs, and Firestone, Mr. Ford added to his own brain power, the sum and substance of the intelligence, experience, knowledge, and spiritual forces of these four men. Moreover, he appropriated, and made use of the Master Mind principle through the methods of procedure described in this book.

This principle is available to you!

We have already mentioned Mahatma Gandhi. Perhaps the majority of those who have heard of Gandhi look upon him as merely an eccentric little man, who goes around without formal wearing apparel, and makes trouble for the British Government.

In reality, Gandhi is not eccentric, but he is the most powerful man now living. (Estimated by the number of his followers and their faith in their leader.) Moreover, he is probably the most powerful man who has ever lived. His power is passive, but it is real.

Let us study the method by which he attained his stupendous power. It may be explained in a few words. He came by power through inducing over two hundred million people to coordinate, with mind and body, in a spirit of harmony, for a definite purpose.

In brief, Gandhi has accomplished a miracle, for it is a miracle when two hundred million people can be induced—not forced—to cooperate in a spirit of harmony, for a limitless time. If you doubt that this is a miracle, try to induce any two people to cooperate in a spirit of harmony for *any length of time.*

If there is any one axiom that I have tried to live up to in trying to become successful in business, it is the fact that I have tried to surround myself with associates who know more about business than I do.

—Monte L. Bean

A group of brains coordinated (or connected) in a spirit of harmony will provide more thought-energy than a single brain, just as a group of electric batteries will provide more energy than a single battery.

Every man who manages a business knows what a difficult matter it is to get employees to work together in a spirit even remotely resembling harmony.

The list of the chief sources from which power may be attained is, as you have seen, headed by Infinite Intelligence. When two or more people coordinate in a spirit of harmony, and work toward a definite objective, they place themselves in position, through that alliance, to absorb power directly from the great universal storehouse of Infinite Intelligence. This is the greatest of all sources of power. It is the source to which the genius turns. It is the source to which every great leader turns (whether he may be conscious of the fact or not).

The other two major sources from which the knowledge necessary for the accumulation of power may be obtained are no more reliable than the five senses of man. The senses are not always reliable. Infinite Intelligence does not err.

In subsequent chapters, the methods by which Infinite Intelligence may be most readily contacted will be adequately described.

This is not a course on religion. No fundamental principle described in this book should be interpreted as being intended to interfere either directly, or indirectly, with any man's religious habits. This book has been confined, exclusively, to instructing the reader how to transmute the definite purpose of desire for money, into its monetary equivalent.

Read, *think,* and meditate as you read. Soon, the entire subject will unfold, and you will see it in perspective. You are now seeing the detail of the individual chapters.

Money is as shy and elusive as the "old time" maiden. It must be wooed and won by methods not unlike those used by a determined lover, in pursuit of the girl of his choice. And, coincidental as it is, the power used in the "wooing" of money is not greatly different from that used in wooing a maiden. That power, when successfully used in the pursuit of money must be mixed with faith. It must be mixed with desire. It must be mixed with persistence. It must be applied through a plan, and that plan must be set into action.

When money comes in quantities known as "the big money," it flows to the one who accumulates it, as easily as water flows downhill. There exists a great unseen stream of power, which may be compared to a river; except that one side flows in one direction, carrying all who get into that side of the stream, onward and upward to wealth—and the other side flows in the opposite direc-

Feedback is the breakfast of champions.

—Ken Blanchard and
Spencer Johnson

Poverty needs no plan. It needs no one to aid it, because it is bold and ruthless. Riches are shy and timid. They have to be "attracted."

tion, carrying all who are unfortunate enough to get into it (and not able to extricate themselves from it), downward to misery and poverty.

Every man who has accumulated a great fortune has recognized the existence of this stream of life. It consists of one's thinking process. The positive emotions of thought form the side of the stream which carries one to fortune. The negative emotions form the side which carries one down to poverty.

This carries a thought of stupendous importance to the person who is following this book with the object of accumulating a fortune.

If you are in the side of the stream of power which leads to poverty, this may serve as an oar, by which you may propel yourself over into the other side of the stream. It can serve you only through application and use. Merely reading, and passing judgment on it, either one way or another, will in no way benefit you.

Some people undergo the experience of alternating between the positive and negative sides of the stream, being at times on the positive side, and at times on the negative side. The Wall Street crash of '29 swept millions of people from the positive to the negative side of the stream. These millions are struggling, some of them in desperation and fear, to get back to the positive side of the stream. This book was written especially for those millions.

Poverty and riches often change places. The crash taught the world this truth, although the world will not long remember the lesson. Poverty may, and generally does, voluntarily take the place of riches. When riches take the place of poverty, the change is usually brought about through well-conceived and carefully executed PLANS. Poverty needs no plan. It needs no one to aid it, because it is bold and ruthless. Riches are shy and timid. They have to be "attracted."

I've learned that people will forget what you said, people will forget what you did, but people will never forget how you made them feel.
—Maya Angelou

Anybody can wish for riches, and most people do, but only a few know that a definite plan, plus a burning desire for wealth, are the only dependable means of accumulating wealth.

Anybody can wish for riches, and most people do, but only a few know that a definite plan, plus a burning desire for wealth, are the only dependable means of accumulating wealth.

QUESTIONS FOR SUCCESS

- *What is the most helpful idea from this chapter for you?*

- *How does Napoleon Hill define "power" (page 191)?*

- *What are the "sources of knowledge" (pages 191–192)?*

- *How can you gain power through a Master Mind?*

YOUR SUCCESS STEPS

☐ _____

☐ _____

☐ _____

☐ _____

☐ _____

☐ _____

CHAPTER 11

THE MYSTERY OF SEX TRANSMUTATION

The Tenth Step Toward Riches

The meaning of the word "transmute" is, in simple language, "the changing, or transferring of one element, or form of energy, into another."

The emotion of sex brings into being a state of mind.

Because of ignorance on the subject, this state of mind is generally associated with the physical, and because of improper influences, to which most people have been subjected, in acquiring knowledge of sex, things essentially physical have highly biased the mind.

The emotion of sex has back of it the possibility of three constructive potentialities; they are:—

1. The perpetuation of mankind.
2. The maintenance of health (as a therapeutic agency, it has no equal).
3. The transformation of mediocrity into genius through transmutation.

Sex transmutation is simple and easily explained. It means the switching of the mind from thoughts of physical expression, to thoughts of some other nature.

The first and the best victory is to conquer self.

—Plato

The meaning of the word "transmute" is, in simple language, "the changing, or transferring of one element, or form of energy, into another."

Genius is only the power of making continuous efforts.

—Elbert Hubbard

Sex desire is the most powerful of human desires. When driven by this desire, men develop keenness of imagination, courage, will-power, persistence, and creative ability unknown to them at other times. So strong and impelling is the desire for sexual contact that men freely run the risk of life and reputation to indulge it. When harnessed, and redirected along other lines, this motivating force maintains all of its attributes of keenness of imagination, courage, etc., which may be used as powerful creative forces in literature, art, or in any other profession or calling, including, of course, the accumulation of riches.

The transmutation of sex energy calls for the exercise of will-power, to be sure, but the reward is worth the effort. The desire for sexual expression is inborn and natural. The desire cannot, and should not be submerged or eliminated. But it should be given an outlet through forms of expression which enrich the body, mind, and spirit of man. If not given this form of outlet, through transmutation, it will seek outlets through purely physical channels.

A river may be dammed, and its water controlled for a time, but eventually, it will force an outlet. The same is true of the emotion of sex. It may be submerged and controlled for a time, but its very nature causes it to be ever seeking means of expression. If it is not transmuted into some creative effort it will find a less worthy outlet.

Fortunate, indeed, is the person who has discovered how to give sex emotion an outlet through some form of creative effort, for he has, by that discovery, lifted himself to the status of a genius.

Scientific research has disclosed these significant facts:

1. The men of greatest achievement are men with highly developed sex natures; men who have learned the art of sex transmutation.
2. The men who have accumulated great fortunes and achieved outstanding recognition in literature, art, industry, architecture, and the professions were motivated by the influence of a woman.

The research from which these astounding discoveries were made went back through the pages of biography and history for more than two thousand years. Wherever there was evidence available in connection with the lives of men and

Sex transmutation is simple and easily explained. It means the switching of the mind from thoughts of physical expression, to thoughts of some other nature.

women of great achievement, it indicated most convincingly that they possessed highly developed sex natures.

The emotion of sex is an "irresistible force," against which there can be no such opposition as an "immovable body." When driven by this emotion, men become gifted with a super power for action. Understand this truth, and you will catch the significance of the statement that sex transmutation will lift one to the status of a genius.

The emotion of sex contains the secret of creative ability.

Destroy the sex glands, whether in man or beast, and you have removed the major source of action. For proof of this, observe what happens to any animal after it has been castrated. A bull becomes as docile as a cow after it has been altered sexually. Sex alteration takes out of the male, whether man or beast, all the fight that was in him. Sex alteration of the female has the same effect.

Nothing great was ever achieved without enthusiasm.

—Ralph Waldo Emerson

THE TEN MIND STIMULI

The human mind responds to stimuli, through which it may be "keyed up" to high rates of vibration, known as enthusiasm, creative imagination, intense desire, etc. The stimuli to which the mind responds most freely are:—

1. The desire for sex expression
2. Love
3. A burning desire for fame, power, or financial gain, money
4. Music
5. Friendship between either those of the same sex, or those of the opposite sex
6. A Master Mind alliance based upon the harmony of two or more people who ally themselves for spiritual or temporal advancement
7. Mutual suffering, such as that experienced by people who are persecuted
8. Auto-suggestion

Sex desire is the most powerful of human desires. When driven by this desire, men develop keenness of imagination, courage, willpower, persistence, and creative ability unknown to them at other times.

9. Fear

10. Narcotics and alcohol

The desire for sex expression comes at the head of the list of stimuli, which most effectively "step-up" the vibrations of the mind and start the "wheels" of physical action. Eight of these stimuli are natural and constructive. Two are destructive. The list is here presented for the purpose of enabling you to make a comparative study of the major sources of mind stimulation. From this study, it will be readily seen that the emotion of sex is, by great odds, the most intense and powerful of all mind stimuli.

This comparison is necessary as a foundation for proof of the statement that transmutation of sex energy may lift one to the status of a genius. Let us find out what constitutes a genius.

Some wiseacre has said that a genius is a man who "wears long hair, eats queer food, lives alone, and serves as a target for the joke makers." A better definition of a genius is "a man who has discovered how to increase the vibrations of thought to the point where he can freely communicate with sources of knowledge not available through the ordinary rate of vibration of thought."

The person who thinks will want to ask some questions concerning this definition of genius. The first question will be "How may one communicate with sources of knowledge which are not available through the ordinary rate of vibration of thought?"

The next question will be "Are there known sources of knowledge which are available only to genii, and if so, what are these sources, and exactly how may they be reached?"

We shall offer proof of the soundness of some of the more important statements made in this book—or at least we shall offer evidence through which you may secure your own proof through experimentation, and in doing so, we shall answer both of these questions.

When harnessed, and redirected along other lines, this motivating force maintains all of its attributes of keenness of imagination, courage, etc., which may be used as powerful creative forces in . . . the accumulation of riches.

"GENIUS" IS DEVELOPED THROUGH THE SIXTH SENSE

The reality of a "sixth sense" has been fairly well established. This sixth sense is "Creative Imagination." The faculty of creative imagination is one which the majority of people never use during an entire lifetime, and if used at all, it usually happens by mere accident. A relatively small number of people use, with deliberation and purpose aforethought, the faculty of creative imagination. Those who use this faculty voluntarily, and with understanding of its functions, are genii.

The faculty of creative imagination is the direct link between the finite mind of man and Infinite Intelligence. All so-called revelations, referred to in the realm of religion, and all discoveries of basic or new principles in the field of invention take place through the faculty of creative imagination.

When ideas or concepts flash into one's mind, through what is popularly called a "hunch," they come from one or more of the following sources:—

1. Infinite Intelligence
2. One's subconscious mind, wherein is stored every sense impression and thought impulse which ever reached the brain through any of the five senses
3. From the mind of some other person who has just released the thought, or picture of the idea or concept, through conscious thought, or
4. From the other person's subconscious storehouse.

There are no other known sources from which "inspired" ideas or "hunches" may be received.

The creative imagination functions best when the mind is vibrating (due to some form of mind stimulation) at an exceedingly high rate. That is, when the mind is functioning at a rate of vibration higher than that of ordinary, normal thought.

When brain action has been stimulated, through one or more of the ten mind stimulants, it has the effect of lifting the individual far above the horizon of ordinary thought, and permits him to envision distance, scope, and quality

In reading the lives of great men, I found that the first victory they won was over themselves; self-discipline with all of them came first.

—Harry S. Truman

The desire cannot, and should not be submerged or eliminated. But it should be given an outlet through forms of expression which enrich the body, mind, and spirit of man.

of thoughts not available on the lower plane, such as that occupied while one is engaged in the solution of the problems of business and professional routine.

When lifted to this higher level of thought, through any form of mind stimulation, an individual occupies, relatively, the same position as one who has ascended in an airplane to a height from which he may see over and beyond the horizon line which limits his vision, while on the ground. Moreover, while on this higher level of thought, the individual is not hampered or bound by any of the stimuli which circumscribe and limit his vision while wrestling with the problems of gaining the three basic necessities of food, clothing, and shelter. He is in a world of thought in which the ordinary, work-a-day thoughts have been as effectively removed as are the hills and valleys and other limitations of physical vision, when he rises in an airplane.

While on this exalted plane of thought, the creative faculty of the mind is given freedom for action. The way has been cleared for the sixth sense to function; it becomes receptive to ideas which could not reach the individual under any other circumstances. The "sixth sense" is the faculty which marks the difference between a genius and an ordinary individual.

The creative faculty becomes more alert and receptive to vibrations, originating outside the individual's subconscious mind, the more this faculty is used, and the more the individual relies upon it, and makes demands upon it for thought impulses. This faculty can be cultivated and developed only through use.

That which is known as one's "conscience" operates entirely through the faculty of the sixth sense.

The great artists, writers, musicians, and poets become great, because they acquire the habit of relying upon the "still, small voice" which speaks from within, through the faculty of creative imagination. It is a fact well known to people who have "keen" imaginations that their best ideas come through so-called "hunches."

There is a great orator who does not attain to greatness, until he closes his eyes and begins to rely entirely upon the faculty of Creative Imagination. When asked why he closed his eyes just before the climaxes of his oratory, he replied, "I do it because then I speak through ideas which come to me from within."

One of America's most successful and best-known financiers followed the habit of closing his eyes for two or three minutes before making a decision.

If we don't discipline ourselves, the world will do it for us.

—William Feather

Fortunate, indeed, is the person who has discovered how to give sex emotion an outlet through some form of creative effort, for he has, by that discovery, lifted himself to the status of a genius.

When asked why he did this, he replied, "With my eyes closed, I am able to draw upon a source of superior intelligence."

The late Dr. Elmer R. Gates, of Chevy Chase, Maryland, created more than two hundred useful patents, many of them basic, through the process of cultivating and using the creative faculty. His method is both significant and interesting to one interested in attaining to the status of genius, in which category Dr. Gates unquestionably belonged. Dr. Gates was one of the really great, though less publicized scientists of the world.

In his laboratory, he had what he called his "personal communication room." It was practically sound proof, and so arranged that all light could be shut out. It was equipped with a small table, on which he kept a pad of writing paper. In front of the table, on the wall, was an electric pushbutton, which controlled the lights. When Dr. Gates desired to draw upon the forces available to him through his Creative Imagination, he would go into this room, seat himself at the table, shut off the lights, and concentrate upon the known factors of the invention on which he was working, remaining in that position until ideas began to "flash" into his mind in connection with the unknown factors of the invention.

On one occasion, ideas came through so fast that he was forced to write for almost three hours. When the thoughts stopped flowing, and he examined his notes, he found they contained a minute description of principles which had not a parallel among the known data of the scientific world. Moreover, the answer to his problem was intelligently presented in those notes. In this manner Dr. Gates completed over two hundred patents, which had been begun, but not completed, by "half-baked" brains. Evidence of the truth of this statement is in the United States Patent Office.

Dr. Gates earned his living by "sitting for ideas" for individuals and corporations. Some of the largest corporations in America paid him substantial fees, by the hour, for "sitting for ideas."

The reasoning faculty is often faulty, because it is largely guided by one's accumulated experience. Not all knowledge, which one accumulates through "experience," is accurate. Ideas received through the creative faculty are much more reliable, for the reason that they come from sources more reliable than any which are available to the reasoning faculty of the mind.

Discipline is the bridge between goals and accomplishments.

—Jim Rohn

A better definition of a genius is "a man who has discovered how to increase the vibrations of thought to the point where he can freely communicate with sources of knowledge not available through the ordinary rate of vibration of thought."

If getting rich is the result of doing things in a Certain Way, and if like causes always produce like effects, then any man or woman who can do things in that way can become rich, and the whole matter is brought within the domain of exact science.

—Wallace D. Wattles

The major difference between the genius and the ordinary "crank" inventor may be found in the fact that the genius works through his faculty of creative imagination, while the "crank" knows nothing of this faculty. The scientific inventor (such as Mr. Edison, and Dr. Gates) makes use of both the synthetic and the creative faculties of imagination.

For example, the scientific inventor, or "genius," begins an invention by organizing and combining the known ideas, or principles accumulated through experience, through the synthetic faculty (the reasoning faculty). If he finds this accumulated knowledge to be insufficient for the completion of his invention, he then draws upon the sources of knowledge available to him through his *creative* faculty. The method by which he does this varies with the individual, but this is the sum and substance of his procedure:

1. He stimulates his mind so that it vibrates on a higher-than-average plane, using one or more of the ten mind stimulants or some other stimulant of his choice.
2. He concentrates upon the known factors (the finished part) of his invention, and creates in his mind a perfect picture of unknown factors (the unfinished part) of his invention. He holds this picture in mind until it has been taken over by the subconscious mind, then relaxes by clearing his mind of all thought, and waits for his answer to "flash" into his mind.

Sometimes the results are both definite and immediate. At other times, the results are negative, depending upon the state of development of the "sixth sense," or creative faculty.

Mr. Edison tried out more than ten thousand different combinations of ideas through the synthetic faculty of his imagination before he "tuned in" through the creative faculty, and got the answer which perfected the incandescent light. His experience was similar when he produced the talking machine.

There is plenty of reliable evidence that the faculty of creative imagination exists. This evidence is available through accurate analysis of men who have become leaders in their respective callings, without having had extensive edu-

A relatively small number of people use, with deliberation and purpose aforethought, the faculty of creative imagination. Those who use this faculty voluntarily, and with understanding of its functions, are genii.

cations. Lincoln was a notable example of a great leader who achieved greatness, through the discovery, and use of his faculty of creative imagination. He discovered, and began to use this faculty as the result of the stimulation of love which he experienced after he met Anne Rutledge, a statement of the highest significance, in connection with the study of the source of genius.

The pages of history are filled with the records of great leaders whose achievements may be traced directly to the influence of women who aroused the creative faculties of their minds, through the stimulation of sex desire. Napoleon Bonaparte was one of these. When inspired by his first wife, Josephine, he was irresistible and invincible. When his "better judgment" or reasoning faculty prompted him to put Josephine aside, he began to decline. His defeat and St. Helena were not far distant.

If good taste would permit, we might easily mention scores of men, well known to the American people, who climbed to great heights of achievement under the stimulating influence of their wives, only to drop back to destruction after money and power went to their heads, and they put aside the old wife for a new one. Napoleon was not the only man to discover that sex influence, *from the right source,* is more powerful than any substitute of expediency, which may be created by mere reason.

The human mind responds to stimulation!

Among the greatest and most powerful of these stimuli is the urge of sex. When harnessed and transmuted, this driving force is capable of lifting men into that higher sphere of thought which enables them to master the sources of worry and petty annoyance which beset their pathway on the lower plane.

Unfortunately, only the genii have made the discovery. Others have accepted the experience of sex urge, without discovering one of its major potentialities—a fact which accounts for the great number of "others" as compared to the limited number of genii.

For the purpose of refreshing the memory, in connection with the facts available from the biographies of certain men, we here present the names of a few men of outstanding achievement, each of whom was known to have been of a highly sexed nature. The genius which was theirs, undoubtedly found its source of power in transmuted sex energy:

The difference between failure and success is doing a thing nearly right and doing a thing exactly right.

—Edward Simmons

The great artists, writers, musicians, and poets become great, because they acquire the habit of relying upon the "still small voice," which speaks from within, through the faculty of creative imagination.

George Washington	Thomas Jefferson
Napoleon Bonaparte	Elbert Hubbard
William Shakespeare	Elbert H. Gary
Abraham Lincoln	Oscar Wilde
Ralph Waldo Emerson	Woodrow Wilson
Robert Burns	John H. Patterson
Andrew Jackson	Enrico Caruso

No one ever attains very eminent success by simply doing what is required of him; it is the amount and excellence of what is over and above the required that determines the greatness of ultimate distinction.
—Charles Kendall Adams

Your own knowledge of biography will enable you to add to this list. Find, if you can, a single man, in all history of civilization, who achieved outstanding success in any calling, who was not driven by a well-developed sex nature.

If you do not wish to rely upon biographies of men not now living, take inventory of those whom you know to be men of great achievement, and see if you can find one among them who is not highly sexed.

Sex energy is the creative energy of all genii. *There never has been, and never will be a great leader, builder, or artist lacking in this driving force of sex.*

Surely no one will misunderstand these statements to mean that all who are highly sexed are genii! Man attains to the status of a genius only when, and if, he stimulates his mind so that it draws upon the forces available, through the creative faculty of the imagination. Chief among the stimuli with which this "stepping up" of the vibrations may be produced is sex energy. The mere *possession of* this energy is not sufficient to produce a genius. The energy must be *transmuted* from desire for physical contact, into some other form of desire and action, before it will lift one to the status of a genius.

Far from becoming genii, because of great sex desires, the majority of men *lower* themselves, through misunderstanding and misuse of this great force, to the status of the lower animals.

WHY MEN SELDOM SUCCEED BEFORE FORTY

I discovered, from the analysis of over 25,000 people, that men who succeed in an outstanding way, seldom do so before the age of forty, and more often they

The reasoning faculty is often faulty, because it is largely guided by one's accumulated experience. Not all knowledge, which one accumulates through "experience" is accurate.

do not strike their real pace until they are well beyond the age of fifty. This fact was so astounding that it prompted me to go into the study of its cause most carefully, carrying the investigation over a period of more than twelve years.

This study disclosed the fact that the major reason why the majority of men who succeed do not begin to do so before the age of forty to fifty, is their tendency to dissipate their energies through over-indulgence in physical expression of the emotion of sex. The majority of men *never* learn that the urge of sex has other possibilities, which far transcend in importance, that of mere physical expression. The majority of those who make this discovery, do so *after having wasted many years* at a period when the sex energy is at its height, prior to the age of forty-five to fifty. This usually is followed by noteworthy achievement.

The lives of many men up to, and sometimes well past the age of forty, reflect a continued dissipation of energies, which could have been more profitably turned into better channels. Their finer and more powerful emotions are sown wildly to the four winds. Out of this habit of the male grew the term "sowing his wild oats."

The desire for sexual expression is by far the strongest and most impelling of all the human emotions, and for this very reason this desire, when *harnessed and transmuted* into action, other than that of physical expression, may raise one to the status of a genius.

One of America's most able business men frankly admitted that his attractive secretary was responsible for most of the plans he created. He admitted that her presence lifted him to heights of creative imagination, such as he could experience under no other stimulus.

One of the most successful men in America owes most of his success to the influence of a very charming young woman, who has served as his source of inspiration for more than twelve years. Everyone knows the man to whom this reference is made, but not everyone knows the real source of his achievements.

History is not lacking in examples of men who attained to the status of genii, as the result of the use of artificial mind stimulants in the form of alcohol and narcotics. Edgar Allan Poe wrote the "Raven" while under the influence of liquor, "dreaming dreams that mortal never dared to dream before." James Whitcomb Riley did his best writing while under the influence of alcohol.

Nothing can stop the man with the right mental attitude from achieving his goal; nothing on earth can help the man with the wrong mental attitude.

—W. W. Ziege

Ideas received through the creative faculty are much more reliable, for the reason that they come from sources more reliable than any which are available to the reasoning faculty of the mind.

Perhaps it was thus he saw "the ordered intermingling of the real and the dream, the mill above the river, and the mist above the stream." Robert Burns wrote best when intoxicated, "For Auld Lang Syne, my dear, we'll take a cup of kindness yet, for Auld Lang Syne."

But let it be remembered that many such men have destroyed themselves in the end. Nature has prepared her own potions with which men may safely stimulate their minds so they vibrate on a plane that enables them to tune in to fine and rare thoughts which come from—no man knows where! No satisfactory substitute for Nature's stimulants has ever been found.

It is a fact well known to psychologists that there is a very close relationship between sex desires and spiritual urges—a fact which accounts for the peculiar behavior of people who participate in the orgies known as religious "revivals," common among the primitive types.

The world is ruled, and the destiny of civilization is established, by the human emotions. People are influenced in their actions, not by reason so much as by "feelings." The creative faculty of the mind is set into action entirely by emotions, and *not by cold reason.* The most powerful of all human emotions is that of sex. There are other mind stimulants, some of which have been listed, but no one of them, nor all of them combined, can equal the driving power of sex.

A mind stimulant is any influence which will either temporarily, or permanently, increase the vibrations of thought. The ten major stimulants, described, are those most commonly resorted to. Through these sources one may commune with Infinite Intelligence, or enter, at will, the storehouse of the subconscious mind, either one's own, or that of another person, a procedure *which is all there is of genius.*

A teacher, who has trained and directed the efforts of more than thirty thousand sales people, made the astounding discovery that highly sexed men are the most efficient salesmen. The explanation is, that the factor of personality known as "personal magnetism" is nothing more nor less than sex energy. Highly sexed people always have a plentiful supply of magnetism. Through cultivation and understanding, this vital force may be drawn upon and used to great advantage in the relationships between people. This energy may be communicated to others through the following media:

You cannot always control circumstances, but you can control your own thoughts.

—Charles Popplestown

The mere possession of this energy is not sufficient to produce a genius. The energy must be transmuted from desire for physical contact, into some other form of desire and action, before it will lift one to the status of a genius.

1. The hand-shake. The touch of the hand indicates, instantly, the presence of magnetism, or the lack of it.
2. The tone of voice. Magnetism, or sex energy, is the factor with which the voice may be colored, or made musical and charming.
3. Posture and carriage of the body. Highly sexed people move briskly, and with grace and ease.
4. The vibrations of thought. Highly sexed people mix the emotion of sex with their thoughts, or may do so at will, and in that way, may influence those around them.
5. Body adornment. People who are highly sexed are usually very careful about their personal appearance. They usually select clothing of a style becoming to their personality, physique, complexion, etc.

Success is not the key to happiness. Happiness is the key to success. If you love what you are doing, you will be successful.

—Herman Cain

When employing salesmen, the more capable sales manager looks for the quality of personal magnetism as the *first requirement* of a salesman. People who lack sex energy will never become enthusiastic nor inspire others with enthusiasm, and enthusiasm is one of the most important requisites in salesmanship, no matter what one is selling.

The public speaker, orator, preacher, lawyer, or salesman who is lacking in sex energy is a "flop," as far as being able to influence others is concerned. Couple with this the fact that most people can be influenced only through an appeal to their emotions, and you will understand the importance of sex energy as a part of the salesman's native ability. Master salesmen attain the status of mastery in selling, because they, either consciously, or unconsciously, *transmute* the energy of sex into sales enthusiasm! In this statement may be found a very practical suggestion as to the actual meaning of sex transmutation.

The salesman who knows how to take his mind off the subject of sex, and direct it in sales effort with as much enthusiasm and determination as he would apply to its original purpose, has acquired the art of sex transmutation, whether he knows it or not. The majority of salesmen who transmute their sex energy do so without being in the least aware of what they are doing, or how they are doing it.

Transmutation of sex energy calls for more will-power than the average

The majority of men never learn that the urge of sex has other possibilities, which far transcend in importance, that of mere physical expression.

Destiny is not a matter of chance, it is a matter of choice; it is not a thing to be waited for, it is a thing to be achieved.

—Winston Churchill

person cares to use for this purpose. Those who find it difficult to summon will-power sufficient for transmutation, may gradually acquire this ability. Though this requires will-power, the reward for the practice is more than worth the effort.

The entire subject of sex is one with which the majority of people appear to be unpardonably ignorant. The urge of sex has been grossly misunderstood, slandered, and burlesqued by the ignorant and the evil minded, for so long that the very word "sex" is seldom used in polite society. Men and women who are known to be blessed—yes, blessed—with highly sexed natures, are usually looked upon as being people who will bear watching. Instead of being called blessed, they are usually called cursed.

Millions of people, even in this age of enlightenment, have inferiority complexes which they developed because of this false belief that a highly sexed nature is a curse. These statements, of the virtue of sex energy, should not be construed as justification for the libertine. The emotion of sex is a virtue only when used intelligently, and with discrimination. It may be misused, and often is, to such an extent that it debases, instead of enriches, both body and mind. The better use of this power is the burden of this chapter.

It seemed quite significant to the author, when he made the discovery that practically every great leader whom he had the privilege of analyzing, was a man whose achievements were largely inspired by a woman. In many instances, the "woman in the case" was a modest, self-denying wife, of whom the public had heard but little or nothing. In a few instances, the source of inspiration has been traced to the "other woman." Perhaps such cases may not be entirely unknown to you.

Intemperance in sex habits is just as detrimental as intemperance in habits of drinking and eating. In this age in which we live, an age which began with the world war, intemperance in habits of sex is common. This orgy of indulgence may account for the shortage of great leaders. No man can avail himself of the forces of his creative imagination, while dissipating them. Man is the only creature on earth which violates Nature's purpose in this connection. Every other animal indulges its sex nature in moderation, and with purpose which harmonizes with the laws of nature. Every other animal responds to the call of sex only in "season." Man's inclination is to declare "open season."

People are influenced in their actions, not by reason so much as by "feelings." The creative faculty of the mind is set into action entirely by emotions, and not by cold reason.

Every intelligent person knows that stimulation in excess, through alcoholic drink and narcotics, is a form of intemperance which destroys the vital organs of the body, including the brain. Not every person knows, however, that over-indulgence in sex expression may become a habit as destructive and as detrimental to creative effort as narcotics or liquor.

A sex-mad man is not essentially different than a dope-mad man! Both have lost control over their faculties of reason and will-power. Sexual over-indulgence may not only destroy reason and will-power, but it may also lead to either temporary or permanent insanity. Many cases of hypochondria (imaginary illness) grow out of habits developed in ignorance of the true function of sex.

From these brief references to the subject, it may be readily seen that ignorance on the subject of sex transmutation forces stupendous penalties upon the ignorant on the one hand, and withholds from them equally stupendous benefits, on the other.

Widespread ignorance on the subject of sex is due to the fact that the subject has been surrounded with mystery and beclouded by dark silence. The conspiracy of mystery and silence has had the same effect upon the minds of young people that the psychology of prohibition had. The result has been increased curiosity, and desire to acquire more knowledge on this "verboten" subject; and to the shame of all lawmakers, and most physicians—by training best qualified to educate youth on that subject—information has not been easily available.

Seldom does an individual enter upon highly creative effort in any field of endeavor before the age of forty. The average man reaches the period of his greatest capacity to create between forty and sixty. These statements are based upon analysis of thousands of men and women who have been carefully observed. They should be encouraging to those who fail to arrive before the age of forty, and to those who become frightened at the approach of "old age," around the forty-year mark. The years between forty and fifty are, as a rule, the most fruitful. Man should approach this age not with fear and trembling, but with hope and eager anticipation.

If you want evidence that most men do not begin to do their best work before the age of forty, study the records of the most successful men known to

History records the successes of men with objectives and a sense of direction. Oblivion is the position of small men overwhelmed by obstacles.

—William H. Danforth

Those who find it difficult to summon will-power sufficient for transmutation, may gradually acquire this ability. Though this requires will-power, the reward for the practice is more than worth the effort.

We must not, in trying to think about how we can make a big difference, ignore the small daily differences we can make which, over time, add up to big differences that we often cannot foresee.

—Marian Wright Edelman

the American people, and you will find it. Henry Ford had not "hit his pace" of achievement until he had passed the age of forty. Andrew Carnegie was well past forty before he began to reap the reward of his efforts. James J. Hill was still running a telegraph key at the age of forty. His stupendous achievements took place after that age. Biographies of American industrialists and financiers are filled with evidence that the period from forty to sixty is the most productive age of man.

Between the ages of thirty and forty, man begins to learn (if he ever learns) the art of sex transmutation. This discovery is generally accidental, and more often than otherwise, the man who makes it is totally unconscious of his discovery. He may observe that his powers of achievement have increased around the age of thirty-five to forty, but in most cases, he is not familiar with the cause of this change; that Nature begins to harmonize the emotions of love and sex in the individual, between the ages of thirty and forty, so that he may draw upon these great forces, and apply them jointly as stimuli to action.

Sex, alone, is a mighty urge to action, but its forces are like a cyclone—they are often uncontrollable. When the emotion of love begins to mix itself with the emotion of sex, the result is calmness of purpose, poise, accuracy of judgment, and balance. What person, who has attained to the age of forty, is so unfortunate as to be unable to analyze these statements, and to corroborate them by his own experience?

When driven by his desire to please a woman, based solely upon the emotion of sex, a man may be, and usually is, capable of great achievement, but his actions may be disorganized, distorted, and totally destructive. When driven by his desire to please a woman, based upon the motive of sex alone, a man may steal, cheat, and even commit murder. But when the emotion of love is mixed with the emotion of sex, that same man will guide his actions with more sanity, balance, and reason.

Criminologists have discovered that the most hardened criminals can be reformed through the influence of a woman's *love.* There is no record of a criminal having been reformed solely through the sex influence. These facts are well known, but their cause is not. Reformation comes, if at all, through the *heart,* or the emotional side of man, *not* through his head, or reasoning side. Reformation means "a change of heart." It does not mean a "change of head." A man

No man can avail himself of the forces of his creative imagination, while dissipating them.

may, because of reason, make certain changes in his personal conduct to avoid the consequences of undesirable effects, but genuine reformation comes only through a change of heart—through a desire to change.

Love, romance, and sex are all emotions capable of driving men to heights of super achievement. Love is the emotion which serves as a safety valve, and insures balance, poise, and constructive effort. When combined, these three emotions may lift one to an altitude of a genius. There are genii, however, who know but little of the emotion of love. Most of them may be found engaged in some form of action which is destructive, or at least, not based upon justice and fairness toward others. If good taste would permit, a dozen genii could be named in the field of industry and finance, who ride ruthlessly over the rights of their fellow men. They seem totally lacking in conscience. The reader can easily supply his own list of such men.

The emotions are states of mind. Nature has provided man with a "chemistry of the mind" which operates in a manner similar to the principles of chemistry of matter. It is a well-known fact that, through the aid of chemistry of matter, a chemist may create a deadly poison by mixing certain elements, none of which are—in themselves—harmful in the right proportions. The emotions may, likewise, be combined so as to create a deadly poison. The emotions of sex and jealousy, when mixed, may turn a person into an insane beast.

The presence of any one or more of the destructive emotions in the human mind, through the chemistry of the mind, sets up a poison which may destroy one's sense of justice and fairness. In extreme cases, the presence of any combination of these emotions in the mind may destroy one's reason.

The road to genius consists of the development, control, and use of sex, love, and romance. Briefly, the process may be stated as follows:

Encourage the presence of these emotions as the dominating thoughts in one's mind, and discourage the presence of all the destructive emotions. The mind is a creature of habit. It thrives upon the *dominating* thoughts fed it. Through the faculty of will-power, one may discourage the presence of any emotion, and encourage the presence of any other. Control of the mind, through the power of will, is not difficult. Control comes from persistence, and habit. The secret of control lies in understanding the process of transmutation. When any negative emotion presents itself in one's mind, it can be transmuted into a

Everyone thinks of changing the world, but no one thinks of changing himself.

—Leo Tolstoy

Love, romance, and sex are all emotions capable of driving men to heights of super achievement. . . . When combined, these three emotions may lift one to an altitude of a genius.

Progress is impossible without change; and those who cannot change their minds cannot change anything.

—George Bernard Shaw

positive, or constructive emotion, by the simple procedure of changing one's thoughts.

There is no other road to genius than through voluntary self-effort! A man may attain to great heights of financial or business achievement, solely by the driving force of sex energy, but history is filled with evidence that he may, and usually does, carry with him certain traits of character which rob him of the ability to either hold or enjoy his fortune. This is worthy of analysis, thought, and meditation, for it states a truth, the knowledge of which may be helpful to women as well as men. Ignorance of this has cost thousands of people their privilege of happiness, even though they possessed riches.

The emotions of love and sex leave their unmistakable marks upon the features. Moreover, these signs are so visible, that all who wish may read them. The man who is driven by the storm of passion, based upon sex desires alone, plainly advertises that fact to the entire world, by the expression of his eyes, and the lines of his face. The emotion of love, when mixed with the emotion of sex, softens, modifies, and beautifies the facial expression. No character analyst is needed to tell you this—you may observe it for yourself.

The emotion of love brings out, and develops, the artistic and the aesthetic nature of man. It leaves its impress upon one's very soul, even after the fire has been subdued by time and circumstance.

Memories of love never pass. They linger, guide, and influence long after the source of stimulation has faded. There is nothing new in this. Every person, who has been moved by genuine love, knows that it leaves enduring traces upon the human heart. The effect of love endures, because love is spiritual in nature. The man who cannot be stimulated to great heights of achievement by love, is hopeless—he is dead, though he may seem to live.

Even the memories of love are sufficient to lift one to a higher plane of creative effort. The major force of love may spend itself and pass away, like a fire which has burned itself out, but it leaves behind indelible marks as evidence that it passed that way. Its departure often prepares the human heart for a still greater love.

Go back into your yesterdays, at times, and bathe your mind in the beautiful memories of past love. It will soften the influence of the present worries and annoyances. It will give you a source of escape from the unpleasant realities of

When any negative emotion presents itself in one's mind, it can be transmuted into a positive, or constructive emotion, by the simple procedure of changing one's thoughts.

life, and maybe—who knows?—your mind will yield to you, during this temporary retreat into the world of fantasy, ideas or plans which may change the entire financial or spiritual status of your life.

If you believe yourself unfortunate, because you have "loved and lost," perish the thought. One who has loved truly can never lose entirely. Love is whimsical and temperamental. Its nature is ephemeral, and transitory. It comes when it pleases, and goes away without warning. Accept and enjoy it while it remains, but spend no time worrying about its departure. Worry will never bring it back.

Dismiss, also, the thought that love never comes but once. Love may come and go, times without number, but there are no two love experiences which affect one in just the same way. There may be, and there usually is, one love experience which leaves a deeper imprint on the heart than all the others, but all love experiences are beneficial, except to the person who becomes resentful and cynical when love makes its departure.

There should be no disappointment over love, and there would be none if people understood the difference between the emotions of love and sex. The major difference is that love is spiritual, while sex is biological. No experience, which touches the human heart with a spiritual force, can possibly be harmful, except through ignorance, or jealousy.

Love is, without question, life's greatest experience. It brings one into communion with Infinite Intelligence. When mixed with the emotions of romance and sex, it may lead one far up the ladder of creative effort. The emotions of love, sex, and romance are sides of the eternal triangle of achievement-building genius. Nature creates genii through no other force.

Love is an emotion with many sides, shades, and colors. The love which one feels for parents or children is quite different from that which one feels for one's sweetheart. The one is mixed with the emotion of sex, while the other is not.

The love which one feels in true friendship is not the same as that felt for one's sweetheart, parents, or children, but it, too, is a form of love.

Then, there is the emotion of love for things inanimate, such as the love of Nature's handiwork. But the most intense and burning of all these various kinds of love is that experienced in the blending of the emotions of love and sex. Marriages, not blessed with the eternal affinity of love, properly balanced and proportioned, with sex, cannot be happy ones—and seldom endure. Love,

When you always do your best, you take action. Doing your best is taking action because you love it, not because you're expecting a reward.

—Don Miguel Ruiz

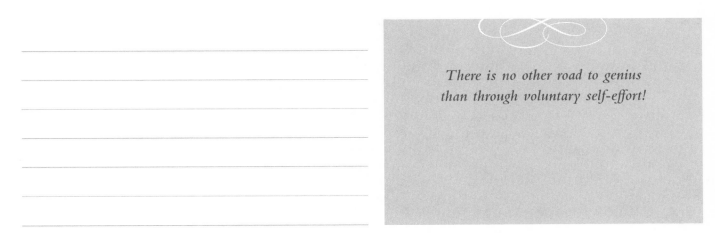

There is no other road to genius than through voluntary self-effort!

There are risks and costs to a program of action, but they are far less than the long-range risks and costs of comfortable inaction.

—John F. Kennedy

alone, will not bring happiness in marriage, nor will sex alone. When these two beautiful emotions are blended, marriage may bring about a state of mind, closest to the spiritual that one may ever know on this earthly plane.

When the emotion of romance is added to those of love and sex, the obstructions between the finite mind of man and Infinite Intelligence are removed. Then a genius has been born!

What a different story is this, than those usually associated with the emotion of sex. Here is an interpretation of the emotion which lifts it out of the commonplace, and makes of it potter's clay in the hands of God, from which He fashions all that is beautiful and inspiring. It is an interpretation which would, when properly understood, bring harmony out of the chaos which exists in too many marriages. The disharmonies often expressed in the form of nagging may usually be traced to *lack of knowledge* on the subject of sex. Where love, romance and the proper understanding of the emotion and function of sex abide, there is no disharmony between married people.

Fortunate is the husband whose wife understands the true relationship between the emotions of love, sex, and romance. When motivated by this holy triumvirate, no form of labor is burdensome, because even the most lowly form of effort takes on the nature of a labor of love.

It is a very old saying that "a man's wife may either make him or break him," but the reason is not always understood. The "making" and "breaking" is the result of the wife's understanding, or lack of understanding of the emotions of love, sex, and romance.

Despite the fact that men are polygamous, by the very nature of their biological inheritance, it is true that no woman has as great an influence on a man as his wife, unless he is married to a woman totally unsuited to his nature. If a woman permits her husband to lose interest in her, and become more interested in other women, it is usually because of her ignorance, or indifference toward the subjects of sex, love, and romance. This statement presupposes, of course, that genuine love once existed between a man and his wife. The facts are equally applicable to a man who permits his wife's interest in him to die.

Married people often bicker over a multitude of trivialities. If these are analyzed accurately, the real cause of the trouble will often be found to be indifference, or ignorance on these subjects.

The major force of love may spend itself and pass away, like a fire which has burned itself out, but it leaves behind indelible marks as evidence that it passed that way. Its departure often prepares the human heart for a still greater love.

Man's greatest motivating force is his desire to please woman! The hunter who excelled during prehistoric days, before the dawn of civilization, did so, because of his desire to appear great in the eyes of woman. Man's nature has not changed in this respect. The "hunter" of today brings home no skins of wild animals, but he indicates his desire for her favor by supplying fine clothes, motor cars, and wealth. Man has the same desire to please woman that he had before the dawn of civilization. The only thing that has changed is his method of pleasing. Men who accumulate large fortunes, and attain to great heights of power and fame, do so, mainly, to satisfy their *desire to please women.* Take women out of their lives, and great wealth would be useless to most men. *It is this inherent desire of man to please woman, which gives woman the power to make or break a man.*

The woman who understands man's nature and tactfully caters to it, need have no fear of competition from other women. Men may be "giants" with indomitable will-power when dealing with other men, but they are easily managed by the women of their choice.

Most men will not admit that they are easily influenced by the women they prefer, because it is in the nature of the male to want to be recognized as the stronger of the species. Moreover, the intelligent woman recognizes this "manly trait" and very wisely makes no issue of it.

Some men know that they are being influenced by the women of their choice—their wives, sweethearts, mothers or sisters—but they tactfully refrain from rebelling against the influence because they are intelligent enough to know that no man is happy or complete without the modifying influence of the right woman. The man who does not recognize this important truth deprives himself of the power which has done more to help men achieve success than all other forces combined.

What it lies in our power to do, it lies in our power not do.

—Aristotle

The emotion of love brings out, and develops, the artistic and the aesthetic nature of man. It leaves its impress upon one's very soul, even after the fire has been subdued by time and circumstance.

QUESTIONS FOR SUCCESS

- *What is the most helpful idea from this chapter for you?*

- *What does Napoleon Hill mean by "sex transmutation"?*

- *What are the "Ten Mind Stimuli"?*

- *What is the "sixth sense" and how does it develop genius?*

- *Where do ideas or "hunches" come from?*

- *Review the story about Dr. Elmer R. Gates (page 205), and how he would "sit for ideas." How can you do this in your life?*

- *Napoleon Hill writes, "No man can avail himself of the forces of his creative imagination, while dissipating them." How have you dissipated rather than used your creative forces in the past?*

YOUR SUCCESS STEPS

☐ _____

☐ _____

☐ _____

☐ _____

☐ _____

☐ _____

CHAPTER 12

THE SUBCONSCIOUS MIND

The Connecting Link

The Eleventh Step Toward Riches

The subconscious mind consists of a field of consciousness, in which every impulse of thought that reaches the objective mind through any of the five senses is classified and recorded, and from which thoughts may be recalled or withdrawn as letters may be taken from a filing cabinet.

It receives, and files, sense impressions or thoughts, regardless of their nature. You may voluntarily plant in your subconscious mind any plan, thought, or purpose which you desire to, translate into its physical or monetary equivalent. The subconscious acts first on the dominating desires which have been mixed with emotional feeling, such as faith.

Consider this in connection with the instructions given in the chapter on desire, for taking the six steps there outlined, and the instructions given in the chapter on the building and execution of plans, and you will understand the importance of the thought conveyed.

The subconscious mind works day and night. Through a method of procedure, unknown to man, the subconscious mind draws upon the forces of Infinite Intelligence for the power with which it voluntarily transmutes one's desires into their physical equivalent, making use always of the most practical media by which this end may be accomplished.

You cannot *entirely* control your subconscious mind, but you can voluntarily hand over to it any plan, desire, or purpose which you wish transformed into

> *To permit your mind to dwell upon the inferior is to become inferior and to surround yourself with inferior things. On the other hand, to fix your attention on the best is to surround yourself with the best, and to become the best.*
>
> —Wallace D. Wattles

> *The subconscious mind consists of a field of consciousness, in which every impulse of thought that reaches the objective mind through any of the five senses is classified and recorded, and from which thoughts may be recalled or withdrawn.*

concrete form. Read, again, instructions for using the subconscious mind, in the chapter on auto-suggestion.

There is plenty of evidence to support the belief that the subconscious mind is the connecting link between the finite mind of man and Infinite Intelligence. It is the intermediary through which one may draw upon the forces of Infinite Intelligence at will. It, alone, contains the secret process by which mental impulses are modified and changed into their spiritual equivalent. It, alone, is the medium through which prayer may be transmitted to the source capable of answering prayer.

The possibilities of creative effort connected with the subconscious mind are stupendous and imponderable. They inspire one with awe.

I never approach the discussion of the subconscious mind without a feeling of littleness and inferiority due, perhaps, to the fact that man's entire stock of knowledge on this subject is so pitifully limited. The very fact that the subconscious mind is the medium of communication between the thinking mind of man and Infinite Intelligence is, of itself, a thought which almost paralyzes one's reason.

After you have accepted, as a reality, the existence of the subconscious mind, and understand its possibilities, as a medium for transmuting your desires into their physical or monetary equivalent, you will comprehend the full significance of the instructions given in the chapter on desire. You will also understand why you have been repeatedly admonished to make your desires clear, and to reduce them to writing. You will also understand the necessity of persistence in carrying out instructions.

The thirteen principles are the stimuli with which you acquire the ability to reach, and to influence your subconscious mind. Do not become discouraged, if you cannot do this upon the first attempt. Remember that the subconscious mind may be voluntarily directed *only through habit,* under the directions given in the chapter on faith. You have not yet had time to master faith. Be patient. Be persistent.

A good many statements in the chapters on faith and auto-suggestion will be repeated here, for the benefit of your subconscious mind. Remember, your subconscious mind functions voluntarily, *whether you make any effort to influence it or not.* This, naturally, suggests to you that thoughts of fear and poverty, and all

The way to gain a good reputation is to endeavor to be what you desire to appear.

—Socrates

The subconscious mind will not remain idle! If you fail to plant desires in your subconscious mind, it will feed upon the thoughts which reach it as the result of your neglect.

negative thoughts serve as stimuli to your subconscious mind, *unless* you master these impulses and give it more desirable food upon which it may feed.

The subconscious mind will not remain idle! If you fail to plant desires in your subconscious mind, it will feed upon the thoughts which reach it as the *result of your neglect.* We have already explained that thought impulses, both negative and positive, are reaching the subconscious mind continuously, from the four sources which were mentioned in the chapter on sex transmutation.

For the present, it is sufficient if you remember that you are living *daily,* in the midst of all manner of thought impulses which are reaching your subconscious mind, without your knowledge. Some of these impulses are negative, some are positive. You are now engaged in trying to help shut off the flow of negative impulses, and to aid in voluntarily influencing your subconscious mind, through positive impulses of desire.

When you achieve this, you will possess the key which unlocks the door to your subconscious mind. Moreover, you will control that door so completely, that no undesirable thought may influence your subconscious mind.

Everything which man creates begins in the form of a thought impulse. Man can create nothing which he does not first conceive in thought. Through the aid of the imagination, thought impulses may be assembled into plans. The imagination, when under control, may be used for the creation of plans or purposes that lead to success in one's chosen occupation.

All thought impulses, intended for transmutation into their physical equivalent, voluntarily planted in the subconscious mind, must pass through the imagination, and be mixed with faith. The "mixing" of faith with a plan, or purpose, intended for submission to the subconscious mind, may be done only through the imagination.

From these statements, you will readily observe that voluntary use of the subconscious mind calls for coordination and application of all the principles.

Ella Wheeler Wilcox gave evidence of her understanding of the power of the subconscious mind when she wrote:

> *You never can tell what a thought will do*
> *In bringing you hate or love—*
> *For thoughts are things, and their airy wings*

Your disposition will be suitable to that which you most frequently think on; for the soul is, as it were, tinged with the color and complexions of its own thoughts. Your life is what your thoughts make it.

—Marcus Aurelius

Everything which man creates begins in the form of a thought impulse. Man can create nothing which he does not first conceive in thought.

Are swifter than carrier doves.
They follow the law of the universe—
Each thing creates its kind,
And they speed o'er the track to bring you back
Whatever went out from your mind.

It takes as much hard mental work
to fail as it does to succeed. Failure
is actually a success negative.

—Raymond Charles Barker

Mrs. Wilcox understood the truth, that thoughts which go out from one's mind, also imbed themselves deeply in one's subconscious mind, where they serve as a magnet, pattern, or blueprint by which the subconscious mind is influenced while translating them into their physical equivalent. Thoughts are truly things, for the reason that every material thing begins in the form of thought-energy.

The subconscious mind is more susceptible to influence by impulses of thought mixed with "feeling" or emotion, than by those originating solely in the reasoning portion of the mind. In fact, there is much evidence to support the theory that only emotionalized thoughts have any action influence upon the subconscious mind. It is a well-known fact that emotion or feeling rules the majority of people. If it is true that the subconscious mind responds more quickly to and is influenced more readily by thought impulses which are well mixed with emotion, it is essential to become familiar with the more important of the emotions. There are seven major positive emotions, and seven major negative emotions. The negatives *voluntarily* inject themselves into the thought impulses, which insure passage into the subconscious mind. The positives must be injected, through the principle of auto-suggestion, into the thought impulses which an individual wishes to pass on to his subconscious mind. (Instructions have been given in the chapter on auto-suggestion.)

These emotions, or feeling impulses, may be likened to yeast in a loaf of bread, because they constitute the action element, which transforms thought impulses from the passive to the active state. Thus may one understand why thought impulses, which have been well mixed with emotion, are acted upon more readily than thought impulses originating in "cold reason."

You are preparing yourself to influence and control the "inner audience" of your subconscious mind, in order to hand over to it the desire for money, which you wish transmuted into its monetary equivalent. It is essential, therefore, that

The subconscious mind is more susceptible to influence by impulses of thought mixed with "feeling" or emotion, than by those originating solely in the reasoning portion of the mind.

you understand the method of approach to this "inner audience." You must speak its language, or it will not heed your call. It understands best the language of emotion or feeling. Let us, therefore, describe here the seven major positive emotions, and the seven major negative emotions, so that you may draw upon the positives, and avoid the negatives, when giving instructions to your subconscious mind.

Success is blocked by concentrating on it and planning for it. . . . Success is shy—it won't come out while you're watching.

—Tennessee Williams

THE SEVEN MAJOR POSITIVE EMOTIONS

The emotion of DESIRE
The emotion of FAITH
The emotion of LOVE
The emotion of SEX
The emotion of ENTHUSIASM
The emotion of ROMANCE
The emotion of HOPE

There are other positive emotions, but these are the seven most powerful, and the ones most commonly used in creative effort. Master these seven emotions (they can be mastered only by use) and the other positive emotions will be at your command when you need them. Remember, in this connection, that you are studying a book which is intended to help you develop a "money consciousness" *by filling your mind with positive emotions.* One does not become money conscious by filling one's mind with negative emotions.

THE SEVEN MAJOR NEGATIVE EMOTIONS
(TO BE AVOIDED)

The emotion of FEAR
The emotion of JEALOUSY
The emotion of HATRED
The emotion of REVENGE

Remember . . . that you are studying a book which is intended to help you develop a "money consciousness" by filling your mind with positive emotions. One does not become money conscious by filling one's mind with negative emotions.

The emotion of GREED

The emotion of SUPERSTITION

The emotion of ANGER

Your own mind is a sacred enclosure into which nothing harmful can enter except by your promotion.

—Ralph Waldo Emerson

Positive and negative emotions cannot occupy the mind at the same time. One or the other must dominate. It is your responsibility to make sure that positive emotions constitute the dominating influence of your mind. Here the law of habit will come to your aid. *Form the habit* of applying and using the positive emotions! Eventually, they will dominate your mind so completely, that the negatives *cannot enter it.*

Only by following these instructions literally, and continuously, can you gain control over your subconscious mind. The presence of a single negative in your conscious mind is sufficient to *destroy* all chances of constructive aid from your subconscious mind.

If you are an observing person, you must have noticed that most people resort to prayer only after everything else has failed! Or else they pray by a ritual of meaningless words. And because it is a fact that most people who pray do so only after everything else has failed, they go to prayer with their minds filled with fear and doubt, *which are the emotions the subconscious mind acts upon,* and passes on to Infinite Intelligence. Likewise, that is the emotion which Infinite Intelligence receives, and acts upon.

If you pray for a thing, but have fear as you pray, that you may not receive it, or that your prayer will not be acted upon by Infinite Intelligence, your prayer *will have been in vain.*

Prayer does, sometimes, result in the realization of that for which one prays. If you have ever had the experience of receiving that for which you prayed, go back in your memory, and recall your actual state of mind, while you were praying, and you will know, for sure, that the theory here described is more than a theory.

The time will come when the schools and educational institutions of the country will teach the "science of prayer." Moreover, then prayer may be, and will be reduced to a science. When that time comes (it will come as soon as mankind is ready for it, and demands it), no one will approach the Universal Mind in a state of fear, for the very good reason that there will be no such

Positive and negative emotions cannot occupy the mind at the same time. *One or the other must dominate. It is your responsibility to make sure that positive emotions constitute the dominating influence of your mind.*

emotion as fear. Ignorance, superstition, and false teaching will have disappeared, and man will have attained his true status as a child of Infinite Intelligence. A few have already attained this blessing.

If you believe this prophesy is far-fetched, take a look at the human race in retrospect. Less than a hundred years ago, men believed the lightning to be evidence of the wrath of God, and feared it. Now, thanks to the power of faith, men have harnessed the lightning and made it turn the wheels of industry. Much less than a hundred years ago, men believed the space between the planets to be nothing but a great void, a stretch of dead nothingness. Now, thanks to this same power of faith, men know that far from being either dead or a void, the space between the planets is very much alive, that it is the highest form of vibration known, excepting, perhaps, the vibration of thought. Moreover, men know that this living, pulsating, vibratory energy which permeates every atom of matter, and fills every niche of space, connects every human brain with every other human brain.

What reason have men to believe that this same energy does not connect every human brain with Infinite Intelligence?

There are no toll-gates between the finite mind of man and Infinite Intelligence. The communication costs nothing except Patience, Faith, Persistence, Understanding, and a sincere desire to communicate. Moreover, the approach can be made only by the individual himself. Paid prayers are worthless. Infinite Intelligence does no business by proxy. You either go direct, or you do not communicate.

You may buy prayer books and repeat them until the day of your doom, without avail. Thoughts which you wish to communicate to Infinite Intelligence must undergo transformation, such as can be given only through your own subconscious mind.

The method by which you may communicate with Infinite Intelligence is very similar to that through which the vibration of sound is communicated by radio. If you understand the working principle of radio, you of course, know that sound cannot be communicated through the ether until it has been "stepped up," or changed into a rate of vibration which the human ear cannot detect. The radio sending station picks up the sound of the human voice, and "scrambles," or modifies it by stepping up the vibration millions of times. Only

You do not need to know how the final result will come to pass. That is the function of the subconscious. It has ways and means that, if they were known, would stagger the intellect.

—Raymond Charles Barker

Form the habit *of applying and using the positive emotions! Eventually, they will dominate your mind so completely, that the negatives cannot enter it.*

in this way, can the vibration of sound be communicated through the ether. After this transformation has taken place, the ether "picks up" the energy (which originally was in the form of vibrations of sound), carries that energy to radio receiving stations, and these receiving sets "step" that energy back down to its original rate of vibration so it is recognized as sound.

The subconscious mind is the intermediary, which translates one's prayers into terms which Infinite Intelligence can recognize, presents the message, and brings back the answer in the form of a definite plan or idea for procuring the object of the prayer. Understand this principle, and you will know why mere words read from a prayer book cannot, and will never serve as an agency of communication between the mind of man and Infinite Intelligence.

Before your prayer will reach Infinite Intelligence (a statement of the author's theory only), it probably is transformed from its original thought vibration into terms of spiritual vibration. Faith is the only known agency which will give your thoughts a spiritual nature. Faith and fear make poor bedfellows. *Where one is found, the other cannot exist.*

The power which is in you is in the things around you, and when you begin to move forward, the things will arrange themselves for your advantage.

—Wallace D. Wattles

If you pray for a thing, but have fear as you pray that you may not receive it, or that your prayer will not be acted upon by Infinite Intelligence, your prayer will have been in vain.

QUESTIONS FOR SUCCESS

- *What is the most helpful idea from this chapter for you?*

- *What is the subconscious mind, and how does it affect your life?*

- *How can you plant a plan, desire, or purpose into your subconscious mind?*

- *Why is it important to guard your mind from negative thoughts? How do you do that?*

- *Napoleon Hill writes, "There are seven major positive emotions, and seven major negative emotions. The negatives* voluntarily *inject themselves into the thought impulses, which insure passage into the subconscious mind. The positives must be injected, through the principle of auto-suggestion, into the thought impulses which an individual wishes to pass on to his subconscious mind." Why do negative emotions enter our thought impulses voluntarily, while positive ones must be injected?*

- *What are "The Seven Major Positive Emotions" and "The Seven Major Negative Emotions"?*

- "Positive and negative emotions cannot occupy the mind at the same time," *says Napoleon Hill. Which is your mind filled more with—positive or negative emotions?*

YOUR SUCCESS STEPS

- ☐ _____
- ☐ _____
- ☐ _____
- ☐ _____
- ☐ _____
- ☐ _____

CHAPTER 13

THE BRAIN

A Broadcasting and Receiving
Station for Thought

The Twelfth Step Toward Riches

More than twenty years ago, the author, working in conjunction with the late Dr. Alexander Graham Bell, and Dr. Elmer R. Gates, observed that every human brain is both a broadcasting and receiving station for the vibration of thought.

Through the medium of the ether, in a fashion similar to that employed by the radio broadcasting principle, every human brain is capable of picking up vibrations of thought which are being released by other brains.

In connection with the statement in the preceding paragraph, compare, and consider the description of the Creative Imagination, as outlined in the chapter on imagination. The Creative Imagination is the "receiving set" of the brain, which receives thoughts, released by the brains of others. It is the agency of communication between one's conscious, or reasoning mind, and the four sources from which one may receive thought stimuli.

When stimulated, or "stepped up" to a high rate of vibration, the mind becomes more receptive to the vibration of thought which reaches it through the ether from outside sources. This "stepping up" process takes place through the positive emotions, or the negative emotions. Through the emotions, the vibrations of thought may be increased.

Vibrations of an exceedingly high rate are the only vibrations picked up and

Success is a state of mind. If you want success, start thinking of yourself as a success.

—Dr. Joyce Brothers

Every human brain is both a broadcasting and receiving station for the vibration of thought.

An unintelligent use of mind can only produce an unintelligent result.
—Raymond Charles Barker

carried, by the ether, from one brain to another. Thought is energy travelling at an exceedingly high rate of vibration. Thought, which has been modified or "stepped up" by any of the major emotions, vibrates at a much higher rate than ordinary thought, and it is this type of thought which passes from one brain to another, through the broadcasting machinery of the human brain.

The emotion of sex stands at the head of the list of human emotions, as far as intensity and driving force are concerned. The brain which has been stimulated by the emotion of sex, vibrates at a much more rapid rate than it does when that emotion is quiescent or absent.

The result of sex transmutation is the increase of the rate of vibration of thoughts to such a pitch that the Creative Imagination becomes highly receptive to ideas, which it picks up from the ether. On the other hand, when the brain is vibrating at a rapid rate, it not only attracts thoughts and ideas released by other brains through the medium of the ether, but it gives to one's own thoughts that "feeling" which is essential before those thoughts will be picked up and acted upon by one's subconscious mind.

Thus, you will see that the broadcasting principle is the factor through which you mix feeling, or emotion with your thoughts and pass them on to your subconscious mind.

The subconscious mind is the "sending station" of the brain, through which vibrations of thought are broadcast. The Creative Imagination is the "receiving set," through which the vibrations of thought are picked up from the ether.

Along with the important factors of the subconscious mind, and the faculty of the Creative Imagination, which constitute the sending and receiving sets of your mental broadcasting machinery, consider now the principle of auto-suggestion, which is the medium by which you may put into operation your "broadcasting" station.

Through the instructions described in the chapter on auto-suggestion, you were definitely informed of the method by which desire may be transmuted into its monetary equivalent.

Operation of your mental "broadcasting" station is a comparatively simple procedure. You have but three principles to bear in mind, and to apply, when you wish to use your broadcasting station—the subconscious mind, creative

Through the medium of the ether, in a fashion similar to that employed by the radio broadcasting principle, every human brain is capable of picking up vibrations of thought which are being released by other brains.

imagination, and auto-suggestion. The stimuli through which you put these three principles into action have been described—the procedure begins with desire.

GREATEST FORCES ARE "INTANGIBLE"

The depression brought the world to the very border-line of understanding of the forces which are intangible and unseen. Through the ages which have passed, man has depended too much upon his physical senses, and has limited his knowledge to physical things, which he could see, touch, weigh, and measure.

We are now entering the most marvelous of all ages—an age which will teach us something of the intangible forces of the world about us. Perhaps we shall learn, as we pass through this age, that the "other self" is more powerful than the physical self we see when we look into a mirror.

Sometimes men speak lightly of the intangibles—the things which they cannot perceive through any of their five senses, and when we hear them, it should remind us that *all of us are controlled by forces which are unseen and intangible.*

The whole of mankind has not the power to cope with, nor to control the intangible force wrapped up in the rolling waves of the oceans. Man has not the capacity to understand the intangible force of gravity, which keeps this little earth suspended in mid-air, and keeps man from falling from it, much less the power to control that force. Man is entirely subservient to the intangible force which comes with a thunder storm, and he is just as helpless in the presence of the intangible force of electricity—nay, he does not even know what electricity is, where it comes from, or what is its purpose!

Nor is this by any means the end of man's ignorance in connection with things unseen and intangible. He does not understand the intangible force (and intelligence) wrapped up in the soil of the earth—*the force which provides him with every morsel of food he eats, every article of clothing he wears, every dollar he carries in his pockets.*

A man may have a large brain and a good mind, strong faculties, and brilliant talents, and yet he is not a great man unless he uses all these in a great way.

—Wallace D. Wattles

The Creative Imagination is the "receiving set" of the brain, which receives thoughts released by the brains of others.

THE DRAMATIC STORY OF THE BRAIN

Let not your mind run on what you lack as much as on what you have already. Of the things you have, select the best; and then reflect how eagerly they would have been sought if you did not have them.

—Marcus Aurelius

Last, but not least, man, with all of his boasted culture and education, understands little or nothing of the intangible force (the greatest of all the intangibles) of *thought*. He knows but little concerning the physical brain, and its vast network of intricate machinery through which the power of thought is translated into its material equivalent, but he is now entering an age which shall yield enlightenment on the subject. Already men of science have begun to turn their attention to the study of this stupendous thing called a brain, and, while they are still in the kindergarten stage of their studies, they have uncovered enough knowledge to know that the central switchboard of the human brain, the number of lines which connect the brain cells one with another, equal the figure one, followed by fifteen million ciphers.

"The figure is so stupendous," said Dr. C. Judson Herrick, of the University of Chicago, "that astronomical figures dealing with hundreds of millions of light years, become insignificant by comparison. . . . It has been determined that there are from 10 billion to 14 billion nerve cells in the human cerebral cortex, and we know that these are arranged in definite patterns. These arrangements are not haphazard. They are orderly. Recently developed methods of electro-physiology draw off action currents from very precisely located cells, or fibers with micro-electrodes, amplify them with radio tubes, and record potential differences to a millionth of a volt."

It is inconceivable that such a network of intricate machinery should be in existence for the sole purpose of carrying on the physical functions incidental to growth and maintenance of the physical body. Is it not likely that the same system, which gives billions of brain cells the media for communication one with another, provides, also, the means of communication with other intangible forces?

After this book had been written, just before the manuscript went to the publisher, there appeared in the *New York Times* an editorial showing that at least one great university, and one intelligent investigator in the field of mental phenomena, are carrying on an organized research through which conclusions have been reached that parallel many of those described in this and the follow-

Vibrations of an exceedingly high rate are the only vibrations picked up and carried, by the ether, from one brain to another. Thought is energy travelling at an exceedingly high rate of vibration.

ing chapter. The editorial briefly analyzed the work carried on by Dr. Rhine, and his associates at Duke University, viz:—

WHAT IS "TELEPATHY"?

"A month ago we cited on this page some of the remarkable results achieved by Professor Rhine and his associates in Duke University from more than a hundred thousand tests to determine the existence of 'telepathy' and 'clairvoyance.' These results were summarized in the first two articles in *Harper's Magazine.* In the second which has now appeared, the author, E. H. Wright, attempts to summarize what has been learned, or what it seems reasonable to infer, regarding the exact nature of these 'extrasensory' modes of perception.

"The actual existence of telepathy and clairvoyance now seems to some scientists enormously probable as the result of Rhine's experiments. Various percipients were asked to name as many cards in a special pack as they could without looking at them and without other sensory access to them. About a score of men and women were discovered who could regularly name so many of the cards correctly that 'there was not one chance in many a million million of their having done their feats by luck or accident.'

"But how did they do them? These powers, assuming that they exist, do not seem to be sensory. There is no known organ for them. The experiments worked just as well at distances of several hundred miles as they did in the same room. These facts also dispose, in Mr. Wright's opinion, of the attempt to explain telepathy or clairvoyance through any physical theory of radiation. All known forms of radiant energy decline inversely as the square of the distance traversed. Telepathy and clairvoyance do not. But they do vary through physical causes as our other mental powers do. Contrary to widespread opinion, they do not improve when the percipient is asleep or half-asleep, but, on the contrary, when he is most wide-awake and alert. Rhine discovered that a narcotic will invariably lower a percipient's score, while a stimulant will always send it higher. The most reliable performer apparently cannot make a good score unless he tries to do his best.

"One conclusion that Wright draws with some confidence is that telepathy

Always bear in mind that your own resolution to succeed is more important than any other.
—Abraham Lincoln

Thought, which has been modified or "stepped up" by any of the major emotions, vibrates at a much higher rate than ordinary thought.

Self-trust is the first secret of success.
—Ralph Waldo Emerson

and clairvoyance are really one and the same gift. That is, the faculty that 'sees' a card face down on a table seems to be exactly the same one that 'reads' a thought residing only in another mind. There are several grounds for believing this. So far, for example, the two gifts have been found in every person who enjoys either of them. In every one so far the two have been of equal vigor, almost exactly. Screens, walls, distances have no effect at all on either. Wright advances from this conclusion to express what he puts forward as no more than the mere 'hunch' that other extrasensory experiences, prophetic dreams, premonitions of disaster, and the like, may also prove to be part of the same faculty. The reader is not asked to accept any of these conclusions unless he finds it necessary, but the evidence that Rhine has piled up must remain impressive."

In view of Dr. Rhine's announcement in connection with the conditions under which the mind responds to what he terms "extrasensory" modes of perception, I now feel privileged to add to his testimony by stating that my associates and I have discovered what we believe to be the ideal conditions under which the mind can be stimulated so that the sixth sense described in the next chapter can be made to function in a practical way.

The conditions to which I refer consist of a close working alliance between myself and two members of my staff. Through experimentation and practice, we have discovered how to stimulate our minds (by applying the principle used in connection with the "Invisible Counselors" described in the next chapter) so that we can, by a process of blending our three minds into one, find the solution to a great variety of personal problems which are submitted by my clients.

The procedure is very simple. We sit down at a conference table, clearly state the nature of the problem we have under consideration, then begin discussing it. Each contributes whatever thoughts that may occur. The strange thing about this method of mind stimulation is that it places each participant in communication with unknown sources of knowledge definitely outside his own experience.

If you understand the principle described in the chapter on the Master Mind, you of course recognize the round-table procedure here described as being a practical application of the Master Mind.

This method of mind stimulation, through harmonious discussion of defi-

You have but three principles to bear in mind, and to apply, when you wish to use your broadcasting station—the subconscious mind, creative imagination, and auto-suggestion.

nite subjects, between three people, illustrates the simplest and most practical use of the Master Mind.

By adopting and following a similar plan any student of this philosophy may come into possession of the famous Carnegie formula briefly described in the introduction. If it means nothing to you at this time, mark this page and read it again after you have finished the last chapter.

Healthy minds do not ignore negative conditions; they proceed to overcome them.
—Raymond Charles Barker

The "depression" was a blessing in disguise.
It reduced the whole world
to a new starting point that gives
every one a new opportunity.

We sit down . . . clearly state the nature of the problem we have under consideration, then begin discussing it. Each contributes whatever thoughts that may occur. . . . This method of mind stimulation . . . illustrates the simplest and most practical use of the Master Mind.

QUESTIONS FOR SUCCESS

- *What is the most helpful idea from this chapter for you?*

- *Why does Napoleon Hill call the brain "both a broadcasting and receiving station for the vibration of thought"?*

- *Napoleon Hill describes a "method of mind stimulation, through harmonious discussion of definite subjects" between members of a Master Mind. How have you experienced this form of "telepathy" in your life?*

YOUR SUCCESS STEPS

- ☐ _____
- ☐ _____
- ☐ _____
- ☐ _____
- ☐ _____
- ☐ _____

CHAPTER 14

THE SIXTH SENSE

The Door to the Temple of Wisdom

The Thirteenth Step Toward Riches

The "thirteenth" principle is known as the sixth sense, through which Infinite Intelligence may, and will communicate voluntarily, without any effort from, or demands by, the individual.

This principle is the apex of the philosophy. It can be assimilated, understood, and applied only by first mastering the other twelve principles.

The sixth sense is that portion of the subconscious mind which has been referred to as the Creative Imagination. It has also been referred to as the "receiving set" through which ideas, plans, and thoughts flash into the mind. The "flashes" are sometimes called "hunches" or "inspirations."

The sixth sense defies description! It cannot be described to a person who has not mastered the other principles of this philosophy, because such a person has no knowledge, and no experience with which the sixth sense may be compared. Understanding of the sixth sense comes only by meditation through mind development *from within*. The sixth sense probably is the medium of contact between the finite mind of man and Infinite Intelligence, and for this reason, *it is a mixture of both the mental and the spiritual*. It is believed to be the point at which the mind of man contacts the Universal Mind.

After you have mastered the principles described in this book, you will be prepared to accept as truth a statement which may, otherwise, be incredible to you, namely:

If any man seeks for greatness, let him forget greatness and ask for truth, and he will find both.

—Horace Mann

> The "thirteenth" principle is known as the sixth sense, through which Infinite Intelligence may, and will communicate voluntarily, without any effort from, or demands by, the individual.

Average people accept the good that others tell them is good. The Infinite did not create you to be an average person.

—Raymond Charles Barker

Through the aid of the sixth sense, you will be warned of impending dangers in time to avoid them, and notified of opportunities in time to embrace them.

There comes to your aid, and to do your bidding, with the development of the sixth sense, a "guardian angel" who will open to you at all times the door to the Temple of Wisdom.

Whether or not this is a statement of truth, you will never know, except by following the instructions described in the pages of this book, or some similar method of procedure.

The author is not a believer in, nor an advocate of "miracles," for the reason that he has enough knowledge of Nature to understand that Nature *never deviates from her established laws.* Some of her laws are so incomprehensible that they produce what appear to be "miracles." The sixth sense comes as near to being a miracle as anything I have ever experienced, and it appears so, only because I do not understand the method by which this principle is operated.

This much the author does know—that there is a power, or a First Cause, or an Intelligence, which permeates every atom of matter, and embraces every unit of energy perceptible to man—that this Infinite Intelligence converts acorns into oak trees, causes water to flow downhill in response to the law of gravity, follows night with day, and winter with summer, each maintaining its proper place and relationship to the other. This Intelligence may, through the principles of this philosophy, be induced to aid in transmuting desires into concrete, or material form. The author has this knowledge, because he has experimented with it—and has experienced it.

Step by step, through the preceding chapters, you have been led to this, the last principle. If you have mastered each of the preceding principles, you are now prepared to accept, *without being skeptical,* the stupendous claims made here. If you have not mastered the other principles, you must do so before you may determine, definitely, whether or not the claims made in this chapter are fact or fiction.

While I was passing through the age of "hero-worship" I found myself trying to imitate those whom I most admired. Moreover, I discovered that the element of faith, with which I endeavored to imitate my idols, gave me great capacity to do so quite successfully.

I have never entirely divested myself of this habit of hero-worship, although

The sixth sense is that portion of the subconscious mind which has been referred to as the Creative Imagination. It has also been referred to as the "receiving set" through which ideas, plans, and thoughts flash into the mind. The "flashes" are sometimes called "hunches" or "inspirations."

I have passed the age commonly given over to such. My experience has taught me that the next best thing to being truly great, is to emulate the great, by feeling and action, as nearly as possible.

Long before I had ever written a line for publication, or endeavored to deliver a speech in public, I followed the habit of reshaping my own character, by trying to imitate the nine men whose lives and life-works had been most impressive to me. These nine men were Emerson, Paine, Edison, Darwin, Lincoln, Burbank, Napoleon, Ford, and Carnegie. Every night, over a long period of years, I held an imaginary Council meeting with this group whom I called my "Invisible Counselors."

The procedure was this. Just before going to sleep at night, I would shut my eyes, and see, in my imagination, this group of men seated with me around my Council Table. Here I had not only an opportunity to sit among those whom I considered to be great, but I actually dominated the group, by serving as the Chairman.

I had a very definite purpose in indulging my imagination through these nightly meetings. My purpose was to rebuild my own character so it would represent a composite of the characters of my imaginary counselors. Realizing, as I did, early in life, that I had to overcome the handicap of birth in an environment of ignorance and superstition, I deliberately assigned myself the task of voluntary rebirth through the method here described.

There is nothing noble in being superior to some other man. The true nobility is in being superior to your previous self.

—Hindu proverb

BUILDING CHARACTER THROUGH AUTO-SUGGESTION

Being an earnest student of psychology, I knew, of course, that all men have become what they are, because of their dominating thoughts and desires. I knew that every deeply seated desire has the effect of causing one to seek outward expression through which that desire may be transmuted into reality. I knew that self-suggestion is a powerful factor in building character, that it is, in fact, the sole principle through which character is built.

With this knowledge of the principles of mind operation, I was fairly well armed with the equipment needed in rebuilding my character. In these imag-

Understanding of the sixth sense comes only by meditation through mind development from within.

Much may be depending on your doing some simple act; it may be the very thing which is to open the door of opportunity to very great possibilities.

—Wallace D. Wattles

inary Council meetings I called on my Cabinet members for the knowledge I wished each to contribute, addressing myself to each member in audible words, as follows:—

"Mr. Emerson, I desire to acquire from you the marvelous understanding of Nature which distinguished your life. I ask that you make an impress upon my subconscious mind, of whatever qualities you possessed, which enabled you to understand and adapt yourself to the laws of Nature. I ask that you assist me in reaching and drawing upon whatever sources of knowledge are available to this end.

"Mr. Burbank, I request that you pass on to me the knowledge which enabled you to so harmonize the laws of Nature that you caused the cactus to shed its thorns, and become an edible food. Give me access to the knowledge which enabled you to make two blades of grass grow where but one grew before, and helped you to blend the coloring of the flowers with more splendor and harmony, for you, alone, have successfully gilded the lily.

"Napoleon, I desire to acquire from you, by emulation, the marvelous ability you possessed to inspire men, and to arouse them to greater and more determined spirit of action. Also to acquire the spirit of enduring faith, which enabled you to turn defeat into victory, and to surmount staggering obstacles. Emperor of Fate, King of Chance, Man of Destiny, I salute you!

"Mr. Paine, I desire to acquire from you the freedom of thought and the courage and clarity with which to express convictions, which so distinguished you!

"Mr. Darwin, I wish to acquire from you the marvelous patience, and ability to study cause and effect, without bias or prejudice, so exemplified by you in the field of natural science.

"Mr. Lincoln, I desire to build into my own character the keen sense of justice, the untiring spirit of patience, the sense of humor, the human understanding, and the tolerance, which were your distinguishing characteristics.

"Mr. Carnegie, I am already indebted to you for my choice of a life-work, which has brought me great happiness and peace of mind. I wish to acquire a thorough understanding of the principles of *organized effort,* which you used so effectively in the building of a great industrial enterprise.

"Mr. Ford, you have been among the most helpful of the men who have

Through the aid of the sixth sense, you will be warned of impending dangers in time to avoid them, and notified of opportunities in time to embrace them.

supplied much of the material essential to my work. I wish to acquire your spirit of persistence, the determination, poise, and self-confidence which have enabled you to master poverty, organize, unify, and simplify human effort, so I may help others to follow in your footsteps.

"Mr. Edison, I have seated you nearest to me, at my right, because of the personal cooperation you have given me, during my research into the causes of success and failure. I wish to acquire from you the marvelous spirit of faith, with which you have uncovered so many of Natures secrets, the spirit of unremitting toil with which you have so often wrested victory from defeat."

My method of addressing the members of the imaginary Cabinet would vary, according to the traits of character in which I was, for the moment, most interested in acquiring. I studied the records of their lives with painstaking care. After some months of this nightly procedure, I was astounded by the discovery that these imaginary figures became, apparently *real*.

Each of these nine men developed individual characteristics, which surprised me. For example, Lincoln developed the habit of always being late, then walking around in solemn parade. When he came, he walked very slowly, with his hands clasped behind him, and once in a while, he would stop as he passed, and rest his hand, momentarily, upon my shoulder. He always wore an expression of seriousness upon his face. Rarely did I see him smile. The cares of a sundered nation made him grave.

That was not true of the others. Burbank and Paine often indulged in witty repartee which seemed, at times, to shock the other members of the Cabinet. One night Paine suggested that I prepare a lecture on "The Age of Reason," and deliver it from the pulpit of a church which I formerly attended. Many around the table laughed heartily at the suggestion. Not Napoleon! He drew his mouth down at the corners and groaned so loudly that all turned and looked at him with amazement. To him the Church was but a pawn of the State, not to be reformed, but to be used, as a convenient inciter to mass activity by the people.

On one occasion Burbank was late. When he came, he was excited with enthusiasm, and explained that he had been late, because of an experiment he was making, through which he hoped to be able to grow apples on any sort of tree. Paine chided him by reminding him that it was an apple which started all

Develop success from failures. Discouragement and failure are two of the surest stepping-stones to success.

—Dale Carnegie

The author is not a believer in, nor an advocate of "miracles," for the reason that he has enough knowledge of Nature to understand that Nature never deviates from her established laws. Some of her laws are so incomprehensible that they produce what appear to be "miracles."

*Defeat never comes to any man
until he admits it.*

—Josephus Daniels

the trouble between man and woman. Darwin chuckled heartily as he suggested that Paine should watch out for little serpents, when he went into the forest to gather apples, as they had the habit of growing into big snakes. Emerson observed, "No serpents, no apples," and Napoleon remarked, "No apples, no state!"

Lincoln developed the habit of always being the last one to leave the table after each meeting. On one occasion, he leaned across the end of the table, his arms folded, and remained in that position for many minutes. I made no attempt to disturb him. Finally, he lifted his head slowly, got up and walked to the door, then turned around, came back, and laid his hand on my shoulder and said, "My boy, you will need much courage if you remain steadfast in carrying out your purpose in life. But remember, when difficulties overtake you, the common people have common sense. Adversity will develop it."

One evening Edison arrived ahead of all the others. He walked over and seated himself at my left, where Emerson was accustomed to sit, and said, "You are destined to witness the discovery of the secret of life. When the time comes, you will observe that life consists of great swarms of energy, or entities, each as intelligent as human beings *think* themselves to be. These units of life group together like hives of bees, and remain together until they disintegrate, *through lack of harmony*. These units have differences of opinion, the same as human beings, and often fight among themselves. These meetings which you are conducting will be very helpful to you. They will bring to your rescue some of the same units of life which served the members of your Cabinet, during their lives. These units are eternal. They never die! Your own thoughts and desires serve as the magnet which attracts units of life, from the great ocean of life out there. Only the friendly units are attracted—the ones which harmonize with the nature of your desires."

The other members of the Cabinet began to enter the room. Edison got up, and slowly walked around to his own seat. Edison was still living when this happened. It impressed me so greatly that I went to see him, and told him about the experience. He smiled broadly, and said, "Your dream was more a reality than you may imagine it to have been." He added no further explanation to his statement.

These meetings became so realistic that I became fearful of their consequences, and discontinued them for several months. The experiences were so uncanny,

*My experience has taught me that
the next best thing to being truly great,
is to emulate the great, by feeling and
action, as nearly as possible.*

I was afraid if I continued them I would lose sight of the fact that the meetings were purely *experiences of my imagination.*

Some six months after I had discontinued the practice I was awakened one night, or thought I was, when I saw Lincoln standing at my bedside. He said, "The world will soon need your services. It is about to undergo a period of chaos which will cause men and women to lose faith, and become panic stricken. Go ahead with your work and complete your philosophy. That is your mission in life. If you neglect it, for any cause whatsoever, you will be reduced to a primal state, and be compelled to retrace the cycles through which you have passed during thousands of years."

I was unable to tell, the following morning, whether I had dreamed this, or had actually been awake, and I have never since found out which it was, but I do know that the dream, if it were a dream, was so vivid in my mind the next day that I resumed my meetings the following night.

At our next meeting, the members of my Cabinet all filed into the room together, and stood at their accustomed places at the Council Table, while Lincoln raised a glass and said, "Gentlemen, let us drink a toast to a friend who has returned to the fold."

After that, I began to add new members to my Cabinet, until now it consists of more than fifty, among them Christ, St. Paul, Galileo, Copernicus, Aristotle, Plato, Socrates, Homer, Voltaire, Bruno, Spinoza, Drummond, Kant, Schopenhauer, Newton, Confucius, Elbert Hubbard, Brann, Ingersoll, Wilson, and William James.

This is the first time that I have had the courage to mention this. Heretofore, I have remained quiet on the subject, because I knew, from my own attitude in connection with such matters, that I would be misunderstood if I described my unusual experience. I have been emboldened now to reduce my experience to the printed page, because I am now less concerned about what "they say" than I was in the years that have passed. One of the blessings of maturity is that it sometimes brings one greater courage to be truthful, regardless of what those who do not understand may think or say.

Lest I be misunderstood, I wish here to state most emphatically, that I still regard my Cabinet meetings as being purely imaginary, but I feel entitled to suggest that, while the members of my Cabinet may be purely fictional, and

The toughest thing about success is that you've got to keep on being a success. Talent is only a starting point in business. You've got to keep working that talent.

—Irving Berlin

The procedure was this. Just before going to sleep at night, I would shut my eyes, and see, in my imagination, this group of men seated with me around my Council Table. I actually dominated the group by serving as Chairman.

Whatever is true, whatever is honorable, whatever is just, whatever is pure, whatever is lovely, whatever is gracious . . . think about these things.

—Philippians 4:8

the meetings existent only in my own imagination, they have led me into glorious paths of adventure, rekindled an appreciation of true greatness, encouraged creative endeavor, and emboldened the expression of honest thought.

Somewhere in the cell-structure of the brain is located an organ which receives vibrations of thought ordinarily called "hunches." So far, science has not discovered where this organ of the sixth sense is located, but this is not important. The fact remains that human beings do receive accurate knowledge, through sources other than the physical senses. Such knowledge, generally, is received when the mind is under the influence of extraordinary stimulation. Any emergency which arouses the emotions, and causes the heart to beat more rapidly than normal may, and generally does, bring the sixth sense into action. Anyone who has experienced a near accident while driving, knows that on such occasions, the sixth sense often comes to one's rescue, and aids, by split seconds, in avoiding the accident.

These facts are mentioned preliminary to a statement of fact which I shall now make, namely, that during my meetings with the "Invisible Counselors" I find my mind most receptive to ideas, thoughts, and knowledge which reach me through the sixth sense. I can truthfully say that I owe entirely to my "Invisible Counselors" full credit for such ideas, facts, or knowledge as I received through "inspiration."

On scores of occasions, when I have faced emergencies, some of them so grave that my life was in jeopardy, I have been miraculously guided past these difficulties through the influence of my "Invisible Counselors."

My original purpose in conducting Council meetings with imaginary beings was solely that of impressing my own subconscious mind, through the principle of auto-suggestion, with certain characteristics which I desired to acquire. In more recent years, my experimentation has taken on an entirely different trend. I now go to my imaginary counselors with every difficult problem which confronts me and my clients. The results are often astonishing, although I do not depend entirely on this form of counsel.

You, of course, have recognized that this chapter covers a subject with which a majority of people are not familiar. The sixth sense is a subject that will be of great interest and benefit to the person whose aim is to accumulate vast wealth, but it need not claim the attention of those whose desires are more modest.

I had a very definite purpose in indulging my imagination through these nightly meetings. My purpose was to rebuild my own character so it would represent a composite of the characters of my imaginary counselors.

Henry Ford undoubtedly understands and makes practical use of the sixth sense. His vast business and financial operations make it necessary for him to understand and use this principle. The late Thomas A. Edison understood and used the sixth sense in connection with the development of inventions, especially those involving basic patents, in connection with which he had no human experience and no accumulated knowledge to guide him, as was the case while he was working on the talking machine, and the moving-picture machine.

Nearly all great leaders, such as Napoleon, Bismarck, Joan of Arc, Christ, Buddha, Confucius, and Mohammed, understood, and probably made use of the sixth sense almost continuously. The major portion of their greatness consisted of their knowledge of this principle.

The sixth sense is not something that one can take off and put on at will. Ability to use this great power comes slowly, through application of the other principles outlined in this book. Seldom does any individual come into workable knowledge of the sixth sense before the age of forty. More often the knowledge is not available until one is well past fifty, and this, for the reason that the spiritual forces, with which the sixth sense is so closely related, do not mature and become usable except through years of meditation, self-examination, and serious thought.

No matter who you are, or what may have been your purpose in reading this book, you can profit by it without understanding the principle described in this chapter. This is especially true if your major purpose is that of accumulation of money or other material things.

The chapter on the sixth sense was included, because the book is designed for the purpose of presenting a complete philosophy by which individuals may unerringly guide themselves in attaining whatever they ask of life. The starting point of all achievement is desire. The finishing point is that brand of knowledge which leads to understanding—understanding of self, understanding of others, understanding of the laws of Nature, recognition and understanding of happiness.

This sort of understanding comes in its fullness only through familiarity with, and use of the principle of the sixth sense, hence that principle had to be included as a part of this philosophy, for the benefit of those who demand more than money.

The man who will use his skill and constructive imagination to see how much he can give for a dollar, instead of how little he can give for a dollar, is bound to succeed.

—Henry Ford

During my meetings with the "Invisible Counselors" I find my mind most receptive to ideas, thoughts, and knowledge which reach me through the sixth sense.

When written in Chinese, the word "crisis" is composed of two characters. One represents danger and the other represents opportunity.
—John F. Kennedy

Having read the chapter, you must have observed that while reading it, you were lifted to a high level of mental stimulation. Splendid! Come back to this again a month from now, read it once more, and observe that your mind will soar to a still-higher level of stimulation. Repeat this experience from time to time, giving no concern as to how much or how little you learn at the time, and eventually you will find yourself in possession of a power that will enable you to throw off discouragement, master fear, overcome procrastination, and draw freely upon your imagination. Then you will have felt the touch of that unknown "something" which has been the moving spirit of every truly great thinker, leader, artist, musician, writer, statesman. Then you will be in position to transmute your desires into their physical or financial counterpart as easily as you may lie down and quit at the first sign of opposition.

FAITH VS. FEAR!

Previous chapters have described how to develop faith, through auto-suggestion, desire, and the subconscious. The next chapter presents detailed instructions for the mastery of fear.

Here will be found a full description of the six fears which are the cause of all discouragement, timidity, procrastination, indifference, indecision, and the lack of ambition, self-reliance, initiative, self-control, and enthusiasm.

Search yourself carefully as you study these six enemies, as they may exist only in your subconscious mind, where their presence will be hard to detect.

Remember, too, as you analyze the "Six Ghosts of Fear," that they are nothing but ghosts because they exist only in one's mind.

Remember, also, that ghosts—creations of uncontrolled imagination—have caused most of the damage people have done to their own minds, therefore, ghosts can be as dangerous as if they lived and walked on the earth in physical bodies.

The Ghost of the Fear of Poverty, which seized the minds of millions of people in 1929, was so real that it caused the worst business depression this country has ever known. Moreover, this particular ghost still frightens some of us out of our wits.

I can truthfully say that I owe entirely to my "Invisible Counselors" full credit for such ideas, facts, or knowledge as I received through "inspiration."

QUESTIONS FOR SUCCESS

- *What is the most helpful idea from this chapter for you?*

- *How does Napoleon Hill describe the "sixth sense" and how it can work in your life?*

- *Napoleon Hill writes about "Infinite Intelligence." What does this term mean?*

- *What is an "Imaginary Council" and how did it affect the author's life?*

- *If you were to form an Imaginary Council, whom would you invite to be on it?*

- *Napoleon Hill writes, "[D]uring my meetings with the 'Invisible Counselors' I find my mind most receptive to ideas, thoughts, and knowledge which reach me through the sixth sense. I can truthfully say that I owe entirely to my 'Invisible Counselors' full credit for such ideas, facts, or knowledge as I received through 'inspiration.'" How might an Imaginary Council aid you in your obtaining your goal or desire?*

YOUR SUCCESS STEPS

☐ _____

☐ _____

☐ _____

☐ _____

☐ _____

☐ _____

CHAPTER 15

HOW TO OUTWIT THE SIX GHOSTS OF FEAR

Take Inventory of Yourself, As You Read This Closing Chapter, and Find Out How Many of the "Ghosts" Are Standing in Your Way

Before you can put any portion of this philosophy into successful use, your mind must be prepared to receive it. The preparation is not difficult. It begins with study, analysis, and understanding of three enemies which you shall have to clear out. These are indecision, doubt, and fear!

The sixth sense will never function while these three negatives, or any of them remain in your mind. The members of this unholy trio are closely related; where one is found, the other two are close at hand.

Indecision is the seedling of fear! Remember this, as you read. Indecision crystallizes into doubt; the two blend and become fear! The "blending" process often is slow. This is one reason why these three enemies are so dangerous. They germinate and grow *without their presence being observed*.

The remainder of this chapter describes an end which must be attained before the philosophy, as a whole, can be put into practical use. It also analyzes a condition which has, but lately, reduced huge numbers of people to poverty, and it states a truth which must be understood by all who accumulate riches, whether measured in terms of money or a state of mind of far greater value than money.

The purpose of this chapter is to turn the spotlight of attention upon the cause

There is no failure except in no longer trying.

—Elbert Hubbard

Before you can put any portion of this philosophy into successful use, your mind must be prepared to receive it.

and the cure of the six basic fears. Before we can master an enemy, we must know its name, its habits, and its place of abode. As you read, analyze yourself carefully, and determine which, if any, of the six common fears have attached themselves to you.

Do not be deceived by the habits of these subtle enemies. Sometimes they remain hidden in the subconscious mind, where they are difficult to locate, and still more difficult to eliminate.

THE SIX BASIC FEARS

There are six basic fears, with some combination of which every human suffers at one time or another. Most people are fortunate if they do not suffer from the entire six. Named in the order of their most common appearance, they are:—

The fear of POVERTY
The fear of CRITICISM   } at the bottom of
The fear of ILL HEALTH   most of one's worries
The fear of LOSS OF LOVE OF SOMEONE
The fear of OLD AGE
The fear of DEATH

All other fears are of minor importance; they can be grouped under these six headings.

The prevalence of these fears, as a curse to the world, runs in cycles. For almost six years, while the depression was on, we floundered in the cycle of fear of poverty. During the world war, we were in the cycle of fear of death. Just following the war, we were in the cycle of fear of ill health, as evidenced by the epidemic of disease which spread itself all over the world.

Fears are nothing more than states of mind. One's state of mind is subject to control and direction. Physicians, as everyone knows, are less subject to attack by disease than ordinary laymen, for the reason that physicians do not fear disease. Physicians, without fear or hesitation, have been known to physically contact hundreds of people, daily, who were suffering from such contagious diseases as

The preparation is not difficult. It begins with study, analysis, and understanding of three enemies which you shall have to clear out. These are indecision, doubt, and fear!

small-pox, without becoming infected. Their immunity against the disease consisted, largely, if not solely, in their absolute lack of fear.

Man can create nothing which he does not first conceive in the form of an impulse of thought. Following this statement comes another of still greater importance, namely man's thought impulses begin immediately to translate themselves into their physical equivalent, whether those thoughts are voluntary or involuntary. Thought impulses which are picked up through the ether, by mere chance (thoughts which have been released by other minds) may determine one's financial, business, professional, or social destiny just as surely as do the thought impulses which one creates by intent and design.

We are here laying the foundation for the presentation of a fact of great importance to the person who does not understand why some people appear to be "lucky" while others of equal or greater ability, training, experience, and brain capacity seem destined to ride with misfortune. This fact may be explained by the statement that *every human being has the ability to completely control his own mind,* and with this control, obviously, every person may open his mind to the tramp thought impulses which are being released by other brains, or close the doors tightly and admit only thought impulses of his own choice.

Nature has endowed man with absolute control over but one thing, and that is thought. This fact, coupled with the additional fact that everything which man creates begins in the form of a thought, leads one very near to the principle by which fear may be mastered.

If it is true that all thought has a tendency to clothe itself in its physical equivalent (and this is true, beyond any reasonable room for doubt), it is equally true that thought impulses of fear and poverty cannot be translated into terms of courage and financial gain.

The people of America began to think of poverty, following the Wall Street crash of 1929. Slowly, but surely that mass thought was crystallized into its physical equivalent, which was known as a "depression." This had to happen; it is in conformity with the laws of Nature.

Thank God every morning when you get up that you have something to do which must be done, whether you like it or not. Being forced to work, and forced to do your best, will breed in you temperance, self-control, diligence, strength of will, content, and a hundred other virtues which the idle never know.

—Charles Kingsley

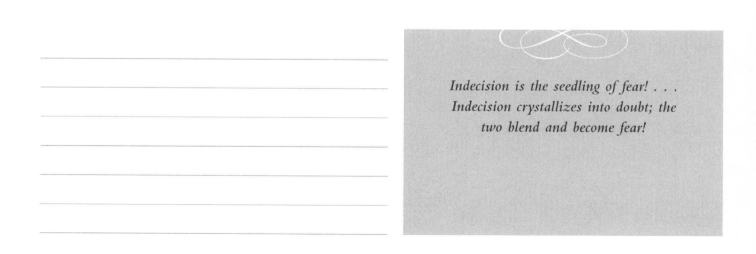

Indecision is the seedling of fear! . . . Indecision crystallizes into doubt; the two blend and become fear!

THE FEAR OF POVERTY

Men were born to succeed, not to fail.

　　　　—Henry David Thoreau

There can be no compromise between poverty and riches! The two roads that lead to poverty and riches travel in opposite directions. If you want riches, you must refuse to accept any circumstance that leads toward poverty. (The word "riches" is here used in its broadest sense, meaning financial, spiritual, mental, and material estates.) The starting point of the path that leads to riches is desire. In chapter two, you received full instructions for the proper use of desire. In this chapter, on fear, you have complete instructions for preparing your mind to make practical use of desire.

Here, then, is the place to give yourself a challenge which will definitely determine how much of this philosophy you have absorbed. Here is the point at which you can turn prophet and foretell, accurately, what the future holds in store for you. If, after reading this chapter, you are willing to accept poverty, you may as well make up your mind to receive poverty. This is one decision you cannot avoid.

If you demand riches, determine what form, and how much will be required to satisfy you. You know the road that leads to riches. You have been given a road map which, if followed, will keep you on that road. If you neglect to make the start, or stop before you arrive, no one will be to blame but you. This responsibility is yours. No alibi will save you from accepting the responsibility if you now fail or refuse to demand riches of Life, because the acceptance calls for but one thing—incidentally, the only thing you can control—and that is a state of mind. A state of mind is something that one assumes. It cannot be purchased; it must be created.

Fear of poverty is a state of mind, nothing else! But it is sufficient to destroy one's chances of achievement in any undertaking, a truth which became painfully evident during the depression.

This fear paralyzes the faculty of reason, destroys the faculty of imagination, kills off self-reliance, undermines enthusiasm, discourages initiative, leads to uncertainty of purpose, encourages procrastination, wipes out enthusiasm, and makes self-control an impossibility. It takes the charm from one's personality, destroys the possibility of accurate thinking, diverts concentration of effort; it

As you read, analyze yourself carefully, and determine which, if any, of the six common fears have attached themselves to you.

masters persistence, turns the will-power into nothingness, destroys ambition, beclouds the memory, and invites failure in every conceivable form; it kills love and assassinates the finer emotions of the heart, discourages friendship and invites disaster in a hundred forms, leads to sleeplessness, misery, and unhappiness—and all this despite the obvious truth that we live in a world of over-abundance of everything the heart could desire, with nothing standing between us and our desires, excepting lack of a definite purpose.

The Fear of Poverty is, without doubt, the most destructive of the six basic fears. It has been placed at the head of the list, because it is the most difficult to master. Considerable courage is required to state the truth about the origin of this fear, and still greater courage to accept the truth after it has been stated. The fear of poverty grew out of man's inherited tendency to prey upon his fellow man economically. Nearly all animals lower than man are motivated by instinct, but their capacity to "think" is limited, therefore, they prey upon one another physically. Man, with his superior sense of intuition, with the capacity to think and to reason, does not eat his fellow man bodily; he gets more satisfaction out of "eating" him financially. Man is so avaricious that every conceivable law has been passed to safeguard him from his fellow man.

Of all the ages of the world, of which we know anything, the age in which we live seems to be one that is outstanding because of man's money-madness. A man is considered less than the dust of the earth, unless he can display a fat bank account; but if he has money—never mind how he acquired it—he is a "king" or a "big shot"; he is above the law, he rules in politics, he dominates in business, and the whole world about him bows in respect when he passes.

Nothing brings man so much suffering and humility as poverty! Only those who have experienced poverty understand the full meaning of this.

It is no wonder that man *fears* poverty. Through a long line of inherited experiences man has learned, for sure, that some men cannot be trusted, where matters of money and earthly possessions are concerned. This is a rather stinging indictment, the worst part of it being that it is true.

The majority of marriages are motivated by the wealth possessed by one, or both of the contracting parties. It is no wonder, therefore, that the divorce courts are busy.

So eager is man to possess wealth that he will acquire it in whatever manner

It is only well with me when I have a chisel in my hand.

—Michelangelo

There are six basic fears, with some combination of which every human suffers at one time or another. Most people are fortunate if they do not suffer from the entire six.

he can—through legal methods if possible, through other methods if necessary or expedient.

Self-analysis may disclose weaknesses which one does not like to acknowledge. This form of examination is essential to all who demand of Life more than mediocrity and poverty. Remember, as you check yourself point by point, that you are both the court and the jury, the prosecuting attorney and the attorney for the defense, and that you are the plaintiff and the defendant, also, that you are on trial. Face the facts squarely. Ask yourself definite questions and demand direct replies. When the examination is over, you will know more about yourself. If you do not feel that you can be an impartial judge in this self-examination, call upon someone who knows you well to serve as judge while you cross-examine yourself. You are after the truth. *Get it, no matter at what cost, even though it may temporarily embarrass you!*

The majority of people, if asked what they fear most, would reply, "I fear nothing." The reply would be inaccurate, because few people realize that they are bound, handicapped, whipped spiritually and physically through some form of fear. So subtle and deeply seated is the emotion of fear that one may go through life burdened with it, never recognizing its presence. Only a courageous analysis will disclose the presence of this universal enemy. When you begin such an analysis, search deeply into your character. Here is a list of the symptoms for which you should look:

SYMPTOMS OF THE FEAR OF POVERTY

INDIFFERENCE. Commonly expressed through lack of ambition; willingness to tolerate poverty; acceptance of whatever compensation life may offer without protest; mental and physical laziness; lack of initiative, imagination, enthusiasm and self-control.

INDECISION. The habit of permitting others to do one's thinking. Staying "on the fence."

DOUBT. Generally expressed through alibis and excuses designed to cover up, explain away, or apologize for one's failures, sometimes expressed in the form of envy of those who are successful, or by criticising them.

Fears are nothing more than states of mind. *One's state of mind is subject to control and direction.*

WORRY. Usually expressed by finding fault with others, a tendency to spend beyond one's income, neglect of personal appearance, scowling and frowning; intemperance in the use of alcoholic drink, sometimes through the use of narcotics; nervousness, lack of poise, self-consciousness and lack of self-reliance.

OVER-CAUTION. The habit of looking for the negative side of every circumstance, thinking and talking of possible failure instead of concentrating upon the means of succeeding. Knowing all the roads to disaster, but never searching for the plans to avoid failure. Waiting for "the right time" to begin putting ideas and plans into action, until the waiting becomes a permanent habit. Remembering those who have failed, and forgetting those who have succeeded. Seeing the hole in the doughnut, but overlooking the doughnut. Pessimism, leading to indigestion, poor elimination, auto-intoxication, bad breath, and bad disposition.

PROCRASTINATION. The habit of putting off until tomorrow that which should have been done last year. Spending enough time in creating alibis and excuses to have done the job. This symptom is closely related to over-caution, doubt and worry. Refusal to accept responsibility when it can be avoided. Willingness to compromise rather than put up a stiff fight. Compromising with difficulties instead of harnessing and using them as stepping stones to advancement. Bargaining with Life for a penny, instead of demanding prosperity, opulence, riches, contentment and happiness. Planning what to do if and when overtaken by failure, instead of burning all bridges and making retreat impossible. Weakness of, and often total lack of self-confidence, definiteness of purpose, self-control, initiative, enthusiasm, ambition, thrift, and sound reasoning ability. Expecting poverty instead of demanding riches. Association with those who accept poverty instead of seeking the company of those who demand and receive riches.

If a man does not keep pace with his companions, perhaps it is because he hears a different drummer. Let him keep step to music which he hears, however measured or far away.

—Henry David Thoreau

Man can create nothing which he does not first conceive in the form of an impulse of thought. . . . Man's thought impulses begin immediately to translate themselves into their physical equivalent, whether those thoughts are voluntary or involuntary.

MONEY TALKS!

The very best thing you can do for the whole world is to make the most of yourself.

—Wallace D. Wattles

Some will ask, "Why did you write a book about money? Why measure riches in dollars, alone?" Some will believe, and rightly so, that there are other forms of riches more desirable than money. Yes, there are riches which cannot be measured in terms of dollars, but there are millions of people who will say, "Give me all the money I need, and I will find everything else I want."

The major reason why I wrote this book on how to get money is the fact that the world has but lately passed through an experience that left millions of men and women paralyzed with the fear of poverty. What this sort of fear does to one was well described by Westbrook Pegler, in the *New York World-Telegram*, viz:

"Money is only clam shells or metal discs or scraps of paper, and there are treasures of the heart and soul which money cannot buy, but most people, being broke, are unable to keep this in mind and sustain their spirits. When a man is down and out and on the street, unable to get any job at all, something happens to his spirit which can be observed in the droop of his shoulders, the set of his hat, his walk and his gaze. He cannot escape a feeling of inferiority among people with regular employment, even though he knows they are definitely not his equals in character, intelligence or ability.

"These people—even his friends—feel, on the other hand, a sense of superiority and regard him, perhaps unconsciously, as a casualty. He may borrow for a time, but not enough to carry on in his accustomed way, and he cannot continue to borrow very long. But borrowing in itself, when a man is borrowing merely to live, is a depressing experience, and the money lacks the power of earned money to revive his spirits. Of course, none of this applies to bums or habitual ne'er-do-wells, but only to men of normal ambitions and self-respect.

WOMEN CONCEAL DESPAIR

"Women in the same predicament must be different. We somehow do not think of women at all in considering the down-and-outers. They are scarce in the breadlines, they rarely are seen begging on the streets, and they are not recognizable in crowds by the same plain signs which identify busted men. Of course,

> Every human being has the ability to completely control his own mind. . . . *Nature has endowed man with absolute control over but one thing, and that is thought.*

I do not mean the shuffling hags of the city streets who are the opposite number of the confirmed male bums. I mean reasonably young, decent and intelligent women. There must be many of them, but their despair is not apparent. Maybe they kill themselves.

"When a man is down and out he has time on his hands for brooding. He may travel miles to see a man about a job and discover that the job is filled or that it is one of those jobs with no base pay but only a commission on the sale of some useless knickknack which nobody would buy except out of pity. Turning that down, he finds himself back on the street with nowhere to go but just anywhere. So he walks and walks. He gazes into store windows at luxuries which are not for him, and feels inferior and gives way to people who stop to look with an active interest. He wanders into the railroad station or puts himself down in the library to ease his legs and soak up a little heat, but that isn't looking for a job, so he gets going again. He may not know it, but his aimlessness would give him away even if the very lines of his figure did not. He may be well dressed in the clothes left over from the days when he had a steady job, but the clothes cannot disguise the droop.

MONEY MAKES DIFFERENCE

"He sees thousands of other people, bookkeepers or clerks or chemists or wagon hands, busy at their work and envies them from the bottom of his soul. They have their independence, their self-respect and manhood, and he simply cannot convince himself that he is a good man, too, though he argue it out and arrive at a favorable verdict hour after hour.

"It is just money which makes this difference in him. With a little money he would be himself again.

"Some employers take the most shocking advantage of people who are down and out. The agencies hang out little colored cards offering miserable wages to busted men—$12 a week, $15 a week. A $17 a week job is a plum, and anyone with $25 a week to offer does not hang the job in front of an agency on a colored card. I have a want ad clipped from a local paper demanding a clerk, a good, clean penman, to take telephone orders for a sandwich shop from 11 a.m. to 2 p.m. for $8 a month—not $8 a week but $8 a month. The ad says also, 'State religion.' Can you imagine the brutal effrontery of anyone who demands a

In this world it is not what we take up, but what we give up, that makes us rich.

—Henry Ward Beecher

If it is true that all thought has a tendency to clothe itself in its physical equivalent (and this is true, beyond any reasonable room for doubt), it is equally true that thought impulses of fear and poverty cannot be translated into terms of courage and financial gain.

good, clean penman for 11 cents an hour inquiring into the victim's religion? But that is what busted people are offered."

A successful man is one who can lay a firm foundation with the bricks others have thrown at him.

—David Brinkley

THE FEAR OF CRITICISM

Just how man originally came by this fear, no one can state definitely, but one thing is certain—he has it in a highly developed form. Some believe that this fear made its appearance about the time that politics became a "profession." Others believe it can be traced to the age when women first began to concern themselves with "styles" in wearing apparel.

This author, being neither a humorist nor a prophet, is inclined to attribute the basic fear of criticism to that part of man's inherited nature which prompts him not only to take away his fellow man's goods and wares, but to justify his action by criticism of his fellow man's character. It is a well-known fact that a thief will criticise the man from whom he steals—that politicians seek office, not by displaying their own virtues and qualifications, but by attempting to besmirch their opponents.

The fear of criticism takes on many forms, the majority of which are petty and trivial. Baldheaded men, for example, are bald for no other reason than their fear of criticism. Heads become bald because of the tight-fitting bands of hats which cut off the circulation from the roots of the hair. Men wear hats, not because they actually need them, but mainly because "everyone is doing it." The individual falls into line and does likewise, lest some other individual criticise him. Women seldom have bald heads, or even thin hair, because they wear hats which fit their heads loosely, the only purpose of the hats being adornment.

But, it must not be supposed that women are free from the fear of criticism. If any woman claims to be superior to man with reference to this fear, ask her to walk down the street wearing a hat of the vintage of 1890.

The astute manufacturers of clothing have not been slow to capitalize on this basic fear of criticism, with which all mankind has been cursed. Every season the styles in many articles of wearing apparel change. Who establishes

There can be no compromise between poverty and riches! The two roads that lead to poverty and riches travel in opposite directions.

the styles? Certainly not the purchaser of clothing, but the manufacturer. Why does he change the styles so often? The answer is obvious. He changes the styles so he can sell more clothes.

For the same reason the manufacturers of automobiles (with a few rare and very sensible exceptions) change styles of models every season. No man wants to drive an automobile which is not of the latest style, although the older model may actually be the better car.

We have been describing the manner in which people behave under the influence of fear of criticism as applied to the small and petty things of life. Let us now examine human behavior when this fear affects people in connection with the more important events of human relationship. Take for example practically any person who has reached the age of "mental maturity" (from thirty-five to forty years of age, as a general average), and if you could read the secret thoughts of his mind, you would find a very decided disbelief in most of the fables taught by the majority of the dogmatists and theologians a few decades back.

Not often, however, will you find a person who has the courage to openly state his belief on this subject. Most people will, if pressed far enough, tell a lie rather than admit that they do not believe the stories associated with that form of religion which held people in bondage prior to the age of scientific discovery and education.

Why does the average person, even in this day of enlightenment, shy away from denying his belief in the fables which were the basis of most of the religions a few decades ago? The answer is "because of the fear of criticism." Men and women have been burned at the stake for daring to express disbelief in ghosts. It is no wonder we have inherited a consciousness which makes us fear criticism. The time was, and not so far in the past, when criticism carried severe punishments—it still does in some countries.

The fear of criticism robs man of his initiative, destroys his power of imagination, limits his individuality, takes away his self-reliance, and does him damage in a hundred other ways. Parents often do their children irreparable injury by criticising them. The mother of one of my boyhood chums used to punish him with a switch almost daily, always completing the job with the statement,

Success is dependent on effort.

—Sophocles

If you want riches, you must refuse to accept any circumstance that leads toward poverty. . . . The starting point of the path that leads to riches is desire.

"You'll land in the penitentiary before you are twenty." He was sent to a reformatory at the age of seventeen.

Criticism is the one form of service, of which everyone has too much. Everyone has a stock of it which is handed out, gratis, whether called for or not. One's nearest relatives often are the worst offenders. It should be recognized as a crime (in reality it is a crime of the worst nature) for any parent to build inferiority complexes in the mind of a child, through unnecessary criticism. Employers who understand human nature, get the best there is in men, not by criticism, but by constructive suggestion. Parents may accomplish the same results with their children. Criticism will plant fear in the human heart, or resentment, but it will not build love or affection.

Symptoms of the Fear of Criticism

This fear is almost as universal as the fear of poverty, and its effects are just as fatal to personal achievement, mainly because this fear destroys initiative, and discourages the use of imagination. The major symptoms of the fear are:

SELF-CONSCIOUSNESS. Generally expressed through nervousness, timidity in conversation and in meeting strangers, awkward movement of the hands and limbs, shifting of the eyes.

LACK OF POISE. Expressed through lack of voice control, nervousness in the presence of others, poor posture of body, poor memory.

PERSONALITY. Lacking in firmness of decision, personal charm, and ability to express opinions definitely. The habit of sidestepping issues instead of meeting them squarely. Agreeing with others without careful examination of their opinions.

INFERIORITY COMPLEX. The habit of expressing self-approval by word of mouth and by actions, as a means of covering up a feeling of inferiority. Using "big words" to impress others (often without knowing the real meaning of the words). Imitating others in dress, speech, and manners.

The common idea that success spoils people by making them vain, egotistic, and self-complacent is erroneous; on the contrary it makes them, for the most part, humble, tolerant and kind.

—W. Somerset Maugham

Here, then, is the place to give yourself a challenge which will definitely determine how much of this philosophy you have absorbed. Here is the point at which you can turn prophet and foretell, accurately, what the future holds in store for you.

Boasting of imaginary achievements. This sometimes gives a surface appearance of a feeling of superiority.

EXTRAVAGANCE. The habit of trying to "keep up with the Joneses," spending beyond one's income.

LACK OF INITIATIVE. Failure to embrace opportunities for self-advancement, fear to express opinions, lack of confidence in one's own ideas, giving evasive answers to questions asked by superiors, hesitancy of manner and speech, deceit in both words and deeds.

LACK OF AMBITION. Mental and physical laziness, lack of self-assertion, slowness in reaching decisions, easily influenced by others, the habit of criticising others behind their backs and flattering them to their faces, the habit of accepting defeat without protest, quitting an undertaking when opposed by others, suspicious of other people without cause, lacking in tactfulness of manner and speech, unwillingness to accept the blame for mistakes.

The person who gets the farthest is generally the one who is willing to do and dare. The sure-thing boat never gets far from shore.

—Dale Carnegie

THE FEAR OF ILL HEALTH

This fear may be traced to both physical and social heredity. It is closely associated, as to its origin, with the causes of fear of Old Age and the fear of Death, because it leads one closely to the border of "terrible worlds" of which man knows not, but concerning which he has been taught some discomforting stories. The opinion is somewhat general, also, that certain unethical people engaged in the business of "selling health" have had not a little to do with keeping alive the fear of ill health.

In the main, man fears ill health because of the terrible pictures which have been planted in his mind of what may happen if death should overtake him. He also fears it because of the economic toll which it may claim.

A reputable physician estimated that 75 percent of all people who visit phy-

If, after reading this chapter, you are willing to accept poverty, you may as well make up your mind to receive poverty. This is one decision you cannot avoid.

sicians for professional service are suffering with hypochondria (imaginary illness). It has been shown most convincingly that the fear of disease, even where there is not the slightest cause for fear, often produces the physical symptoms of the disease feared.

Powerful and mighty is the human mind! It builds or it destroys.

Playing upon this common weakness of fear of ill health, dispensers of patent medicines have reaped fortunes. This form of imposition upon credulous humanity became so prevalent some twenty years ago that *Collier's Weekly* magazine conducted a bitter campaign against some of the worst offenders in the patent medicine business.

During the "flu" epidemic which broke out during the world war, the mayor of New York City took drastic steps to check the damage which people were doing themselves through their inherent fear of ill health. He called in the newspaper men and said to them, "Gentlemen, I feel it necessary to ask you not to publish any *scare headlines* concerning the 'flu' epidemic. Unless you cooperate with me, we will have a situation which we cannot control." The newspapers quit publishing stories about the "flu," and within one month the epidemic had been successfully checked.

Through a series of experiments conducted some years ago, it was proved that people may be made ill by suggestion. We conducted this experiment by causing three acquaintances to visit the "victims," each of whom asked the question, "What ails you? You look terribly ill." The first questioner usually provoked a grin, and a nonchalant "Oh, nothing, I'm all right," from the victim. The second questioner usually was answered with the statement, "I don't know exactly, but I do feel badly." The third questioner was usually met with the frank admission that the victim was actually feeling ill.

Try this on an acquaintance if you doubt that it will make him uncomfortable, but do not carry the experiment too far. There is a certain religious sect whose members take vengeance upon their enemies by the "hexing" method. They call it "placing a spell" on the victim.

There is overwhelming evidence that disease sometimes begins in the form of negative thought impulse. Such an impulse may be passed from one mind to another, by suggestion, or created by an individual in his own mind.

A man who was blessed with more wisdom than this incident might indi-

The secret of success is constancy of purpose.

—Benjamin Franklin

No alibi will save you from accepting the responsibility if you now fail or refuse to demand riches of Life, because the acceptance calls for but one thing— incidentally, the only thing you can control—and that is a state of mind.

cate, once said, "When anyone asks me how I feel, I always want to answer by knocking him down."

Doctors send patients into new climates for their health, because a change of "mental attitude" is necessary. The seed of fear of ill health lives in every human mind. Worry, fear, discouragement, disappointment in love and business affairs, cause this seed to germinate and grow. The recent business depression kept the doctors on the run, because every form of negative thinking may cause ill health.

Disappointments in business and in love stand at the head of the list of causes of fear of ill health. A young man suffered a disappointment in love which sent him to a hospital. For months he hovered between life and death. A specialist in suggestive therapeutics was called in. The specialist changed nurses, placing him in charge of a very *charming young woman* who began (by pre-arrangement with the doctor) to make love to him the first day of her arrival on the job. Within three weeks the patient was discharged from the hospital, still suffering, but with an entirely different malady. He was in love again. The remedy was a hoax, but the patient and the nurse were later married. Both are in good health at the time of this writing.

You can do anything you wish to do, have anything you wish to have, be anything you wish to be.

—Robert Collier

Symptoms of the Fear of Ill Health

The symptoms of this almost universal fear are:

AUTO-SUGGESTION. The habit of negative use of self-suggestion by looking for, and expecting to find the symptoms of all kinds of disease. "Enjoying" imaginary illness and speaking of it as being real. The habit of trying all "fads" and "isms" recommended by others as having therapeutic value. Talking to others of operations, accidents and other forms of illness. Experimenting with diets, physical exercises, reducing systems, without professional guidance. Trying home remedies, patent medicines and "quack" remedies.

HYPOCHONDRIA. The habit of talking of illness, concentrating the mind upon disease, and expecting its appearance until a nervous break occurs. Nothing that comes in bottles can cure this condition. It is brought on

A state of mind is something that one assumes. It cannot be purchased; it must be created.

by negative thinking and nothing but positive thought can effect a cure. Hypochondria (a medical term for imaginary disease) is said to do as much damage on occasion, as the disease one fears might do. Most so-called cases of "nerves" come from imaginary illness.

EXERCISE. Fear of ill health often interferes with proper physical exercise, and results in over-weight, by causing one to avoid outdoor life.

SUSCEPTIBILITY. Fear of ill health breaks down Nature's body resistance, and creates a favorable condition for any form of disease one may contact.

The fear of ill health often is related to the fear of poverty, especially in the case of the hypochondriac, who constantly worries about the possibility of having to pay doctor's bills, hospital bills, etc. This type of person spends much time preparing for sickness, talking about death, saving money for cemetery lots, and burial expenses, etc.

SELF-CODDLING. The habit of making a bid for sympathy, using imaginary illness as the lure. (People often resort to this trick to avoid work.) The habit of feigning illness to cover plain laziness, or to serve as an alibi for lack of ambition.

INTEMPERANCE. The habit of using alcohol or narcotics to destroy pains such as headaches, neuralgia, etc., instead of eliminating the cause.

The habit of reading about illness and worrying over the possibility of being stricken by it. The habit of reading patent medicine advertisements.

THE FEAR OF LOSS OF LOVE

The original source of this inherent fear needs but little description, because it obviously grew out of man's polygamous habit of stealing his fellow man's mate, and his habit of taking liberties with her whenever he could.

Jealousy, and other similar forms of dementia praecox grow out of man's inherited fear of the loss of love of someone. This fear is the most painful of all the six basic fears. It probably plays more havoc with the body and mind than any of the other basic fears, as it often leads to permanent insanity.

The fear of the loss of love probably dates back to the stone age, when men stole women by brute force. They continue to steal females, but their technique has changed. Instead of force, they now use persuasion, the promise of pretty clothes, motor cars, and other "bait" much more effective than physical force. Man's habits are the same as they were at the dawn of civilization, but he expresses them differently.

Careful analysis has shown that women are more susceptible to this fear than men. This fact is easily explained. Women have learned, from experience, that men are polygamous by nature, that they are not to be trusted in the hands of rivals.

The price of greatness is responsibility.

—Winston Churchill

Symptoms of the Fear of Loss of Love
The distinguishing symptoms of this fear are:—

JEALOUSY. The habit of being suspicious of friends and loved ones without any reasonable evidence of sufficient grounds. (Jealousy is a form of dementia praecox which sometimes becomes violent without the slightest cause.) The habit of accusing wife or husband of infidelity without grounds. General suspicion of everyone, absolute faith in no one.

FAULT FINDING. The habit of finding fault with friends, relatives, business associates and loved ones upon the slightest provocation, or without any cause whatsoever.

GAMBLING. The habit of gambling, stealing, cheating, and otherwise taking hazardous chances to provide money for loved ones, with the belief that love can be bought. The habit of spending beyond one's means, or incurring debts, to provide gifts for loved ones, with the object of making a favorable showing. Insomnia, nervousness, lack of persistence, weakness of will, lack of self-control, lack of self-reliance, bad temper.

The Fear of Poverty is, without doubt, the most destructive of the six basic fears. It has been placed at the head of the list, because it is the most difficult to master.

THE FEAR OF OLD AGE

Every great man is always being helped by everybody, for his gift is to get good out of all things and all persons.

—John Ruskin

In the main, this fear grows out of two sources. First, the thought that old age may bring with it poverty. Secondly, and by far the most common source of origin, from false and cruel teachings of the past which have been too well mixed with "fire and brimstone," and other bogies cunningly designed to enslave man through fear.

In the basic fear of old age, man has two very sound reasons for his apprehension—one growing out of his distrust of his fellow man, who may seize whatever worldly goods he may possess, and the other arising from the terrible pictures of the world beyond, which were planted in his mind, through social heredity before he came into full possession of his mind.

The possibility of ill health, which is more common as people grow older, is also a contributing cause of this common fear of old age. Eroticism also enters into the cause of the fear of old age, as no man cherishes the thought of diminishing sex attraction.

The most common cause of fear of old age is associated with the possibility of poverty. "Poorhouse" is not a pretty word. It throws a chill into the mind of every person who faces the possibility of having to spend his declining years on a poor farm.

Another contributing cause of the fear of old age is the possibility of loss of freedom and independence, as old age may bring with it the loss of both physical and economic freedom.

Symptoms of the Fear of Old Age

The commonest symptoms of this fear are:

The tendency to slow down and develop an inferiority complex at the age of mental maturity, around the age of forty, falsely believing oneself to be "slipping" because of age. (The truth is that man's most useful years, mentally and spiritually, are those between forty and sixty.)

The habit of speaking apologetically of one's self as "being old" merely because one has reached the age of forty, or fifty, instead of reversing the

Nothing brings man so much suffering and humility as poverty! Only those who have experienced poverty understand the full meaning of this.

rule and expressing gratitude for having reached the age of wisdom and understanding.

The habit of killing off initiative, imagination, and self-reliance by falsely believing one's self too old to exercise these qualities. The habit of the man or woman of forty dressing with the aim of trying to appear much younger, and affecting mannerisms of youth; thereby inspiring ridicule by both friends and strangers.

First we form habits, then they form us. Conquer your bad habits or they will conquer you.

—Rob Gilbert

THE FEAR OF DEATH

To some this is the cruelest of all the basic fears. The reason is obvious. The terrible pangs of fear associated with the thought of death, in the majority of cases, may be charged directly to religious fanaticism. So-called "heathen" are less afraid of death than the more "civilized." For hundreds of millions of years man has been asking the still-unanswered questions "whence" and "whither." Where did I come from, and where am I going?

During the darker ages of the past, the more cunning and crafty were not slow to offer the answer to these questions, for a price. Witness, now, the major source of origin of the fear of death.

"Come into my tent, embrace my faith, accept my dogmas, and I will give you a ticket that will admit you straightaway into heaven when you die," cries a leader of sectarianism. "Remain out of my tent," says the same leader, "and may the devil take you and burn you throughout eternity."

Eternity is a long time. Fire is a terrible thing. The thought of eternal punishment, with fire, not only causes man to fear death, it often causes him to lose his reason. It destroys interest in life and makes happiness impossible.

During my research, I reviewed a book entitled *A Catalogue of the Gods,* in which were listed the *thirty thousand gods* which man has worshiped. Think of it! Thirty thousand of them, represented by everything from a crawfish to a man. It is little wonder that men have become frightened at the approach of death.

While the religious leader may not be able to provide safe conduct into heaven, nor, by lack of such provision, allow the unfortunate to descend into

The majority of people, if asked what they fear most, would reply, "I fear nothing." The reply would be inaccurate, because few people realize that they are bound, handicapped, whipped spiritually and physically through some form of fear.

Your net worth to the world is usually determined by what remains after your bad habits are subtracted from your good ones.

—Benjamin Franklin

hell, the possibility of the latter seems so terrible that the very thought of it lays hold of the imagination in such a realistic way that it paralyzes reason, and sets up the fear of death.

In truth, no man knows, and no man has ever known, what heaven or hell is like, nor does any man know if either place actually exists. This very lack of positive knowledge opens the door of the human mind to the charlatan so he may enter and control that mind with his stock of legerdemain and various brands of pious fraud and trickery.

The fear of death is not as common now as it was during the age when there were no great colleges and universities. Men of science have turned the spotlight of truth upon the world, and this truth is rapidly freeing men and women from this terrible fear of death. The young men and young women who attend the colleges and universities are not easily impressed by "fire" and "brimstone." Through the aid of biology, astronomy, geology, and other related sciences, the fears of the dark ages which gripped the minds of men and destroyed their reason have been dispelled.

Insane asylums are filled with men and women who have gone mad, because of the fear of death.

This fear is useless. Death will come, no matter what anyone may think about it. Accept it as a necessity, and pass the thought out of your mind. It must be a necessity, or it would not come to all. Perhaps it is not as bad as it has been pictured.

The entire world is made up of only two things, energy and matter. In elementary physics we learn that neither matter nor energy (the only two realities known to man) can be created or destroyed. Both matter and energy can be transformed, but neither can be destroyed.

Life is energy, if it is anything. If neither energy nor matter can be destroyed, of course life cannot be destroyed. Life, like other forms of energy, may be passed through various processes of transition, or change, but it cannot be destroyed. Death is mere transition.

If death is not mere change, or transition, then nothing comes after death except a long, eternal, peaceful sleep, and sleep is nothing to be feared. Thus you may wipe out, forever, the fear of Death.

The fear of criticism takes on many forms, the majority of which are petty and trivial.

Symptoms of the Fear of Death

The general symptoms of this fear are:—

The habit of thinking about dying instead of making the most of life, due, generally, to lack of purpose, or lack of a suitable occupation. This fear is more prevalent among the aged, but sometimes the more youthful are victims of it. The greatest of all remedies for the fear of death is a burning desire for achievement, backed by useful service to others. A busy person seldom has time to think about dying. He finds life too thrilling to worry about death. Sometimes the fear of death is closely associated with the Fear of Poverty, where one's death would leave loved ones poverty-stricken. In other cases, the fear of death is caused by illness and the consequent breaking down of physical body resistance. The commonest causes of the fear of death are: ill health, poverty, lack of appropriate occupation, disappointment over love, insanity, religious fanaticism.

Once you learn to quit, it becomes a habit.

—Vincent T. Lombardi

OLD MAN WORRY

Worry is a state of mind based upon fear. It works slowly, but persistently. It is insidious and subtle. Step by step it "digs itself in" until it paralyzes one's reasoning faculty, destroys self-confidence and initiative. Worry is a form of sustained fear caused by indecision; therefore it is a state of mind which can be controlled.

An unsettled mind is helpless. Indecision makes an unsettled mind. Most individuals lack the will-power to reach decisions promptly, and to stand by them after they have been made, even during normal business conditions. During periods of economic unrest (such as the world recently experienced), the individual is handicapped, not alone by his inherent nature to be slow at reaching decisions, but he is influenced by the indecision of others around him who have created a state of "mass indecision."

During the depression the whole atmosphere, all over the world, was filled with "Fearenza" and "Worryitis," the two mental disease germs which began

In the main, man fears ill health because of the terrible pictures which have been planted in his mind of what may happen if death should overtake him. He also fears it because of the economic toll which it may claim.

I never could have done what I have done without the habits of punctuality, order, and diligence, without the determination to concentrate myself on one subject at a time.

—Charles Dickens

to spread themselves after the Wall Street frenzy in 1929. There is only one known antidote for these germs; it is the habit of prompt and firm decision. Moreover, it is an antidote which every individual must apply for himself.

We do not worry over conditions, once we have reached a decision to follow a definite line of action. I once interviewed a man who was to be electrocuted two hours later. The condemned man was the calmest of some eight men who were in the death-cell with him. His calmness prompted me to ask him how it felt to know that he was going into eternity in a short while. With a smile of confidence on his face, he said, "It feels fine. Just think, brother, my troubles will soon be over. I have had nothing but trouble all my life. It has been a hardship to get food and clothing. Soon I will not need these things. I have felt fine ever since I learned for certain that I must die. I made up my mind then, to accept my fate in good spirit."

As he spoke he devoured a dinner of proportions sufficient for three men, eating every mouthful of the food brought to him, and apparently enjoying it as much as if no disaster awaited him. Decision gave this man resignation to his fate! Decision can also prevent one's acceptance of undesired circumstances.

The six basic fears become translated into a state of worry, through indecision. Relieve yourself, forever of the fear of death, by reaching a decision to accept death as an inescapable event. Whip the fear of poverty by reaching a decision to get along with whatever wealth you can accumulate without worry. Put your foot upon the neck of the fear of criticism by reaching a decision not to worry about what other people think, do, or say. Eliminate the fear of old age by reaching a decision to accept it, not as a handicap, but as a great blessing which carries with it wisdom, self-control, and understanding not known to youth. Acquit yourself of the fear of ill health by the decision to forget symptoms. Master the fear of loss of love by reaching a decision to get along without love, if that is necessary.

Kill the habit of worry, in all its forms, by reaching a general, blanket decision that nothing which life has to offer is worth the price of worry. With this decision will come poise, peace of mind, and calmness of thought which will bring happiness.

A man whose mind is filled with fear not only destroys his own chances of

It has been shown most convincingly that the fear of disease, even where there is not the slightest cause for fear, often produces the physical symptoms of the disease feared.

intelligent action, but he transmits these destructive vibrations to the minds of all who come into contact with him, and destroys, also, their chances.

Even a dog or a horse knows when its master lacks courage; moreover, a dog or a horse will pick up the vibrations of fear thrown off by its master, and behave accordingly. Lower down the line of intelligence in the animal kingdom, one finds this same capacity to pick up the vibrations of fear. A honey-bee immediately senses fear in the mind of a person—for reasons unknown, a bee will sting the person whose mind is releasing vibrations of fear, much more readily than it will molest the person whose mind registers no fear.

The vibrations of fear pass from one mind to another just as quickly and as surely as the sound of the human voice passes from the broadcasting station to the receiving set of a radio—and by the self-same medium.

Mental telepathy is a reality. Thoughts pass from one mind to another, voluntarily, whether or not this fact is recognized by either the person releasing the thoughts, or the persons who pick up those thoughts.

The person who gives expression, by word of mouth, to negative or destructive thoughts is practically certain to experience the results of those words in the form of a destructive "kick-back." The release of destructive thought impulses, alone, without the aid of words, produces also a "kick-back" in more ways than one. First of all, and perhaps most important to be remembered, the person who releases thoughts of a destructive nature must suffer damage through the breaking down of the faculty of creative imagination. Secondly, the presence in the mind of any destructive emotion develops a negative personality which repels people, and often converts them into antagonists. The third source of damage to the person who entertains or releases negative thoughts, lies in this significant fact—these thought-impulses are not only damaging to others, but they imbed themselves in the subconscious mind of the person releasing them, and there become a part of his character.

One is never through with a thought, merely by releasing it. When a thought is released, it spreads in every direction, through the medium of the ether, but it also plants itself *permanently* in the subconscious mind of *the person releasing it.*

Your business in life is presumably to achieve success. To be successful, you must find peace of mind, acquire the material needs of life, and above all, attain

Divide each difficulty into as many parts as necessary to resolve it.

—Descartes

Powerful and mighty is the human mind!
It builds or it destroys.

happiness. All of these evidences of success begin in the form of thought impulses.

You may control your own mind; you have the power to feed it whatever thought impulses you choose. With this privilege goes also the responsibility of using it constructively. You are the master of your own earthly destiny just as surely as you have the power to control your own thoughts. You may influence, direct, and eventually control your own environment, making your life what you want it to be—or, you may neglect to exercise the privilege which is yours, to make your life to order, thus casting yourself upon the broad sea of "Circumstance" where you will be tossed hither and yon, like a chip on the waves of the ocean.

Nothing of importance is ever achieved without discipline.
—Bertrand Russell

THE DEVIL'S WORKSHOP

The Seventh Basic Evil

In addition to the Six Basic Fears, there is another evil by which people suffer. It constitutes a rich soil in which the seeds of failure grow abundantly. It is so subtle that its presence often is not detected. This affliction cannot properly be classed as a fear. It is more deeply seated and more often fatal than all of the six fears. For want of a better name, let us call this evil susceptibility to negative influences.

Men who accumulate great riches always protect themselves against this evil! The poverty stricken never do! Those who succeed in any calling must prepare their minds to resist the evil. If you are reading this philosophy for the purpose of accumulating riches, you should examine yourself very carefully, to determine whether you are susceptible to negative influences. If you neglect this self-analysis, you will forfeit your right to attain the object of your desires.

Make the analysis searching. After you read the questions prepared for this self-analysis, hold yourself to a strict accounting in your answers. Go at the task as carefully as you would search for any other enemy you knew to be awaiting you in ambush and deal with your own faults as you would with a more tangible enemy.

You can easily protect yourself against highway robbers, because the law

Life is energy, if it is anything. If neither energy nor matter can be destroyed, of course life cannot be destroyed.

provides organized cooperation for your benefit, but the "seventh basic evil" is more difficult to master, because it strikes when you are not aware of its presence, when you are asleep, and while you are awake. Moreover, its weapon is intangible, because it consists of merely—a state of mind. This evil is also dangerous because it strikes in as many different forms as there are human experiences. Sometimes it enters the mind through the well-meant words of one's own relatives. At other times, it bores from within, through one's own mental attitude. Always it is as deadly as poison, even though it may not kill as quickly.

Most of the important things in the world have been accomplished by people who have kept on trying when there seemed to be no help at all.

—Dale Carnegie

How to Protect Yourself Against Negative Influences

To protect yourself against negative influences, whether of your own making, or the result of the activities of negative people around you, recognize that you have a will-power, and put it into constant use, until it builds a wall of immunity against negative influences in your own mind.

Recognize the fact that you, and every other human being, are, by nature, lazy, indifferent, and susceptible to all suggestions which harmonize with your weaknesses.

Recognize that you are, by nature, susceptible to all the six basic fears, and set up habits for the purpose of counteracting all these fears.

Recognize that negative influences often work on you through your subconscious mind; therefore they are difficult to detect, and keep your mind closed against all people who depress or discourage you in any way.

Clean out your medicine chest, throw away all pill bottles, and stop pandering to colds, aches, pains and imaginary illness.

Deliberately seek the company of people who influence you to think and act for yourself.

Do not expect troubles as they have a tendency not to disappoint.

Without doubt, the most common weakness of all human beings is the habit of leaving their minds open to the negative influence of other people. This weakness is all the more damaging, because most people do not recognize that they are cursed by it, and many who acknowledge it, neglect or refuse to correct the evil until it becomes an uncontrollable part of their daily habits.

To aid those who wish to see themselves as they really are, the following list of questions has been prepared. Read the questions and state your answers

An unsettled mind is helpless. Indecision makes an unsettled mind. Most individuals lack the will-power to reach decisions promptly, and to stand by them after they have been made, even during normal business conditions.

aloud, so you can hear your own voice. This will make it easier for you to be truthful with yourself.

Some men give up their designs when they have almost reached the goal; while others, on the contrary, obtain a victory by exerting, at the last moment, more vigorous efforts than ever before.

—Herodotus

SELF-ANALYSIS TEST QUESTIONS

Do you complain often of "feeling bad," and if so, what is the cause?

Do you find fault with other people at the slightest provocation?

Do you frequently make mistakes in your work, and if so, why?

Are you sarcastic and offensive in your conversation?

Do you deliberately avoid the association of anyone, and if so, why?

Do you suffer frequently with indigestion? If so, what is the cause?

Does life seem futile and the future hopeless to you? If so, why?

Do you like your occupation? If not, why?

Do you often feel self-pity, and if so why?

Are you envious of those who excel you?

To which do you devote most time, thinking of success, or of failure?

Are you gaining or losing self-confidence as you grow older?

Do you learn something of value from all mistakes? Are you permitting some relative or acquaintance to worry you? If so, why?

Are you sometimes "in the clouds" and at other times in the depths of despondency?

Who has the most inspiring influence upon you? What is the cause?

Do you tolerate negative or discouraging influences which you can avoid?

Are you careless of your personal appearance? If so, when and why?

Have you learned how to "drown your troubles" by being too busy to be annoyed by them?

Would you call yourself a "spineless weakling" if you permitted others to do your thinking for you?

Do you neglect internal bathing until auto-intoxication makes you ill-tempered and irritable?

How many preventable disturbances annoy you, and why do you tolerate them?

Kill the habit of worry, in all its forms, by reaching a general, blanket decision that nothing which life has to offer is worth the price of worry. With this decision will come poise, peace of mind, and calmness of thought which will bring happiness.

Do you resort to liquor, narcotics, or cigarettes to "quiet your nerves"? If so, why do you not try will-power instead?

Does anyone "nag" you, and if so, for what reason?

Do you have a definite major purpose, and if so, what is it, and what plan have you for achieving it?

Do you suffer from any of the Six Basic Fears? If so, which ones?

Have you a method by which you can shield yourself against the negative influence of others?

Do you make deliberate use of auto-suggestion to make your mind positive?

Which do you value most, your material possessions, or your privilege of controlling your own thoughts?

Are you easily influenced by others, against your own judgment?

Has today added anything of value to your stock of knowledge or state of mind?

Do you face squarely the circumstances which make you unhappy, or sidestep the responsibility?

Do you analyze all mistakes and failures and try to profit by them, or do you take the attitude that this is not your duty?

Can you name three of your most damaging weaknesses? What are you doing to correct them?

Do you encourage other people to bring their worries to you for sympathy?

Do you choose, from your daily experiences, lessons or influences which aid in your personal advancement?

Does your presence have a negative influence on other people as a rule?

What habits of other people annoy you most?

Do you form your own opinions or permit yourself to be influenced by other people?

Have you learned how to create a mental state of mind with which you can shield yourself against all discouraging influences?

Does your occupation inspire you with faith and hope?

Good luck is another name for tenacity of purpose.

—Ralph Waldo Emerson

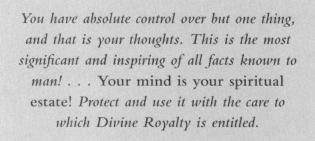

You have absolute control over but one thing, and that is your thoughts. This is the most significant and inspiring of all facts known to man! . . . Your mind is your spiritual estate! Protect and use it with the care to which Divine Royalty is entitled.

Defeat is simply a signal to press onward.

—Helen Keller

Are you conscious of possessing spiritual forces of sufficient power to enable you to keep your mind free from all forms of fear?

Does your religion help you to keep your own mind positive?

Do you feel it your duty to share other people's worries? If so, why?

If you believe that "birds of a feather flock together" what have you learned about yourself by studying the friends whom you attract?

What connection, if any, do you see between the people with whom you associate most closely, and any unhappiness you may experience?

Could it be possible that some person whom you consider to be a friend is, in reality, your worst enemy, because of his negative influence on your mind?

By what rules do you judge who is helpful and who is damaging to you?

Are your intimate associates mentally superior or inferior to you?

How much time out of every twenty-four hours do you devote to

   a. your occupation

   b. sleep

   c. play and relaxation

   d. acquiring useful knowledge

   e. plain waste

Who among your acquaintances

   a. encourages you most

   b. cautions you most

   c. discourages you most

   d. helps you most in other ways

What is your greatest worry? Why do you tolerate it?

When others offer you free, unsolicited advice, do you accept it without question, or analyze their motive?

What, above all else, do you most desire? Do you intend to acquire it? Are you willing to subordinate all other desires for this one? How much time daily do you devote to acquiring it?

Do you change your mind often? If so, why?

Do you usually finish everything you begin?

Mind control is the result of self-discipline and habit. You either control your mind or it controls you. There is no half-way compromise.

Are you easily impressed by other people's business or professional
titles, college degrees, or wealth? Are you easily influenced by
what other people think or say of you?

Do you cater to people because of their social or financial status?

Whom do you believe to be the greatest person living? In what
respect is this person superior to yourself?

How much time have you devoted to studying and answering these
questions? (At least one day is necessary for the analysis and the
answering of the entire list.)

In the middle of difficulty lies opportunity.

—Albert Einstein

If you have answered all these questions truthfully, you know more about
yourself than the majority of people. Study the questions carefully, come back
to them once each week for several months, and be astounded at the amount
of additional knowledge of great value to yourself, you will have gained by the
simple method of answering the questions truthfully. If you are not certain
concerning the answers to some of the questions, seek the counsel of those who
know you well, especially those who have no motive in flattering you, and see
yourself through their eyes. The experience will be astonishing.

You have absolute control over but one thing, and that is your thoughts.
This is the most significant and inspiring of all facts known to man! It reflects
man's Divine nature. This Divine prerogative is the sole means by which you
may control your own destiny. If you fail to control your own mind, you may
be sure you will control nothing else.

If you must be careless with your possessions, let it be in connection with
material things. *Your mind is your spiritual estate!* Protect and use it with the care
to which Divine Royalty is entitled. You were given a will-power for this
purpose.

Unfortunately, there is no legal protection against those who, either by design or ignorance, poison the minds of others by negative suggestion. This form
of destruction should be punishable by heavy legal penalties, because it may
and often does destroy one's chances of acquiring material things which are
protected by law.

Men with negative minds tried to convince Thomas A. Edison that he could
not build a machine that would record and reproduce the human voice,

The most practical of all methods for controlling the mind is the habit of keeping it busy with a definite purpose, backed by a definite plan.

Small opportunities are often the beginning of great enterprises.
—Demosthenes

"because" they said, "no one else had ever produced such a machine." Edison did not believe them. He knew that the mind could produce anything the mind could conceive and believe, and that knowledge was the thing that lifted the great Edison above the common herd.

Men with negative minds told F. W. Woolworth he would go "broke" trying to run a store on five- and ten-cent sales. He did not believe them. He knew that he could do anything, within reason, if he backed his plans with faith. Exercising his right to keep other men's negative suggestions out of his mind, he piled up a fortune of more than a $100 million.

Men with negative minds told George Washington he could not hope to win against the vastly superior forces of the British, but he exercised his Divine right to believe; therefore this book was published under the protection of the Stars and Stripes, while the name of Lord Cornwallis has been all but forgotten.

Doubting Thomases scoffed scornfully when Henry Ford tried out his first crudely built automobile on the streets of Detroit. Some said the thing never would become practical. Others said no one would pay money for such a contraption. Ford said, "I'll belt the earth with dependable motor cars," and he did! His decision to trust his own judgment has already piled up a fortune far greater than the next five generations of his descendants can squander. For the benefit of those seeking vast riches, let it be remembered that practically the sole difference between Henry Ford and a majority of the more than one hundred thousand men who work for him, is this—Ford has a mind and controls it, the others have minds which they do not try to control.

Henry Ford has been repeatedly mentioned, because he is an astounding example of what a man with a mind of his own, and a will to control it, can accomplish. His record knocks the foundation from under that time-worn alibi, "I never had a chance." Ford never had a chance, either, but he created an opportunity and backed it with persistence until it made him richer than Croesus.

Mind control is the result of self-discipline and habit. You either control your mind or it controls you. There is no half-way compromise. The most practical of all methods for controlling the mind is the habit of keeping it busy with a definite purpose, backed by a definite plan. Study the record of any man who achieves noteworthy success, and you will observe that he has control over his

Building alibis with which to explain away failure is a national pastime. The habit is as old as the human race, and is fatal to success!

own mind, moreover, that he exercises that control and directs it toward the attainment of definite objectives. Without this control, success is not possible.

"FIFTY-SEVEN" FAMOUS ALIBIS
BY OLD MAN IF

People who do not succeed have one distinguishing trait in common. They know *all the reasons for failure,* and have what they believe to be airtight alibis to explain away their own lack of achievement.

Some of these alibis are clever, and a few of them are justifiable by the facts. But alibis cannot be used for money. The world wants to know only one thing— have you achieved success?

A character analyst compiled a list of the most commonly used alibis. As you read the list, examine yourself carefully, and determine how many of these alibis, if any, are your own property. Remember, too, the philosophy presented in this book makes every one of these alibis obsolete.

- ☐ IF I didn't have a wife and family . . .
- ☐ IF I had enough "pull" . . .
- ☐ IF I had money . . .
- ☐ IF I had a good education . . .
- ☐ IF I could get a job . . .
- ☐ IF I had good health . . .
- ☐ IF I only had time . . .
- ☐ IF times were better . . .
- ☐ IF other people understood me . . .
- ☐ IF conditions around me were only different . . .
- ☐ IF I could live my life over again . . .
- ☐ IF I did not fear what "they" would say . . .
- ☐ IF I had been given a chance . . .
- ☐ IF I now had a chance . . .
- ☐ IF other people didn't "have it in for me" . . .

Too many people are thinking of security instead of opportunity. They seem more afraid of life than death.

—James F. Byrnes

Why do people cling to their pet alibis? The answer is obvious. They defend their alibis because they create them! A man's alibi is the child of his own imagination. It is human nature to defend one's own brainchild.

Luck is a matter of preparation meeting opportunity.

—Oprah Winfrey

- ☐ IF nothing happens to stop me . . .
- ☐ IF I were only younger . . .
- ☐ IF I could only do what I want . . .
- ☐ IF I had been born rich . . .
- ☐ IF I could meet "the right people" . . .
- ☐ IF I had the talent that some people have . . .
- ☐ IF I dared assert myself . . .
- ☐ IF I only had embraced past opportunities . . .
- ☐ IF people didn't get on my nerves . . .
- ☐ IF I didn't have to keep house and look after the children . . .
- ☐ IF I could save some money . . .
- ☐ IF the boss only appreciated me . . .
- ☐ IF I only had somebody to help me . . .
- ☐ IF my family understood me . . .
- ☐ IF I lived in a big city . . .
- ☐ IF I could just get started . . .
- ☐ IF I were only free . . .
- ☐ IF I had the personality of some people . . .
- ☐ IF I were not so fat . . .
- ☐ IF my talents were known . . .
- ☐ IF I could just get a "break" . . .
- ☐ IF I could only get out of debt . . .
- ☐ IF I hadn't failed . . .
- ☐ IF I only knew how . . .
- ☐ IF everybody didn't oppose me . . .
- ☐ IF I didn't have so many worries . . .
- ☐ IF I could marry the right person . . .
- ☐ IF people weren't so dumb . . .
- ☐ IF my family were not so extravagant . . .
- ☐ IF I were sure of myself . . .
- ☐ IF luck were not against me . . .
- ☐ IF I had not been born under the wrong star . . .
- ☐ IF it were not true that "what is to be will be" . . .
- ☐ IF I did not have to work so hard . . .

Habits are difficult to break, especially when they provide justification for something we do. Plato had this truth in mind when he said, "The first and best victory is to conquer self. To be conquered by self is, of all things, the most shameful and vile."

☐ IF I hadn't lost my money . . .

☐ IF I lived in a different neighborhood . . .

☐ IF I didn't have a "past" . . .

☐ IF I only had a business of my own . . .

☐ IF other people would only listen to me . . .

☐ IF ★ ★ ★ and this is the greatest of them all ★ ★ ★

> I had the courage to see myself as I really am, I would *find out what is wrong with me, and correct it,* then I might have a chance to profit by my mistakes and learn something from the experience of others, for I know that there is something wrong with me, or I would now be where *I would have been if* I had spent more time analyzing my weaknesses, and less time building alibis to cover them.

A pessimist sees the difficulty in every opportunity; an optimist sees the opportunity in every difficulty.

—Winston Churchill

Building alibis with which to explain away failure is a national pastime. The habit is as old as the human race, and *is fatal to success!* Why do people cling to their pet alibis? The answer is obvious. They defend their alibis because they create them! A man's alibi is the child of his own imagination. It is human nature to defend one's own brainchild.

Building alibis is a deeply rooted habit. Habits are difficult to break, especially when they provide justification for something we do. Plato had this truth in mind when he said, "The first and best victory is to conquer self. To be conquered by self is, of all things, the most shameful and vile."

Another philosopher had the same thought in mind when he said, "It was a great surprise to me when I discovered that most of the ugliness I saw in others was but a reflection of my own nature."

"It has always been a mystery to me," said Elbert Hubbard, "why people spend so much time deliberately fooling themselves by creating alibis to cover their weaknesses. If used differently, this same time would be sufficient to cure the weakness; then no alibis would be needed."

In parting, I would remind you that "Life is a checkerboard, and the player opposite you is time. If you hesitate before moving, or neglect to move promptly, your men will be wiped off the board by time. You are playing against a partner who will not tolerate indecision!"

Previously you may have had a logical excuse for not having forced Life to

"Life is a checkerboard, and the player opposite you is time. If you hesitate before moving, or neglect to move promptly, your men will be wiped off the board by time. You are playing against a partner who will not tolerate indecision!"

come through with whatever you asked, but that alibi is now obsolete, because you are in possession of the Master Key that unlocks the door to Life's bountiful riches.

The Master Key is intangible, but it is powerful! It is the privilege of creating, *in your own mind,* a burning desire for a definite form of riches. There is no penalty for the use of the Key, but there is a price you must pay if you do not use it. The price is failure. There is a reward of stupendous proportions if you put the Key to use. It is the satisfaction that comes to all who *conquer self and force Life to pay whatever is asked.*

The reward is worthy of your effort. Will you make the start and be convinced?

"If we are related," said the immortal Emerson, "we shall meet." In closing, may I borrow his thought, and say, "If we are related, we have, through these pages, met."

Deadlines stop our procrastination; they get our adrenaline pumping; they motivate us.

—Rita Emmett

The Master Key is intangible, but it is powerful! . . . There is a reward of stupendous proportions if you put the Key to use. . . . The reward is worthy of your effort. Will you make the start and be convinced?

QUESTIONS FOR SUCCESS

- *What is the most helpful idea from this chapter for you?*

- *What are the "Six Ghosts of Fear"?*

- *What is the "seventh basic evil"?*

- *Which of these do you identify with the most?*

- *How do you protect yourself against negative influences?*

- *Review the "Self-Analysis Test Questions" (pages 276–279). What did you find most surprising in your answers?*

- *Review the list of the "'Fifty-Seven' Famous Alibis" (pages 281–283) and place a check next to the ones that you have used to limit your potential.*

YOUR SUCCESS STEPS

☐ _____

☐ _____

☐ _____

☐ _____

☐ _____

☐ _____

IV.

CREATING YOUR MASTER MIND

abridged from the Penguin e-book

Creating Your Think and Grow Rich Master Mind

BY JOEL FOTINOS

There is one simple technique that can help you achieve what you want, stay committed and inspired along the way, and create long-lasting relationships that will benefit you for years to come. This technique is using the power of the Master Mind.

One of the most effective and important ideas to come out of Napoleon Hill's classic bestsellers *Think and Grow Rich* and *The Law of Success* is the idea of the Master Mind.

In fact, so key is forming Master Mind partnerships that it is the very first lesson in Napoleon Hill's 1928 motivational book (originally a series of books), *The Law of Success.* In it, Napoleon Hill writes that a Master Mind is "a mind that is developed through the harmonious co-operation of two or more people who ally themselves for the purpose of accomplishing any given task." The term Master Mind first came to Napoleon Hill's awareness through his association with Andrew Carnegie, the great steel magnate and philanthropist, who created Master Mind groups to aid in the expansion of his business empire.

I believe that having a Master Mind, no matter what your goal might be, is one of the most effective success habits that you can acquire. With a Master Mind in action in your life, you'll be more apt to be committed and consistent, you'll probably have more fun, and because of these, you'll no doubt see more results as well.

The information in this section is based on the original editions of Napoleon Hill's aforementioned books, with additional material and updates taken from modern-day experiences, including my own. While Napoleon Hill wrote about Master Mind groups largely for a business-oriented reader, Master Mind partnerships can be beneficial for social and other non-business purposes. Groups as varied as sales teams, religious organizations, parent-teacher groups, artists, weight-loss groups, corporations, and even families have all used the principles of the Master Mind to aid in their success.

The Master Mind that you form should be one that helps foster a creative energy of success for you and your Master Mind partner(s). Take these ideas and instructions, and then expand on them to fit your own needs. Be creative, use the ideas that will work for you, and adapt what doesn't into what does.

Every endeavor of success requires several qualities, including commitment and passion. Make sure that you and all the members of your Master Mind are fully committed to the group. If one person dominates, then usually the other member(s) will be less invested in the process and outcomes in the group. Also, if one person is more passionate about the success of the Master Mind than anyone else, the group is probably not going to create long-lasting success. That is why it is critical to be selective in choosing whom you invite into your group.

WHAT IS A MASTER MIND?

According to Hill, a Master Mind is a coming together of people to help one another achieve goals and attain success. He writes in *The Law of Success*,

A Master Mind may be created through the bringing together or blending, in a spirit of perfect harmony, of two or more minds. Out of this harmonious blending the chemistry of the mind creates a third mind which may be appropriated and used by one or all of the individual minds. This Master Mind will remain available as long as the friendly, harmonious alliance between the individual minds exists. It will disintegrate and all evidence of its former existence will disappear the moment the friendly alliance is broken.

The effect of the meeting of two minds is obvious to even the most casual observer [writes Napoleon Hill]. Every effect must have a cause! What could be more reasonable than to suspect that the cause of the change in mental attitude between two minds which have just come in close contact is none other than the disturbance of the electrons or units of each mind in the process of rearranging themselves in the new field created by the contact?

In other words, a chemical reaction is caused when two or more like-minded people come together, and the effect of their contact is greater than the sum of the individual parts. "That the reaction takes place, in every instance, is a known fact which gives us a starting point from which we may show what is meant by the term 'Master Mind.'"

WHAT IS THE DIFFERENCE BETWEEN A MASTER MIND GROUP AND A MASTER MIND PARTNER?

A "Master Mind" can be two or more people. Many people work best in the context of a formal group, and so a group can be the most effective form of "Master Mind" for them. Others work better one-on-one, so for them a partner will be more effective.

For a Master Mind group, Napoleon Hill suggests having approximately a half dozen people working together in harmony. He writes, "A 'Master Mind' may be created by any group of people who will co-ordinate their minds, in a spirit of perfect harmony. The group may consist of any number from two upward. Best results appear available from the blending of six or seven minds."

A Master Mind partner, however, can be extremely effective version of a Master Mind. A Master Mind partner is a one-on-one relationship, where two people come together to support each other in their journey. Master Mind partners can be a more intense experience, since there is more time to focus on the two people, rather than divvying up time for a larger group. Also, it is even more important with a Master Mind partner to share the time and efforts equally, so one partner does not dominate the meetings.

It's important to find exactly the Master Mind situation that suits you the best. Experiment with different forms of Master Mind until you find what supports you the most.

WHAT ARE THE BENEFITS OF A MASTER MIND?

Master Minds should be formed to increase the opportunities for everyone concerned. Some of the many benefits of having a Master Mind (group and/ or partner) include:

- Support, inspiration and motivation
- Consistency in working toward goals
- A method for networking

- Mentoring by one another, gaining from the experience everyone brings
- Accountability, which is a great motivator
- A spirit of brainstorming solutions to challenges and problems

There are many kinds of Master Mind groups, and you will be able to adapt your own group to fit your needs. In general, these groups are:

- Mutually beneficial for all members—no one person should dominate a Master Mind
- Strictly confidential
- Goal-oriented
- Not a group-therapy session or a place to gossip or chitchat

WHOM SHOULD I INVITE TO MY MASTER MIND?

Choosing your Master Mind group or partnership is key to your success. If you choose based only on emotional factors (i.e., you choose a friend, a spouse, etc.), you may not choose the right person to support your efforts. If you choose based only on rational thought, you might choose someone with whom you have no chemistry. Balance your emotional and rational factors in choosing your Master Mind partner(s), so that you are choosing only those whom you trust and respect, with whom you have a good rapport, and whom you can learn from.

If you want to start a Master Mind group, decide *first* what you want the group for, what kind of support you need, and also what you can offer others in the way of support.

Choosing people who have what Napoleon Hill calls a "pleasing personality" is of the utmost importance. Individuals who are contrary in any way by nature tend not to make positive Master Mind participants.

If a member of your Master Mind displays a spirit of disharmony, lack of commitment, or untrustworthiness, it is best to end his or her association with your Master Mind immediately. As Hill wisely states, "No group of minds can be blended into a Master Mind if one of the individuals of that group possesses one of these extremely negative, repellent minds. The negative and positive minds will not blend in the sense here described as a Master Mind. Lack of knowledge of this fact has brought many an otherwise able leader to defeat."

Think of the qualities you will look for in the people you want to invite:

- Supportive
- Noncompetitive

- Hungry for success
- Consistent
- Reliable
- Positive and willing to be part of the group
- Other _____

Where can you find Master Mind candidates?

- Professional contacts
- Business associations
- Religious organizations
- Internet, including social networking sites (such as LinkedIn, Facebook, and others). While this can be a positive option, please proceed carefully.
- Friends and family. Family and friends can be supportive, but it is important to choose only those who have the same motivation and interest level. Also, choose those family members and friends who want to see you grow and are happy for your success. Avoid those with whom you have a rocky relationship with, those who you want to "save" (rather than help), or those who are (or would be) jealous of your increasing success.
- Other _____

How many people should you have in your group?

As stated earlier, Napoleon Hill suggests that six or seven people are ideal for Master Mind groups. However, that may or may not be a good size for you and your goal. Think about how many people you might feel comfortable with in your group—three to six people is a good place to begin, and then add people as necessary.

WHERE DO WE MEET?

The rule of thumb for a positive Master Mind experience is to have a place that is comfortable, quiet, and easily accessible, and that fits the needs of the group.
Some examples:

- Library
- Church or synagogue
- Someone's home. Remember, no interruptions, which can be tough at a residence.

- Restaurant. Find an accommodating restaurant, one that is quiet, offers privacy, and whose management doesn't mind if you sit there for the length of the meeting. Remember to tip servers appropriately based on time, number of people, and the size of your bill.
- Conference room at place of employment. Check with your human resources department to see what restrictions or guidelines you will need to know about before reserving a workplace room.
- Park, or other outdoor space—weather permitting.
- Other _____

Some groups meet solely online, by video conferencing, or by conference call. All of those options can be good, but there is a certain chemistry that happens when people meet in person. There are a number of websites that offer free conference calls, so that each member can "dial in" to one tele- or video conference. If you choose this option, read the fine print on the website, and also make sure each Master Mind participant has the dial-in information. If you are using a method other than in-person meetings, make sure to have e-mailed each person an agenda, and appoint someone to keep track of time.

WHAT DOES A SUCCESSFUL MASTER MIND MEETING INCLUDE?

Successful Master Mind meetings are usually created over time. Start using some of the suggestions below, and then add or subtract options to fit your needs.

Ideas for a Successful Master Mind Meeting:

- Pick a facilitator. The same person may always facilitate, or you may want to rotate the facilitators for each meeting.
- Set up some initial rules and guidelines, such as:
  - How often you are going to meet—usually once or twice a week is a good maximum number of meetings, and monthly is a good minimum
  - How many meetings people can miss in a given time period before they are asked to leave the group
  - How you will deal with disruptive members
  - The process by which you will invite new members once the group has begun
- Start each meeting with an agenda so the meeting is organized and consistent—and also set a time limit for the meeting. Begin with one-hour meetings, and expand (or shorten) meetings if necessary and mutually agreed upon.
- Have the facilitator run the group and keep track of time so the

meeting moves forward and everyone has the same amount of time to talk. Use a stopwatch or a clock if necessary to stay on track, and to make sure everyone has an equal opportunity to share.

- Begin with a check-in, with each person taking two to three minutes to talk about successes and wins that relate specifically to the Master Mind group.
- Allow each person time to do a goal update for five to ten minutes—talk about what their goal is, what they are doing, what they need, what they've done since the last meeting, and what challenges they are facing. Adjust the amount of time allowed for this according to size of the group.
- Create a time, after each person has talked, where the group can brainstorm and offer one another supportive ideas. Do this until every person has had a chance to talk.
- End the meeting either with the facilitator reading something short and inspirational or everyone saying an agreed-upon affirmation together.
- Send each other supportive e-mails during the week and/or
- Set up an Internet place—like a Yahoo! group—where people can send e-mails or post information privately.
- Other _____

Again, you may have to tinker around with these ideas a bit until they fit you and your group perfectly. Communication and support are the keys here.

Many groups, in an attempt to stay on same page, incorporate an inspirational self-help book into the meetings. It might be wise to start with a Napoleon Hill book to begin with, including:

- *Think and Grow Rich*
- *The Think and Grow Rich Workbook*
- *The Law of Success*
- *The Master-Key to Riches*
- *The Magic Ladder to Success*
- or any other book by Napoleon Hill

Other powerful books can be found in the chapter called "Success Classics Reading List" (page 311).

If you are starting a Master Mind partnership, many of the above guidelines and suggestions will apply. Read through them and see which ones speak to you and the other person in your Master Mind.

For more information, see *Creating Your Think and Grow Rich Master Mind* by Joel Fotinos, available as a Penguin e-book, wherever e-books are sold.

V.

ADDITIONAL INSPIRATION

Welcome to the University of Possibility!

Those who get ignited by the Think and Grow Rich philosophy begin to see Napoleon Hill's ideas expressed everywhere, and want to continue to feed their conscious and subconscious mind with inspirational ideas. Included in this special edition of *Think and Grow Rich* are two exciting tools that can serve to expand your mind and your life.

The first tool is excerpts from *six classic works* on prosperity and success. They can be read as supplemental material to *Think and Grow Rich*, ways to underscore those principles that Hill writes so passionately about. If any of these excerpts seem to speak to you and your experience, we encourage you to go to the source material and read the entire work from which the excerpt was taken. There are literally dozens of books we could have excerpted in this section, but for the sake of length, we have selected a few of our favorite excerpts from six of the most powerful and important success classics we could find.

Once you have read these six excerpts, refer to our second tool: a Success Classics Reading List. Read the works on this list, one by one, to further plant seeds of success and prosperity in your subconscious mind. Make it a goal not only to read each of these books but to distill from each one what it has taught you, what gift it has given you. Don't stop with just this list of books; continue to seek additional books that can uplift you. Make it a lifelong endeavor to read as many inspirational books as you can. As Hill noted, as long as we are alive, we can learn. The more we learn, the more we grow. Reading these books is literally putting the *Think and Grow Rich* philosophy into action in your life.

from

THE SCIENCE OF BEING GREAT

by *Wallace D. Wattles*

Becoming Great

Too many . . . do not understand the necessity for present action in realizing the vision and bringing the thought-form into manifestation. Two things are necessary. First, the making of the thought-form, and, second, the actual appropriation to yourself of all that goes into and around the thought-form. . . . When you have made your thought-form, you are already, in your interior, what you want to be; next you must become externally what you want to be. You are already great within, but you are not yet doing the great things without. You cannot begin, on the instant, to do the great things; you cannot be before the world the great actor, or lawyer, or musician, or personality you know yourself to be; no one will entrust great things to you as yet for you have not made yourself known. But you can always begin to do small things in a great way.

Here lies the whole secret. You can begin to be great today in your own home, in your store or office, on the street, everywhere; you can begin to make yourself known as great, and you can do this by doing everything you do in a great way. You must put the whole power of your great soul into every act, however small and commonplace, and so reveal to your family, your friends, and neighbors what you really are. Do not brag or boast of yourself; do not go about telling people what a great personage you are; simply live in a great way. No one will believe you if you tell him you are a great man, but no one can doubt your greatness if you show it in your actions. In your domestic circle be so just, so generous, so courteous, and kindly that your family, your wife, husband, children, brothers, and sisters shall know that you are a great and noble soul. In all your relations with men be great, just, generous, courteous, and kindly. The great are never otherwise.

Overcoming Habitual Thought

It is probable that your greatest difficulty will be to overcome your old habitual ways of thought, and to form new habits. The world is ruled by habit. Kings, tyrants, masters, and plutocrats hold their positions solely because the people have come to habitually accept them. Things are as they are only because people have formed the habit of accepting them as they are. . . .

You have formed, perhaps, the habit of thinking of yourself as a common person, as one of a limited ability, or as being more or less of a failure. Whatever you habitually think yourself to be, that you are. You must form, now, a greater and better habit; you must form a conception of yourself as a being of limitless power, and habitually think that you are that being. It is the habitual, not the periodical thought that decides your destiny. It will avail you nothing to sit apart for a few moments several times a day to affirm that you are great, if during all the balance of the day, while you are about your regular vocation, you think of yourself as not great. No amount of praying or affirmation will make you great if you still habitually regard yourself as being small. The use of prayer and affirmation is to change your habit of thought. Any act, mental or physical, often repeated, becomes a habit. The purpose of mental exercises is to repeat certain thoughts over and over until the thinking of those thoughts becomes constant and habitual. The thoughts we continually repeat become convictions. What you must do is to repeat the new thought of yourself until it is the only way in which you think of yourself. Habitual thought, and not environment or circumstance, has made you what you are. Every person has some central idea or thought-form of himself, and by this idea he classifies and arranges all his facts and external relationships. You are classifying your facts either according to the idea that you are a great and strong personality, or according to the idea that you are limited, common, or weak. If the latter is the case you must change your central idea. Get a new mental picture of yourself. Do not try to become great by repeating mere strings of words or superficial formulae; but repeat over and over the THOUGHT of your own power and ability until you classify external facts, and decide your place everywhere by this idea.

Great Thinking

Greatness is attained only by the thinking of great thoughts. No man can become great in outward personality until he is great internally; and no man can be great internally until he THINKS. No amount of education, reading, or study can make you great without thought; but thought can make you great with very little study. There are altogether too many people who are trying to make something of themselves by reading books without thinking; all such will fail. You are not mentally developed by what you read, but by what you think about what you read.

Thinking is the hardest and most exhausting of all labor; and hence many people shrink from it. God has so formed us that we are continuously impelled to thought; we must either think or engage in some activity to escape thought. The headlong, continuous chase for pleasure in which most people spend all their leisure time is only an effort to escape thought. If they are alone, or if they have nothing amusing to take their attention, as a novel to read or a show to see, they must think; and to escape from thinking they resort to novels, shows, and all the endless devices of the purveyors of amusement. Most people spend the greater part of their leisure time running away from thought, hence they are where they are. We never move forward until we begin to think.

Thinking, not mere knowledge or information, makes personality. Thinking is growth; you cannot think without growing. Every thought engenders another thought. Write one idea and others will follow until you have written a page. You cannot fathom your own mind; it has neither bottom nor boundaries. . . . Heredity, environment, circumstances—all things must give way before you if you practice sustained and continuous thought. But, on the other hand, if you neglect to think for yourself and only use other people's thought, you will never know what you are capable of; and you will end by being incapable of anything.

There can be no real greatness without original thought. All that a man does outwardly is the expression and completion of his inward thinking. No action is possible without thought, and no great action is possible until a great thought has preceded it. Action is the second form of thought, and personality is the materialization of thought. Environment is the result of thought; things group themselves or arrange themselves around you according to your thought. There is, as Emerson says, some central idea or conception of yourself by which all the facts of your life are arranged and classified. Change this central idea and you change the arrangement or classification of all the facts and circumstances of your life. You are what you are because you think as you do; you are where you are because you think as you do.

Action at Home

Do not merely think that you are going to become great; *think that you are great now.* Do not think that you will begin to act in a great way at some future time; begin now. Do not think that you will act in a great way when you reach a different environment; act in a great way where you are now. Do not think that you will begin to act in a great way when you begin to deal with great things; begin to deal in a great way with small things. Do not think that you will begin to be great when you get among more intelligent people, or among people who understand you better; begin now to deal in a great way with the people around you.

If you are not in an environment where there is scope for your best powers and talents you can move in due time; but meanwhile you can be great where you are. . . . You are not made great by the location in which you happen to be, nor by the things with which you may surround yourself. You are not made great by what you receive from others, and you can never manifest greatness so long as you depend on others. You will manifest greatness only when you begin to stand alone. Dismiss all thought of reliance on externals, whether things, books, or people. As Emerson said, "Shakespeare will never be made by the study of Shakespeare." Shakespeare will be made by the thinking of Shakespearean thoughts.

Never mind how the people around you, including those of your own household, may treat you. That has nothing at all to do with your being great; that is, it cannot hinder you from being great. People may neglect you and be unthankful and unkind in their attitude toward you; does that prevent you from being great in your manner and attitude toward them? . . .

Do not talk about your greatness; you are really, in essential nature, no greater than those around you. You may have entered upon a way of living and thinking which they have not yet found, but they are perfect on their own plane of thought and action. Give yourself no airs; great people never do. Ask no honors and seek for no recognition; honors and recognition will come fast enough if you are entitled to them.

Your Duty to Be Great

When [people] start out to make something of themselves and to practice the science of being great, they find themselves necessarily compelled to rearrange many of their relationships. There are friends who perhaps must be alienated, there are relatives who misunderstand and who feel that they are in some way being slighted; the really great man is often considered selfish by a large circle of people who are connected with him and who feel that he might bestow upon them more benefits than he does. The question at the outset is: Is it my duty to make the most of myself regardless of everything else? Or shall I wait until I can do so without any friction or without causing loss to anyone? This is the question of duty to self vs. duty to others. . . .

Your first duty to God, to yourself, and to the world is to make yourself as great a personality, in every way, as you possibly can. . . .

There is a great mass of men and women who have lived and worked until they are practically incapable of thought along these lines; and they cannot receive the message. Something may be done for them by demonstration, that is, by living the life before them. But that is the only way they can be aroused. The world needs demonstration more than it needs teaching. For this mass of people our duty is to become as great in personality as possible in order that they may see and desire to do likewise. It is our duty to make ourselves great for their sakes, so that we may help prepare the world that the next generation shall have better conditions for thought.

A Mental Exercise

A mental exercise is an exercise, not in repeating words, but in the thinking of certain thoughts. The phrases that we repeatedly hear become convictions, as Goethe says, and the thoughts that we repeatedly think become habitual, and make us what we are. The purpose in taking a mental exercise is that you may think certain thoughts repeatedly until you form a habit of thinking them; then they will be your thoughts all the time.

from

THE SCIENCE OF GETTING RICH

by Wallace D. Wattles

Take Action Now . . . Don't Wait!

There are very many people who, consciously or unconsciously, set the creative forces in action by the strength and persistence of their desires, but who remain poor because they do not provide for the reception of the thing they want when it comes.

By thought, the thing you want is brought to you; by action you receive it.

Whatever your action is to be, it is evident that you must act NOW. You cannot act in the past, and it is essential to the clearness of your mental vision that you dismiss the past from your mind. You cannot act in the future, for the future is not here yet. And you cannot tell how you will want to act in any future contingency until that contingency has arrived.

Because you are not in the right business, or the right environment now, do not think that you must postpone action until you get into the right business or environment. And do not spend time in the present taking thought as to the best course in possible future emergencies; have faith in your ability to meet any emergency when it arrives.

If you act in the present with your mind on the future, your present action will be with a divided mind, and will not be effective.

Put your whole mind into present action.

Do not give your creative impulse to Original Substance, and then sit down and wait for results; if you do, you will never get them. Act now. There is never any time but now, and there never will be any time but now. If you are ever to begin to make ready for the reception of what you want, you must begin now.

And your action, whatever it is, must most likely be in your present business or employment, and must be upon the persons and things in your present environment.

You cannot act where you are not; you cannot act where you have been, and you cannot act where you are going to be; you can act only where you are.

Do not bother as to whether yesterday's work was well done or ill done; do today's work well.

Do not try to do tomorrow's work now; there will be plenty of time to do that when you get to it.

Do not wait for a change of environment, before you act; get a change of environment by action.

You can so act upon the environment in which you are now, as to cause yourself to be transferred to a better environment.

Hold with faith and purpose the vision of yourself in the better environment, but act upon your present environment with all your heat, and with all your strength, and with all your mind.

Do not spend any time in day dreaming or castle building; hold to the one vision of what you want, and act NOW. . . .

If you are engaged in some business, and feel that it is not the right one for you, do not wait until you get into the right business before you begin to act.

Do not feel discouraged, or sit down and lament because you are misplaced. No man was ever so misplaced but that he could not find the right place, and no man ever became so involved in the wrong business but that he could get into the right business.

Hold the vision of yourself in the right business, with the purpose to get into it, and the faith that you will get into it, and are getting into it; but ACT in your present business. Use your present business as the means of getting a better one, and use your present environment as the means of getting into a better one. . . .

Hold the vision of yourself in the job you want, while you ACT with faith and purpose on the job you have, and you will certainly get the job you want.

Become Larger Than Your Present Place

You can advance only by being larger than your present place; and no man is larger than his present place who leaves undone any of the work pertaining to that place.

The world is advanced only by those who more than fill their present places. . . .

Every day is either a successful day or a day of failure; and it is the successful days which get you what you want. If every day is a failure, you can never get rich; while if every day is a success, you cannot fail to get rich.

If there is something that may be done today, and you do not do it, you have failed insofar as that thing is concerned; and the consequences may be more disastrous than you imagine.

You cannot foresee the results of even the most trivial act; you do not know the workings of all the forces that have been set moving in your behalf. Much may be depending on your doing some simple act; it may be the very thing which is to open the door of opportunity to very great possibilities. You can never know all the combinations which Supreme Intelligence is making for you in the world of things and of human affairs; your neglect or failure to do some small thing may cause a long delay in getting what you want.

Do, every day, ALL that can be done that day.

There is, however, a limitation or qualification of the above that you must take into account.

You are not to overwork, nor to rush blindly into your business in the effort to do the greatest possible number of things in the shortest possible time.

You are not to try to do tomorrow's work today, nor to do a week's work in a day.

It is really not the number of things you do, but the EFFICIENCY of each separate action that counts.

Every act is, in itself, either a success or a failure.

Every act is, in itself, either effective or inefficient.

Every inefficient act is a failure, and if you spend your life in doing inefficient acts, your whole life will be a failure.

The more things you do, the worse for you, if all your acts are inefficient ones.

On the other hand, every efficient act is a success in itself, and if every act of your life is an efficient one, your whole life MUST be a success.

The cause of failure is doing too many things in an inefficient manner, and not doing enough things in an efficient manner. . . .

Every action is either strong or weak; and when every one is strong, you are acting in the Certain Way which will make you rich.

Every act can be made strong and efficient by holding your vision while you are doing it, and putting the whole power of your FAITH and PURPOSE into it.

It is at this point that the people fail who separate mental power from personal action. They use the power of mind in one place and at one time, and they act in another place and at another time. So their acts are not successful in themselves; too many of them are inefficient. But if ALL Power goes into every act, no matter how commonplace, every act will be a success in itself; and as in the nature of things every success opens the way to other success, your progress toward what you want, and the progress of what you want toward you, will become increasingly rapid.

Rules for a Great Life

Give no anxious thought to possible disasters, obstacles, panics, or unfavorable combinations of circumstances; it is time enough to meet such things when they present themselves before you in the immediate present, and you will find that every difficulty carries with it the wherewithal for its overcoming.

Guard your speech. Never speak of yourself, your affairs, or of anything else in a discouraged or discouraging way.

Never admit the possibility of failure, or speak in a way that infers failure as a possibility.

Never speak of the times as being hard, or of business conditions as being doubtful. Times may be hard and business doubtful for those who are on the competitive plane, but they can never be so for you [on the creative plane]; you can create what you want, and you are above fear.

When others are having hard times and poor business, you will find your greatest opportunities. . . .

Never allow yourself to feel disappointed. You may expect to have a certain thing at a certain time, and not get it at that time; and this will appear to you like failure.

But if you hold to your faith you will find that the failure is only apparent.

Go on in the Certain Way, and if you do not receive that thing, you will receive something so much better that you will see that the seeming failure was really a great success.

from

AS A MAN THINKETH

by James Allen

A Man is Literally What He Thinks

As the plant springs from, and could not be without, the seed, so every act of a man springs from the hidden seeds of thought, and could not have appeared without them. Action is the blossom of thought, and joy and suffering are its fruits; thus does a man garner in the sweet and bitter fruitage of his own husbandry. . . .

A man's mind may be likened to a garden, which may be intelligently cultivated or allowed to run wild; but whether cultivated or neglected, it must, and will, *bring forth*. If no useful seeds are put into it, then an abundance of useless weed-seeds will *fall* therein; and will continue to produce their kind.

Just as the gardener cultivates his plot, keeping it free from weeds, and growing the flowers and fruits which he requires, so may a man tend the garden of his mind, weeding out all the wrong, useless, and impure thoughts, and cultivating toward perfection the flowers and fruits of right, useful, and pure thoughts. By pursuing this process, a man sooner or later discovers that he is the master-gardener of his soul, the director of his life. He also reveals, within himself, the laws of thought, and understands, with ever-increasing accuracy, how the thought forces operate in the shaping of his character and destiny.

Man is buffeted by circumstances so long as he believes himself to be the creature of outside conditions, but when he realizes that he is a creative power, and that he may command the hidden soil and seeds of his being out of which circumstances grow, he then becomes the rightful master of himself.

Good thoughts bear good fruit, bad thoughts bad fruit.

A man will find that as he alters his thoughts towards things and other people, things and other people will alter towards him. Let a man radically alter his thoughts, and he will be astonished at the rapid transformation it will effect in the material conditions of his life. Men do not attract that which they want, but that which they are. All that a man achieves or fails to achieve is the direct result of his own thoughts. A man can only rise, conquer, and achieve by lifting up his thoughts. He remains weak and abject and miserable by refusing to lift up his thoughts.

A man should conceive of a legitimate purpose in his heart, and set out to accomplish it. He should make this purpose the centralizing point of his thoughts. He should steadily focus his thought forces upon the object which he has set before him. He should make this purpose his supreme duty, and should devote himself to its attainment, not allowing his thoughts to wander away into ephemeral fancies, longings, and imaginings. This is the royal road to self-control and true concentration of thought. Even if he fails again and again to accomplish his purpose (as he necessarily must until weakness is overcome), the strength of character gained will be the measure of his true success, and this will form a new starting point for future power and triumph.

Into your hands will be placed the exact results of your own thoughts; you will receive that which you earn; no more, no less. Whatever your present environment may be, you will fall, remain, or rise with your thoughts, your Vision, your Ideal. You will become as small as your controlling desire; as great as your dominant aspiration.

The thoughtless, the ignorant, and the indolent, seeing only the apparent effects of things and not the things themselves, talk of luck, of fortune, and chance. Seeing a man grow rich, they say, "How lucky he is!" Observing another become intellectual, they exclaim, "How highly favored he is!" And nothing the saintly character and wide influence of another, they remark, "How chance aids him at every turn!" They do not see the trials and failures and struggles which these men have voluntarily encountered in order to gain their experience; have no knowledge of the sacrifices they have made, of the undaunted efforts they have put forth, of the faith they have exercised, that they might overcome the apparently insurmountable and realize the Vision of their heart. They do not know the darkness and the heartaches; they only see the light and joy, and call it "luck"; do not see the long and arduous journey, but only behold the pleasant goal, and call it "good fortune"; do not understand the process, but only perceive the results and call it "chance."

In all human affairs there are efforts, and there are results, and the strength of effort is the measure of the result. The Vision that you glorify in your mind, the Ideal that you enthrone in your heart—this you will build your life by. This you will become.

from

THE POWER OF DECISION

by Raymond Charles Barker

Decide to Control Your Life

You are greater than you think you are. You hold the key to life in your mind. You *can* act intelligently in a universe of Intelligence. You *can* decide what shall go into your subconscious mind. You *can* think what you want and thereby have your subconscious mind produce what you want. You *can* control your present experience and plan and determine your future. Thousands have done this. Other thousands are now doing this. Why not join their ranks and become what you want to be?

The Danger of Procrastination

The present moment is the time for decision. In fact, you are making decisions all the time. . . . [I]ndecision is actually a decision. It is a decision to fail. Right now is the time to move from the level of unintelligent day-by-day drifting to the level of decisive mental action.

[A]ll problems are the result of unintelligent thinking and feeling in a field of Intelligence that must assume what you are thinking and feeling is what you really want to have as your experience. In any problem, a new train of ideas is the beginning of the cure. But the new ideas must fascinate your attention. Old ideas have a tremendous hold in your subconscious mind. They are famil-iar territory. They require no great mental effort to keep them activated. You rethink them with ease. You have already convinced your subconscious mind that they are valid and warrant its continued operation of them.

Such comfortable states of consciousness are hypnotic and should be avoided. It takes courage to shake off the routines of comfort and start adventuring with the control of your own life. Here is where the important role of decision comes in—the decision to stay as you are for you are at home in your present limitation, or the decision to be uncomfortable for a while and gradually enjoy new horizons of living. The Law of Mind leaves you free. Free to stay as you are and keep on patching up the present and living in a false hope that tomor-row will be better. Free also to grasp the reins of your mind and emotions and emerge from the cocoon of the usual into the wide new world of the unusual.

Greatness

You are not an observer of the universe. You are a vital participant of the uni-verse. Let no one ever again tell you of your unimportance. God did not make a mistake when you were born. Intelligence created you to live in these times because you are equipped to meet the challenges of these times. You are the right person, in the right place, to create a right world for yourself. All the resources of the Infinite are already yours. They need you as a means of self-expression.

You are the result of your past decisions. You will become and experience the result of your present decisions. Join me in deciding on the side of greatness.

Indecision

Success and failure are results of the use of mind. Every success-motivated mind has been a decisive mind. Every failure-motivated mind has been an indecisive mind. Only the dreamer who acted with decision on his dream brought forth something new and valuable. It takes as much hard mental work to fail as it does to succeed. Failure is actually a success negative. It is the result of consistent negative patterns in the subconscious mind. Worry always begets indecision.

Your only tools in life are your mind and emotions. The most successful people in all fields of activity use the same mind and the same emotions that you are using. The genius does not have more mind than you do. He consciously or subconsciously knows how to use his mind to get the results he wants. The same is true of his use of emotions. He knows what he wants to do and assumes that he can do it. This assumption is his decision. . . .

Indecision is actually the individual's decision to fail. Many people are indecisive all their lives.

The Danger of Complacency

Complacency is an evil. It has no place in the creative process. When it enthralls your mind, subconscious trouble begins. It may be months or years before you are aware of the disintegration it has produced. You may laugh it off, but the degenerative process continues until you wake up. Eventually, some serious problem arises which stops you short and makes you re-evaluate your consciousness. Suddenly you realize that you have been drifting and not creating. You have relaxed in the false comfort of routines and paid no heed to new ideas. Your thinking and conversation are out-of-date, even though respectable. You are caught in the dying mechanism of mind. This mechanism is working this way because you have unconsciously given up living.

If anyone were to tell you that you had unconsciously given up your reason for living, you would be furious. You would point out all the values you have created in your present life. You would recount your triumphs of the past. Yet, at the center of your thought, there would be a nagging sense of failure. The feeling that all was not right. Truth would be staring you in the face. You might or might not want to see it.

Goals. The word is a taunting one to many. The aged say it is too late. The youth say they have no chance. The middle-aged state their limited aims and think they are sufficient. I dare you to think in great terms. I challenge you to dream a great dream. Nothing is impossible to those who decide upon possibility. The Infinite responds by corresponding, by becoming the thing that you have determined shall be. The framework of your preconceived opinions is the only limitation to your begetting. These are subject to change at a moment's notice when you have arrived at decision.

Decide to Be Happy

Happiness is genuine satisfaction with your present experience. The number of people in today's world who are not happy is shocking. Think of six of your friends and estimate how many of them are satisfied with their current situations. Happiness is not a constant, but satisfaction can be. Satisfaction is a deep underlying sense of fulfillment, a sense of doing a good job with life. It is a good subconscious base which abides in certainty through the many vicissitudes at the conscious mind level of experience. It is a basic wholesomeness which permits a flow of creativity to be in action in both mind and emotions.

Unhappy people think they know why they are unhappy. The number of unhappy people I have listened to and counseled with is legion. Their explanations of the many Causes of their unhappiness are usually incorrect. They do not see themselves correctly. Their disturbed emotions distort their reasoning capacity. They want to change events, situations, conditions, and people in their individual worlds. They do not want to change themselves. They want a rearrangement of facts and dodge the concept of a rearrangement of ideas within their own consciousness. . . .

If things do not make unhappy people happy, then what does? A change of consciousness is the answer, and very few people want to change their consciousness. They want to change situations in their experience while remaining in their present static states of mind. A changed experience can only happen to a changed individual. This is a mental and spiritual law. It is the truth of life, and intuitively every person knows it. Try as we may to avoid this truth, it remains true. The world responds to you by corresponding to your thought. It becomes to you what you are to it. It outpictures your consciousness and can change only when your consciousness changes. Things, situations, and events do not happen. They are caused, and your mentality is a field of causation.

Decide to Live Richly

The grandeur of life is known by the few when it should be known by the many. The majority of people live in part only. They are half-healthy, half-wealthy, half-happy, and half-creative. They have accepted this half way of living as normal. Once in a while, in a rare moment, they glimpse a larger life and wish that it could be so. They then return to their habitual thinking and continue to function in their half-hearted way. Half-living is abnormal and unnecessary.

You can live a much fuller life right where you are in your present circumstances. It does not require more money, a better job, a nicer home, or a different marriage partner. It requires a change of consciousness, and this you can do for you are a thinker. You are the controller of your consciousness. The moment you decided to live a richer life, your consciousness will devise the ways and means of your having it. . . .

It all depends on you, not on the world of events, things, and people. Your mind is where you live. Your world, your body, and your situation react in exact accordance to your mind. Not someone else's mind, *your* mind. An expanded consciousness expresses [itself] in an expanded experience. This is the way the law of mind works, and it works no other way. A greater and happier outward experience requires a larger and fuller knowing in consciousness to precede it.

Many people use this mental law in reverse. They think in smaller terms all the time. They unconsciously lessen their viewpoints, take less and less interest in the business of living, and wonder why they are unhappy and limited in scope. If you were to tell them that it is because of their consciousness, they would be furious. They live in the closed-in belief that nothing is their fault, that somehow the situation developed by its own causation. So they adjust to the lesser life and say that those who are able to live with ease and in order are lucky. The latter are not lucky; they are wise. They see themselves in a larger way. They not only glimpse the greater, they grasp it.

Prosperity

I define prosperity as the ability to do what you want to do at the instant you want to do it. This is living the full life. You will note that the goal is not money. There are as many sick rich people as there are sick poor people. There are as many unhappy rich people as there are unhappy poor people. Money is the means to an end, but it is not the end in and of itself. The belief that money will solve your problems is a delusion. It never has and it never will because your problems arise in and are created by your mind, not your checkbook. The way to solve problems is to change your thought and keep it changed. This is the correct decision to live a full life. . . .

You are a free agent as far as your mind is concerned. You alone decide what shall be. This is the responsibility of life. For one person, it opens the door to limitations and frustration. For another, it opens the wider door to freedom, growth, and true prosperity, which is the ability to do what you want to do when you want to do it.

from

HOW TO LIVE ON 24 HOURS A DAY

by Arnold Bennett

Time is the inexplicable raw material of everything. With it, all is possible; without it, nothing. The supply of time is truly a daily miracle, an affair genuinely astonishing when one examines it.

You wake up in the morning, and lo! your purse is magically filled with twenty-four hours of the unmanufactured tissue of the universe of your life! It is yours. It is the most precious of possessions. No one can take it from you. It is unstealable. And no one receives either more or less than you receive.

In the realm of time there is no aristocracy of wealth, and no aristocracy of intellect. Genius is never rewarded by even an extra hour a day. And there is no punishment. Waste your infinitely precious commodity as much as you will, and the supply will never be withheld from you. Moreover, you cannot draw on the future. Impossible to get into debt! You can only waste the passing moment. You cannot waste tomorrow; it is kept for you. You cannot waste the next hour; it is kept for you.

I have said the affair was a miracle. Is it not?

You have to live on this twenty-four hours of daily time. Out if it you have to spin health, pleasure, money, content, respect, and the evolution of your immortal soul. Its right use, its most effective use, is a matter of the highest urgency and of the most thrilling actuality. All depends on that. Your happiness—the elusive prize that you are all clutching for, my friends!—depends on that.

If one cannot arrange that an income of twenty-four hours a day shall exactly cover all proper items of expenditure, one does muddle one's whole life indefinitely.

We never shall have any more time. We have, and we have always had, all the time there is.

from

THE PATHWAY OF ROSES

by Christian Larson

The Great Idea—Your Great Purpose

Live for a great purpose, and hold the central idea of that purpose constantly before your mind. Do not live for the mere sake of prolonging existence; live for something that magnifies, on the largest possible scale, all the elements of existence. To live for a great purpose is to live a great life, and the greater your life, the greater the good that you will receive from life. The ruling desire of every living soul is to have life, and have it more abundantly; therefore, to fulfill that desire we must continue perpetually to live for that which produces more life. No matter how rich we may become in the real, spiritual life, here is a principle that we must ever remember and apply.

Do not work for yourself; work for the great idea that stands at the apex of your greatest purpose. The greater the idea for which you work, the greater will be your work; and it is he who does the greatest work that does the most for everybody, himself included. When your work is great you become a great power for good among thousands, and at the same time you do more for yourself than you could possibly do in any other manner.

When you begin to live and work for a great purpose, you get into the current of great forces, great minds, and great souls. You gain from every source; all the powerful lives in the world will work with you; you become a living part of that movement in the world that determines the greater destiny of man; you become one of the chief elements upon which will depend the future of countless generations yet to be; you become one of the chosen of the Most High.

To live for a great purpose is to live in the world of great ideas, and great ideas awaken great thoughts. Man is as he thinks. Great thoughts produce great minds; from great minds proceed great works, and great works constitute the building material with which the kingdom upon earth is to be constructed.

When we begin to live for a great and good purpose, we place in action that law that causes all things to work together for good. Henceforth, nothing is in vain; every person, thing, or event that comes into our world will add to the welfare, the richness, and the beauty of that world. All things become ministers of the life that is real life, we have been giving our best everywhere, and we are receiving the best from every source in return.

To live for that which is high, lofty, and sublime is to walk with God; the love, the life, the power, and the wisdom of the Infinite will ever be with us, and to have such companions is to be blessed indeed. Every moment will give us the peace that passeth understanding, every hour will be filled with the joy everlasting, and every day will be as a thousand years in celestial kingdoms on high. . . .

The soul that lives most perfectly in the present creates most nobly for the future. Be yourself today, regardless of what happened yesterday. Be all that you are or can be today, and you will live in a fairer world tomorrow.

VI.

SUCCESS CLASSICS
READING LIST

How many of these motivating books have you read? Seek each of these books, read them, and put them into action in your life. After you have read the book, check the box next to it, and go find the next one. Get a master's degree from Life's University of Possibility! We've also included space for you to write in additional books that are not listed.

☐ *Think and Grow Rich*—Napoleon Hill

EXCERPTED IN THIS BOOK—(NOW READ THE ENTIRE BOOKS)
☐ *The Science of Being Great*—Wallace D. Wattles
☐ *The Science of Getting Rich*—Wallace D. Wattles
☐ *As a Man Thinketh*—James Allen
☐ *The Power of Decision*—Raymond Charles Barker
☐ *How to Live on 24 Hours a Day*—Arnold Bennett
☐ *The Pathway of Roses*—Christian Larson

SELECTED ADDITIONAL TITLES BY NAPOLEON HILL
☐ *The Law of Success*
☐ *The Magic Ladder to Success*
☐ *The Master-Key to Riches*
☐ *Think Your Way to Wealth*
☐ *How to Be Rich* (Napoleon Hill et al.)

☐ *How to Prosper in Hard Times* (Napoleon Hill et al.)
☐ *The Prosperity Bible* (Napoleon Hill et al.)
☐ *Think and Grow Rich Every Day*

SUCCESS CLASSICS

☐ *The Power of Your Subconscious Mind*—Joseph Murphy
☐ *The Master Key System*—Charles F. Haanel
☐ *The Secret of the Ages*—Robert Collier
☐ *Riches Within Your Reach*—Robert Collier
☐ *The Life Magnet*—Robert Collier
☐ *A Message to Garcia*—Elbert Hubbard
☐ *Acres of Diamonds*—Russell Conwell
☐ *In Tune with the Infinite*—Ralph Waldo Trine
☐ *The Game of Life and How to Play It*—Florence Scovel Shinn
☐ *Mind Is the Master*—James Allen
☐ *Prosperity*—Charles Fillmore
☐ *Public Speaking for Success*—Dale Carnegie
☐ *Creative Mind & Success*—Ernest Holmes
☐ *This Thing Called You*—Ernest Holmes

RECENT SUCCESS TITLES

☐ *The Now Habit*—Neil Fiore
☐ *The Prosperity Plan*—Laura B. Fortgang

ADDITIONAL TITLES
(add other titles you would like to read)

_____

_____

_____

_____

_____

_____

VII.

THE THINK AND GROW RICH 90-DAY JOURNEY

To make a big goal come true, you often will need to break it down into smaller, achievable goals. In this way, you can move forward with clarity and confidence, and not get overwhelmed. That is the thought behind the Think and Grow Rich 90-Day Journey.

One of the most effective ways to read *Think and Grow Rich* is to read it slowly, and incorporate the ideas into your life. If you want to delve fully into the philosophy and have a more profound experience of the text, we recommend using the Think and Grow Rich 90-Day Journey as a guide through Hill's thirteen "Steps to Riches." In this, you will be studying one "Step to Riches" each week, for thirteen weeks. This translates to approximately three months, and allows you time to fully grasp and activate the *Think and Grow Rich* philosophy.

Use the following weekly charts as a way to stay focused and motivated through the entire thirteen weeks. Make sure to do all the homework as mentioned, then check off the box once you've completed it, so that you can chart your progress.

For your "Statement of Desire," you can either create your own, or use the one included in this book (on page 8). Napoleon Hill instructs you to read that Statement of Desire twice each day with feeling—and you can keep track of this using these weekly charts.

Each week, create smaller, achievable goals—which we call "Success Steps"—and write them down in the space provided. Check off the box once you accomplish them. Try to get all your Success Steps done each week, and to carry as few of them to the next week as possible.

Also, we've provided check boxes for those who want to also use *The Think and Grow Rich Workbook* and/or *The Think and Grow Rich Success Journal*. Both of those are powerful and important tools taken directly from and inspired by *Think and Grow Rich* to take the ideas even more deeply into your experience. Using them alongside this book is like being on the accelerated path toward your success!

Begin this journey today—don't wait until tomorrow. Be active and committed to your journey, and set aside time each day to studying these life-changing ideas. If you fall behind, don't give up the entire process. Simply start again, wherever you are, and keep moving forward. Every day that you engage in the *Think and Grow Rich* process, you are creating forward momentum in your life.

WEEK ONE:

DESIRE

- ☐ Homework—Read chapters 1 & 2
- ☐ Create your "Statement of Desire" (see page 8)
- ☐ Answer the "Questions for Success" at the end of the chapter
- ☐ Do exercises in *The Think and Grow Rich Workbook*
- ☐ Journal daily in *The Think and Grow Rich Success Journal*

STATEMENT OF DESIRE READING

	DAY 1	DAY 2	DAY 3	DAY 4	DAY 5	DAY 6	DAY 7
am	☐	☐	☐	☐	☐	☐	☐
pm	☐	☐	☐	☐	☐	☐	☐

THIS WEEK'S SUCCESS STEPS

- ☐ _____
- ☐ _____
- ☐ _____

WEEK TWO:

FAITH

- ☐ Homework—Read chapter 3
- ☐ Answer the "Questions for Success" at the end of the chapter
- ☐ Do exercises in *The Think and Grow Rich Workbook*
- ☐ Journal daily in *The Think and Grow Rich Success Journal*

STATEMENT OF DESIRE READING

	DAY 1	DAY 2	DAY 3	DAY 4	DAY 5	DAY 6	DAY 7
am	☐	☐	☐	☐	☐	☐	☐
pm	☐	☐	☐	☐	☐	☐	☐

THIS WEEK'S SUCCESS STEPS

- ☐ _____
- ☐ _____
- ☐ _____

WEEK THREE:
AUTO-SUGGESTION

☐ Homework—Read chapter 4
☐ Answer the "Questions for Success" at the end of the chapter
☐ Do exercises in *The Think and Grow Rich Workbook*
☐ Journal daily in *The Think and Grow Rich Success Journal*

STATEMENT OF DESIRE READING

	DAY 1	DAY 2	DAY 3	DAY 4	DAY 5	DAY 6	DAY 7
am	☐	☐	☐	☐	☐	☐	☐
pm	☐	☐	☐	☐	☐	☐	☐

THIS WEEK'S SUCCESS STEPS

☐ _____

☐ _____

☐ _____

WEEK FOUR:
SPECIALIZED KNOWLEDGE

☐ Homework—Read chapter 5
☐ Answer the "Questions for Success" at the end of the chapter
☐ Do exercises in *The Think and Grow Rich Workbook*
☐ Journal daily in *The Think and Grow Rich Success Journal*

STATEMENT OF DESIRE READING

	DAY 1	DAY 2	DAY 3	DAY 4	DAY 5	DAY 6	DAY 7
am	☐	☐	☐	☐	☐	☐	☐
pm	☐	☐	☐	☐	☐	☐	☐

THIS WEEK'S SUCCESS STEPS

☐ _____

☐ _____

☐ _____

WEEK FIVE:
IMAGINATION

- ☐ Homework—Read chapter 6
- ☐ Answer the "Questions for Success" at the end of the chapter
- ☐ Do exercises in *The Think and Grow Rich Workbook*
- ☐ Journal daily in *The Think and Grow Rich Success Journal*

STATEMENT OF DESIRE READING

	DAY 1	DAY 2	DAY 3	DAY 4	DAY 5	DAY 6	DAY 7
am	☐	☐	☐	☐	☐	☐	☐
pm	☐	☐	☐	☐	☐	☐	☐

THIS WEEK'S SUCCESS STEPS

- ☐ _____
- ☐ _____
- ☐ _____

WEEK SIX:
ORGANIZED PLANNING

- ☐ Homework—Read chapter 7
- ☐ Answer the "Questions for Success" at the end of the chapter
- ☐ Do exercises in *The Think and Grow Rich Workbook*
- ☐ Journal daily in *The Think and Grow Rich Success Journal*

STATEMENT OF DESIRE READING

	DAY 1	DAY 2	DAY 3	DAY 4	DAY 5	DAY 6	DAY 7
am	☐	☐	☐	☐	☐	☐	☐
pm	☐	☐	☐	☐	☐	☐	☐

THIS WEEK'S SUCCESS STEPS

- ☐ _____
- ☐ _____
- ☐ _____

WEEK SEVEN:
DECISION

☐ Homework—Read chapter 8
☐ Answer the "Questions for Success" at the end of the chapter
☐ Do exercises in *The Think and Grow Rich Workbook*
☐ Journal daily in *The Think and Grow Rich Success Journal*

STATEMENT OF DESIRE READING

	DAY 1	DAY 2	DAY 3	DAY 4	DAY 5	DAY 6	DAY 7
am	☐	☐	☐	☐	☐	☐	☐
pm	☐	☐	☐	☐	☐	☐	☐

THIS WEEK'S SUCCESS STEPS

☐ _____

☐ _____

☐ _____

WEEK EIGHT:
PERSISTENCE

☐ Homework—Read chapter 9
☐ Answer the "Questions for Success" at the end of the chapter
☐ Do exercises in *The Think and Grow Rich Workbook*
☐ Journal daily in *The Think and Grow Rich Success Journal*

STATEMENT OF DESIRE READING

	DAY 1	DAY 2	DAY 3	DAY 4	DAY 5	DAY 6	DAY 7
am	☐	☐	☐	☐	☐	☐	☐
pm	☐	☐	☐	☐	☐	☐	☐

THIS WEEK'S SUCCESS STEPS

☐ _____

☐ _____

☐ _____

WEEK NINE:

POWER OF THE MASTER MIND

☐ Homework—Read chapter 10
☐ Answer the "Questions for Success" at the end of the chapter
☐ Do exercises in *The Think and Grow Rich Workbook*
☐ Journal daily in *The Think and Grow Rich Success Journal*

STATEMENT OF DESIRE READING

	DAY 1	DAY 2	DAY 3	DAY 4	DAY 5	DAY 6	DAY 7
am	☐	☐	☐	☐	☐	☐	☐
pm	☐	☐	☐	☐	☐	☐	☐

THIS WEEK'S SUCCESS STEPS

☐ _____

☐ _____

☐ _____

WEEK TEN:

THE MYSTERY OF SEX TRANSMUTATION

☐ Homework—Read chapter 11
☐ Answer the "Questions for Success" at the end of the chapter
☐ Do exercises in *The Think and Grow Rich Workbook*
☐ Journal daily in *The Think and Grow Rich Success Journal*

STATEMENT OF DESIRE READING

	DAY 1	DAY 2	DAY 3	DAY 4	DAY 5	DAY 6	DAY 7
am	☐	☐	☐	☐	☐	☐	☐
pm	☐	☐	☐	☐	☐	☐	☐

THIS WEEK'S SUCCESS STEPS

☐ _____

☐ _____

☐ _____

WEEK ELEVEN:

THE SUBCONSCIOUS MIND

☐ Homework—Read chapter 12

☐ Answer the "Questions for Success" at the end of the chapter

☐ Do exercises in *The Think and Grow Rich Workbook*

☐ Journal daily in *The Think and Grow Rich Success Journal*

STATEMENT OF DESIRE READING

	DAY 1	DAY 2	DAY 3	DAY 4	DAY 5	DAY 6	DAY 7
am	☐	☐	☐	☐	☐	☐	☐
pm	☐	☐	☐	☐	☐	☐	☐

THIS WEEK'S SUCCESS STEPS

☐ _____

☐ _____

☐ _____

WEEK TWELVE:

THE BRAIN

☐ Homework—Read chapter 13

☐ Answer the "Questions for Success" at the end of the chapter

☐ Do exercises in *The Think and Grow Rich Workbook*

☐ Journal daily in *The Think and Grow Rich Success Journal*

STATEMENT OF DESIRE READING

	DAY 1	DAY 2	DAY 3	DAY 4	DAY 5	DAY 6	DAY 7
am	☐	☐	☐	☐	☐	☐	☐
pm	☐	☐	☐	☐	☐	☐	☐

THIS WEEK'S SUCCESS STEPS

☐ _____

☐ _____

☐ _____

WEEK THIRTEEN:

THE SIXTH SENSE

- ☐ Homework—Read chapters 14 & 15
- ☐ Answer the "Questions for Success" at the end of the chapter
- ☐ Do exercises in *The Think and Grow Rich Workbook*
- ☐ Journal daily in *The Think and Grow Rich Success Journal*

STATEMENT OF DESIRE READING

	DAY 1	DAY 2	DAY 3	DAY 4	DAY 5	DAY 6	DAY 7
am	☐	☐	☐	☐	☐	☐	☐
pm	☐	☐	☐	☐	☐	☐	☐

THIS WEEK'S SUCCESS STEPS

☐ _____

☐ _____

☐ _____

VIII.

SUCCESS NOTES

ABOUT THE AUTHORS

NAPOLEON HILL was born in 1883 in Virginia and died in 1970 after a long and successful career as a lecturer, author, and consultant to business leaders. *Think and Grow Rich* is the all-time bestseller in its field, having sold 15 million copies worldwide and setting the standard for today's motivational thinking. Other Tarcher/Penguin books by Napoleon Hill include *The Law of Success, The Master-Key to Riches, The Magic Ladder to Success, Think Your Way to Wealth,* and *Think and Grow Rich Every Day.*

For more information about Napoleon Hill's books, please visit www .tarcherbooks.com.

JOEL FOTINOS is a publisher, author, minister, and speaker. He is the vice president and publisher of the Tarcher imprint at Penguin Group (USA) Inc., and has narrated eight motivational audiobooks on prosperity and success for Penguin audio. Fotinos is the author or coauthor of eight books, including *The Think and Grow Rich Workbook* and two successful e-books on the *Think and Grow Rich* philosophy. He gives *Think and Grow Rich* classes, workshops, and tele-lectures throughout the country, and is also the founder of DebtClear, a program to help individuals in eliminating debt. He lives in New Jersey.

For more information, please visit www.joelfotinos.com.

AUGUST GOLD, cofounder and former spiritual director of Sacred Center New York, is an award-winning author and has served as an inspirational teacher and counselor in New York City for twenty years. She speaks nationally and internationally at conferences and organizations, and is the author or coauthor of several books for adults and children, including *The Prayer Chest, Prayer Partners, Does God Hear My Prayer?* and *Does God Forgive Me?*

For more information, please visit www.augustgold.net.

DISCOVER THE TREASURES OF
NAPOLEON HILL

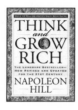

Think and Grow Rich by Napoleon Hill
The groundbreaking classic by the champion wealth-builder of all time—now revised and updated for the twenty-first century.
ISBN 978-1-58542-433-7
Also available from Penguin Audio
ISBN 978-0-14-314374-1

Think and Grow Rich, Deluxe Edition
by Napoleon Hill
A keepsake volume of Napoleon Hill's original masterwork, featuring leather-bound casing, gold stamping, red ribbon place marker, gilded edges, and marbled endpapers. Perfect as a gift and suited to a lifetime of use.
ISBN 978-1-58542-659-1

The Think and Grow Rich Workbook
by Napoleon Hill
For the millions of people who have read and loved *Think and Grow Rich*, here—for the first time—is a workbook and companion to the classic bestseller.
ISBN 978-1-58542-711-6

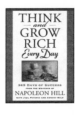

Think and Grow Rich Every Day by Napoleon Hill
Using the most potent writings from Hill's books *Think and Grow Rich* and *The Law of Success*, these daily readings will help turn doubt into confidence, fear into strength, and failure into triumph.
ISBN 978-1-58542-811-3

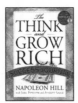

The Think and Grow Rich Success Journal
by Napoleon Hill
with Joel Fotinos and August Gold
This inspiring journal is the ultimate way to add riches
and success to readers' lives. It includes a bonus CD with
powerful motivational affirmations.
ISBN 978-1-58542-839-7

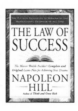

The Law of Success by Napoleon Hill
Here is Napoleon Hill's first pioneering work, featuring
the fullest exploration of his formula for achievement in
fifteen remarkable steps. Newly redesigned and reset.
ISBN 978-1-58542-689-8
Also available from Penguin Audio
ISBN 978-1-58542-689-8

Your Magic Power to Be Rich! by Napoleon Hill
The ultimate Napoleon Hill resource, featuring
updated editions of the master motivator's greatest books:
Think and Grow Rich, The Magic Ladder to Success, and
The Master-Key to Riches.
ISBN 978-1-58542-555-6

Your Magic Ladder to Success by Napoleon Hill
This compact powerful primer in success building is
Napoleon Hill's distillation of his lifetime of learning,
now revised and updated for the twenty-first century.
ISBN 978-1-58542-710-9

The Master-Key to Riches by Napoleon Hill
Her is the actual handbook that Napoleon Hill provided
to certified teachers of his ideas—a master class from
the greatest motivational writer of all time, revised and
updated for the twenty-first century.
ISBN 978-1-58542-709-3
Also available from Penguin Audio
ISBN 978-1-58542-709-3

DON'T MISS THESE PROSPERITY FAVORITES

FROM TARCHER/PENGUIN

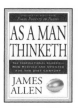

As a Man Thinketh by James Allen
Revised and updated for the twenty-first century,
this is one of the world's most widely loved
inspirational works—as a special bonus it includes
an updated edition of the author's first book, *From
Poverty to Power.*
ISBN 978-1-58542-638-6

The Secret of the Ages by Robert Collier
The classic on how to attain the life you want—
through the incredible visualizing faculties of
your mind.
ISBN 978-1-58542-629-4

The Master Key System by Charles F. Haanel
The legendary guide on how to enact the
"Law of Attraction" in your life.
ISBN 978-1-58542-627-0

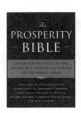

The Prosperity Bible
This beautiful boxed volume features complete
classics by Napoleon Hill, Benjamin Franklin,
James Allen, Florence Scovel Shinn, Ernest
Holmes, and many others.
ISBN 978-1-58542-614-0

A Message to Garcia by Elbert Hubbard
History's greatest motivational lesson, now collected with Elbert Hubbard's most treasured inspirational writings in a signature volume.
ISBN 978-1-58542-691-1

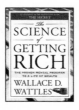

The Science of Getting Rich by Wallace D. Wattles
The time-tested program for a life of prosperity—features the rare bonus work "How to Get What You Want."
ISBN 978-1-58542-601-0

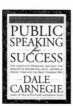

Public Speaking for Success by Dale Carnegie
The definitive, complete edition of Dale Carnegie's public-speaking bible—now revised and updated.
ISBN 978-1-58542-492-4

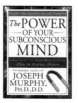

The Power of Your Subconscious Mind by Joseph Murphy, Ph.D., D.D.
The complete, original edition of the million-selling self-help guide that reveals your invisible power to attain any goal.
ISBN 978-1-58542-768-0